HOW TO MAKE IT IN THE NEW MUSIC BUSINESS

Here Are the Tips You've Been Asking for

Inside… Music's Legends Show You How to…

- Write Your Best Song with Diane Warren

- Record and Mix Your Best Sounding Record with Bob Clearmountain

- Master a Hit Record with Bob Ludwig

- Get the Sound You've Always Wanted with Bob Bradshaw

The Music Business Has Completely Changed

It's Time You Take Control of It

THIS IS THE BOOK THAT WILL SHOW YOU HOW

How to Make it in the New Music Business
Robert Wolff

Published by The Creative Syndicate

10400 Overland Road, Suite 143

Boise, Idaho, USA 83709

Copyediting by Lynette Smith

Layout and Design by Betty Abrantes

Book Information: http://RobertWolff.com and

http://amazon.com/author/robertwolff

First Print edition ISBN: 978-0-823079-54-4

Second Print edition ISBN: 978-1-937939-36-6

First Electronic edition ISBN: 978-0-307875-19-8

Second Electronic edition ISBN: 978-1-937939-08-3

First printing 2004

Second printing 2014

Library of Congress Control Number 2003116048

This book is dedicated to my parents,
Adam and Mary Wolff.
Thank you for everything.

CONTENTS

ACKNOWLEDGMENTS

T here are some very special people that I'd like to thank for making this
book a reality.

To Diane Warren: Diane, you are such an inspiration with a talent
unlike anyone else. I want to "Thank You" for choosing me to co-write your
memoirs with you. It was a fantastic experience, and I'm so happy your book
will now touch the lives of so many people all over the world in such amazing
ways. Thank you for being part of this book.

To Bob Bradshaw: When I called you years ago to build my dream guitar
rig, I never knew I'd be getting a great friend to go along with it. Thank you
Bob for that friendship and all your help.

To Steve Lukather: Over the years, your playing has been such a gift to
enjoy. I want to thank you for all of your help with this book and count myself
fortunate as now having the privilege to be your friend.

To Bob Ludwig: Thank you, Bob, for being a part of this book. I always
knew there was a reason why you and your work are so respected. Spending
time with you proved it.

To Bob Clearmountain: Thank you for inviting me to your home and
studio and for taking the time to share your wealth of knowledge. I know readers of this book will be helped and inspired in ways you may never imagine.

To Larry Cohen: To a good friend and trusted advisor. Thank you for
being part of this book.

Special thanks also go to Julie Horton; Realsongs; Bob Nirkind; Christine Wilhemy, Mark Altekruse, Melissa Horn, Nathalie Welch, and Apple; Eric Persing and Spectrasonics; Paul Lefebvre, Rolf Hartley, and Sonic Solutions; Jim Cooper and MOTU; Michael Logue and Antares; Andy Broadaway; Steve Chang and Live 365; Brian McConnon and Steinberg; Peter Maund and Sibelius; Didi Dori, Bob Reardon, and Waves; Marsha Vdovon and Ableton, Cycling '74, and Propellerhead; Bela Canhoto and Native Instruments; Karen Lange and The Company Corporation; Eric Newbauer, Gary Holiday, and Studio Network Solutions; Peter Snell and Tascam; Dave Kerzner, Gary Kerzner, and IK Multimedia; Chandra Lynn and Digidesign; Larry Crane and *TapeOp* magazine; Adrienne Crew and *Salon.com*; and Peter Glanville, Jennifer Wolfe, and Glyph.

INTRODUCTION

It's funny how life works. Just when you think you've got things all figured out, boom… things change. Along comes something new, and it's time to learn all over again.

Take music. Before the digital revolution, unless you had a major label record deal, access to huge piles of cash (courtesy of your record label, to whom you had to pay it all back), a big-name producer (who got a cut of whatever money your record might make), a decent studio (cheap at $2,000 a day), and talented musicians (double and triple scale pay), your chances of making serious money in the music business, even if you sold over a half a million copies of your record, were slim to none.

But then the digital revolution hit. Almost overnight, the way that music was created, recorded, distributed, marketed, and sold was changed forever. The digital revolution has changed something else as well. It has pretty well leveled the playing field for you, for me, and for everyone else. It allows us to make our music, our way.

As my former mentor, the legendary magazine and fitness icon Joe Weider, always said, "You'll never get rich working for anyone else. You've got to do your own thing and be an owner." In music, this means having complete control over your music, your product, and your dream.

So in this book we're going to go to school. I'm going to teach you the lessons of how to achieve this control in today's and tomorrow's digital world. And you're going to learn tips and secrets from many of music's primo players—the people who get paid huge major record label dollars to make the hits. My lessons and their wisdom will help you to get your signature sound. We'll teach you how you can create a business—no, make that an empire, if you like—called You, Inc. And you'll be able to use today's and tomorrow's technology to make it all happen right from your own home.

It's conventional wisdom that musicians can spend countless years becoming good players and singers, but very rarely do they become good businesspeople too. Unfortunately, this has all too often been true, from the brilliant Mozart, who struggled financially and was known for his lack of business acumen, to today's artists, most of whom constantly carp that they need to play out more regularly and wonder why there is always too much month left at the end of the check. That's all about to change.

The idea that there are only a few ways to make money with your music (e.g. perform in clubs, get signed to a record deal, or play on records) has for years been accepted as the gospel truth, but that "truth" is false. There are lots of ways to make money in music, and I'm going to show you some good ones.

I'm also going to teach you how to do what you do now, but better. I think many people would agree that creativity is stifled by pressure—especially when that pressure is financial. It's hard to come up with a great new song when the rent is due tomorrow and your credit cards are maxed out. Follow the strategies in this book and you're going to get some major breathing room in a hurry.

A very rich man once told me, "It's not how much you make, but how much you keep that counts." With the strategies I'm going to teach you, you're going to learn the very things that successful businesspeople do to create wealth and keep it.

I'm going to teach you how to play the major record label game as well, but on your own terms. Let me warn you, though: Many highly respected record business insiders have told me that the record business as we know it is dead. Its years of excess, its lack of creative vision, its inability to promote new sounds and develop enduring artists, and its unwillingness to change, adapt, and ride the Internet/distribution revolution have cut off its lifeline. So far gone is the old record business, my sources say, that in 5 years, the new record business will be composed of independent labels doing distribution deals with key distributors who will get their product to the public.

That said, it must be admitted that there can be benefits to being signed to a major label. However, for every musician who snags a major label deal, there are tens of thousands who don't. And of those who do make the majors, 90 percent of them will never sell more than 10,000 copies of their recordings. Think about it: So many musicians will spend untold precious years of their lives chasing the major label rainbow only to find that at the end of it there's no pot of gold.

Forget those visions of stardom and riches that would be yours if you could only have a gold record (sales of 500,000 units, as certified by the Recording Industry Association of America, or RIAA). The old record business reality is that, after all, expenses are recouped by your label, you'll be lucky to clear $50,000. Make that very lucky. As many who've had huge major label deals have told me, even after selling a million records, you can still owe the record company money.

But don't worry about it. As promised, I'm going to teach you how to create your business—You, Inc.—and as you learn, you're going to get the smarts and the knowledge to take your music as far as you'd like, with or without the support of a major label.

So how am I going to do all this? I'm going to give you specific steps to follow that will give you your best chance for success. We all know that there are no guarantees in life—especially in the music business. Not only are you dealing with fickle public tastes that bend with the wind, as well as a volatile economy that affects individuals' and businesses' spending and saving, but also with a tough career path that can come to a dead end in a heartbeat. Yet if you stick with the plan and follow the steps, you're going to have a great shot at music success.

The first part of this book is all about the new music business. And make no mistake; it is the new music business. As Lesson 1 says, it's old school vs. new reality. For those who think they've got to keep doing things the same old way, the new reality is that it's time for a change.

Take the radio/record label playlist game. Once you learn about how that game is played—Lesson 2—and how incredibly much money it takes to become a player, you'll quickly realize just what little chance you have to win if you play by their rules. But not to worry: I've got a few strategies to get your music on the radio—just like the record companies do—and one of them is going to get you there for a fraction of the old school price.

Ah, I can hear some of you saying, "But, I'd really like to get a major label deal." Just wait until you read Lesson 3, "The Illusion of Needing a Record Deal," and then tell me how badly you want that major label deal. If that doesn't get your attention, then Lesson 4 will. It's a view from both sides of the fence from multi Grammy nominee and 5-time Grammy winner Steve Lukather. Luke's no-holds-barred, tell-it-like-it-is view of the music business—and why it's not just record labels that have caused its demise—is riveting.

After that wake-up call you'll be ready to make your first move: getting the right people to help you. It all begins with Lesson 5, "Building Your A-Team." For years, musicians have made huge mistakes by giving away too much of the income and ownership from their music to people undeserving of it. They've signed bad deals with the wrong people that ceded too much control, and they've overpaid for services that yielded too few results. You're going to find out who you need and who you don't, learn strategies that can save you tens of thousands, if not more, in taxes, and discover how to create your own A-Team without giving away your life, your rights, and your money.

The second part of this book teaches you how to get your music together. It focuses on how the new music business has changed the way music is written and recorded. In order for people to remember you, in order for people to call you and want what you have to offer, you've got to give them something unique. You can either play the music that other people write or you can write the music that other people play. I think you can figure out which has the greatest potential for bringing you the life that you want.

To help you to create your song and develop your sound, I've asked the biggest and best names in music to give you their advice. My basic criterion was simple: Each person chosen had to have been in the music business for a minimum of 20 years and still be at the top of the profession. This was a tough standard to meet. The music business is filled with talented people who were on the scene for only a short while before dropping off the radar screen. I wanted people who had really impacted me and countless others over the years—the ones who, as musical tastes changed, stayed at the top. The individuals you're about to learn from were and still are. We're talking Grammy winners and nominees, industry award winners, and people who still command the utmost respect from the music industry's best.

The first is Diane Warren. In the world of contemporary music and songwriting, Diane is a giant. Her songs have been recorded by the biggest stars in music, and are instantly recognizable and loved by millions of fans all over the world. Diane leads off Part 2 of our book with Lesson 6, "It's All About the Song." Get ready, because I'm taking you into the private songwriting world of the woman many have called "the greatest pop songwriter in the world" and "the premier songwriter of our generation," and whether you write lyrics, music, or both, Diane Warren's words of advice will inspire you.

There's no doubt that with a great song you can go far. But if you also have a great sound, then the chances of your musical success can skyrocket. So how do you get a great sound? There are three steps to developing your own sound. The first is to develop your playing and/or singing ability. When you hear B.B. King, you know it's B.B. King. When you hear Bruce Springsteen, you know it's Bruce Springsteen. If you've already put many years into your music, there's a good chance you're already well on your way to this. If not, you'll find out how to get there.

So the second step is to create your own individual sound, a sound that identifies you. And to help you to create that sound and learn how to use it, Bob Bradshaw, sound designer to the biggest stars in music, gives you advice, tips, and studio tricks people pay big money for. That's Lesson Seven.

Once you have your sound, you need to record it… and that's the third step. Technology is changing so fast that it's nearly impossible to stay up-to-date with all the latest new product releases and updates. Add to it, so many recording platforms to choose from, so Lesson 8 will narrow things down for you a bit by giving you an overview of the equipment that's firmly established and used by the record industry's biggest and best producers, artists, and engineers.

So now that you have your song, have your sound and mastered a few cool tricks on how to use it, and chosen the right recording platform and tools, how do you make your best recording? You wouldn't believe how many demos and potentially great songs and ideas get tossed in the wastebasket each day by people who can give you opportunities, yet are completely turned off by the quality of the recording. As many record industry people have told me, "There are a lot of s*#t songs out there." While it's up to you to make your song the best it can be, you can use some help on the philosophy and mechanics of recording your music. It all starts with the mix, and Lesson 9 gives you mixing advice from one of the world's best: Bob Clearmountain.

You can walk into any major recording studio anywhere in the world and ask if they've heard of Bob Clearmountain, and you'll hear what a recording genius he is. From Bruce Springsteen to The Rolling Stones to Bryan Adams and Def Leppard, to your personal Who's Who of major recording artists who have moved you, Bob Clearmountain is their go-to guy for mixing music. Bob has plenty to say that's going to help you record your best mix and music.

Having your sound and knowing how to mix your recording are only two of the three components needed to having a great sounding record. You also need to master it—the last and crucially important step that most people forget.

If there is one guy who's done it all, and with almost every major artist in the business—from The Beatles to Hendrix to Jim Morrison to Joplin to Frank Sinatra to Phish to Mariah Carey, Whitney Houston, Norah Jones, and Celine Dion, to the best artists of any music genre—it's got to be mastering guru Bob Ludwig. In Lesson 10, he shares his philosophy and some tips that are going to give you a great finished product.

The third part of this book is concerned with the business of the new music business and it's one of my favorite sections. We kick it off with Lesson 11, "Launching the Business of You, Inc." It's full of some of the most powerful strategies you'll ever need for protecting you and your business. It gives you a number of options to make, keep, and leverage wealth, and to legally put you on the same playing field as the major labels.

It's vitally important that, once you have your music ready but before you release it for the world to hear, you protect yourself. I'm talking about being armed with weapons that successful businesses use to protect their company and their assets from people who are ready to rip them off. I'm talking about strategies that'll help you keep more of your hard-earned money. This means having your own business. That's right. It's time for you to get serious about your music and your life, and to become the owner of your own business. It's not as mysterious as it sounds. Think about it: You're already running your own business when you're selling your music, your talents, and your skills to the right buyer. I'm going to teach you how to be legally protected, and along with that how to take advantage of the tremendous tax deductions and investment and saving opportunities unavailable to others who don't use these legal entities. In fact, I'm going to teach you how to form your own corporation or other legal entity of your choosing, over the Internet or over the phone, in 10 minutes or less!

Lesson 12 takes you to boot camp: real-world new music business boot camp, that is. And I've got three subjects to cover: copyrights, protecting your licensing, and protecting your royalties. You're going to learn quickly that getting rich is not about how many gigs you play or hours you work. It's about your creating, owning, licensing, and distributing the intellectual property and copyrights from your music.

The fourth and final section of this book takes a new music business approach to marketing, selling, and distributing your music. It begins in Lesson 13 with how to premier your masterpiece to tens of millions all over the world—which starts with having your own website. Every serious business has one, and your name, time, talent, and music are too valuable for you not to have one, too. And is it ever easy and cheap to do it!

But let's not stop there. Once your website is up, I'll teach you how to Webcast and have your own Internet radio station playing your music 24/7/365 to a global audience of over 500 million people. Imagine the possibilities. And if you've ever dreamed of recording and mixing records with different musicians in another state or country—without having to be there—I'm going to show you how you can do it while sitting in your bedroom.

From there, you're going to read the "Special Report: Capturing Niche Markets" you'll find in Appendix A. It's all about producing & selling music for Niche Markets and the little-known avenues of music opportunities that can pay big rewards.

Finally, it's time to have some fun with "Lessons of Inspiration" in Appendix B and "Dealing with People in the Real World" in Appendix C. I think you'll really like reading these stories and tips.

On the musical road I've traveled, I've had incredible ups and downs. I've toured, lived out of a van, played night-after-thankless-night for not much more money than I could've earned flippin' burgers at McDonald's. As a teen-ager, I knew the adrenaline and excitement of hearing my first record played on the radio. I know what it's like to be nearly broke, to not have money for food and rent, and to have to pawn my guitars just to survive. Yet I also know what it's like to write and produce award-winning music for a major movie studio—Warner Bros.—and to do it in the bedroom studio in my little house in Idaho. So much for having to live in a city where music is made.

I've been employed by a major record label and have met and worked with many of music's biggest stars and hit makers. I've worked for a major market radio station and have seen first-hand how radio re-ally works. I've been involved in many recording sessions as a musi-cian, and I've had my jingle work played on national television. I've lived in and near the three biggest music cities in the United States—Los Angeles, New York, and Nashville—and include among my friends many of the very music stars I grew up reading about.

I tell you these things not to brag or go off on some ego trip. Life's too short for that. I tell you these things because I think I just might be able to relate to where you're coming from.

You see, where I came from is a little midwestern town, and I was given no silver spoon or special favors. My parents, grandparents, aunts, uncles, and cousins weren't musicians. What I've learned—be it how to play an instrument or the real world of people and how business is done—I've learned through many lessons of trial and error, lots of time and money spent, and the amazing predictability of just how wonderfully life can work, how it can open doors and put the right people in your path, at just the right time, when you know what you want and are focused, resilient, and steadfast until you get it.

I came up the hard way, probably just like you, following a dream—a "calling" if you will—that keeps pulling at the heartstrings and says, "Follow your gift wherever and however it leads you and don't be afraid." And you know what else it says? "And don't you dare give up or lose the music—the gift—inside your soul."

With all the experiences I've had during the last few years—the people I've met and the musical awakening I've experienced as to how music is created, made, distributed, and sold—I knew I had to write a book about it. This is that book. It's the book I would've rushed to the bookstore to buy if it had only been there. In a sense, it's the book I always wanted, always needed, but could never find.

Of course, this book shouldn't be the only one in your musical library. The more knowledge you have about the things that you love, the wiser and better off you'll be. There are many other music books out there:

> *This Business of Music (This Business of Music: Definitive Guide to the Music Industry)*

> *All You Need to Know About the Music Business*

> *What They'll Never Tell You About the Music Business: The Myths, the Secrets, the Lies (& a Few Truths)*

These books have solid information on the business and legal aspects of the music industry. But first, you've got to get from dream to reality, and this is the book that's going to take you there.

This is the book that will give you the very tools and knowledge that have helped me and countless others to see the light and that will help you once and for all, as Henry David Thoreau said, to "Live the life you imagine."

Here's to your amazing success,

PART 1

Welcome to the New Music Business

Lesson 1
Old School vs. New Reality: The Digital Revolution
Levels the Playing Field

It's time for a wake-up call. You are one lucky person because you couldn't have picked a better time to follow your musical, singer/songwriting, or recording dreams. The information, new technology, Internet power, untapped markets, and huge potential audience that await your efforts give you more power than ever before to create music in your own way and on your own terms.

Until very recently, songwriters and composers—not just the great classical composers but also the immortal Broadway tunesmiths—had to spend untold hours writing out their music by hand, note by note. No longer. Today, we have music software that notates and automatically scores your music for you, either as you're playing it or after you've recorded it. All you need to do is click the "print" icon on your computer and, voilà, your music is transcribed.

In the days of the Sun, Motown, and Stax sessions, all those immortal record labels had was tape, a limited number of tracks, and a small arsenal of outboard processing gear. And with those tools at their disposal, they made incredible recordings. But today we have over 60 tracks, higher sampling and recording rates, higher fidelity, and amazing editing, processing, and mastering capabilities, and they're all inside that computer, waiting for you to tap into their power.

To make music in the '70s, '80s, and '90s, you needed a major recording studio, a roomful of studio musicians with numerous instruments and racks filled with gear, and a control room with a million or more dollars in consoles, recorders, and processing equipment. Today, you have plug-in capabilities that create and recreate classic models of keyboards, synthesizers, guitars, effects, basses, drums, percussion, horns, orchestras of strings, samplers, and mixers at a touch, generating the same kinds of sounds achieved in those high-priced studios, but now available via computer software, with many in the $200 to $500 price range.

And it doesn't stop there. You can get software that adds vocal harmonies to your song, software that keeps your pitch automatically in tune, software that models classic amps and equipment, and even software that changes the sound of that cheap microphone you love using into the sound of a mic costing thousands of dollars. On a laptop, you can access everything you need to record, mix, and master your music: at home, on a plane, sitting on a boat, or on the beach.

And that's just the beginning.

So why on earth would anyone want a major label deal today? Well, if you are one of the rare few who have the looks, the talent, and the charisma that says star quality, and if a major label is willing to commit big bucks to your promotion and "long term" success, then maybe that's an opportunity too good to pass up. If you're among the rest of us, then you and I need to talk.

Welcome to the Old School Music Business: What Your Record Earns and What You Get to Keep

Let's begin by talking money. As I mentioned in my Introduction, 90 percent of artists with record deals never sell more than 10,000 records. And the big dollars you end up paying back (the label says they pay for it, but at least 50 percent of the cost, if not more, comes out of your royalty) for a chance to be played on the radio could leave you in debt for the rest of your major label life.

So, what if you do get signed and what if you do have a record that starts making money? How much do you think you'll make? Honestly, do you have a clue? Very few people do. Let's do a little real-world record royalty calculation.

Start with the Royalty Rate

Let's say you've signed a standard record deal with standard terms. For the most part, this will be a one-record deal that gives your label first options for perhaps another two or three follow-up albums. Your royalty rate, also known as "points" (a point is a percentage, with 1 point being equal to 1 percent), might be a 10- to 14-point deal. It might be based on the retail selling price of your record. It might also be based on the wholesale price or the price to dealer/price to distributor (a better deal for the label and not a good deal for you, since the royalty is now paid on a lower sales price).

Let's say your royalty is 13 percent based on the retail price of your record, which is $12.98. (Some CDs are priced higher, but there's a lot of consumer pressure on the labels to lower their prices, so $12.98 puts us in the ballpark.) If there weren't any deductions (dream on), you would make approximately $1.69 per record sold. So if you sold 50,000 records, you'd make $84,500, right? Wrong.

Here Come the Deductions

For money earned on each record sold there are deductions, and lots of them. Based on the standard and accepted terms of your record contract, your label can, and most likely will, deduct all of the following.

Recording costs. All expenses having to do with the recording of your record must be paid back by you to your record label. Albums can easily cost $125,000 and up, so those "let's do another take's" end up costing you big time. And these costs are not recouped by the gross money your label receives from your total sales, which would repay your label debt quicker. They are paid back to the label at your royalty rate, which, as you'll recall, is 13 percent. In other words, for every sale of your record, 13 percent (or whatever your royalty rate is) is paid back to the label until your debt is paid off. What about that other 87 percent of the money the label has received that could be used to pay off your debt? The label gets to keep it.

Producer points. Your producer also gets royalties. How much depends on how much in demand he or she is. Producer points range from 2 to 5. These royalties begin with the first record sold and are paid to the producer after your record has recouped its costs. This is not the same deal that you, the artist, receive. You only start receiving royalties on records sold after your debts are recouped. This means that over 100,000 records need to be sold before you're entitled to start receiving any money. Yet while you don't receive any money from those first 100,000 records sold, your producer does. He or she receives a royalty check for every one of those 100,000 records, and for every record sold thereafter as well. Producer royalties are either paid by the label directly to the producer or are paid by you to the producer. They are always paid, though, and they always come from your royalties.

Mixer points. If you use the services of a record mixer, he or she is often offered points from the sale of your music as well. It's not uncommon for good mixers to ask for 1 to 2 points. What is common is that you pay for them.

A&R points. The person at the label who discovers and signs you can also be entitled to a percentage (typically between 1 to 2 percent) of the money that your label makes from your records. Be aware: These "bonuses" can come out of the artist's royalty, and not from the label's portion.

Breakage. Remember the days of vinyl albums and singles? Because a certain percentage of them would be damaged or broken en route to distributors and stores, and thus couldn't be sold, record labels decided to pay royalties on only 90 percent of records sold to offset this potential loss. The 10 percent had nothing to do with how many records were actually broken; it was simply an arbitrary percentage the labels agreed on to give them a cushion against any returns damage. And if you think the breakage deduction went out with vinyl, you're wrong. In effect, it means that the total number of records you sell is automatically decreased by 10 percent right from the start. If you sell 1 million records, your label doesn't have to pay you for the first 100,000.

Foreign sales. Because it takes more time, effort, and expense to promote and distribute your record outside the United States, your record label can reduce your royalty rate for any sales made outside the United States (or outside whatever country where your label is based). The percentages can vary with each country and market. Record companies may accept less of a deduction in countries and territories where they have some ownership in the foreign distributor. In the bigger global markets (also known as "major territories"), the discount can be in the range of 25 to 40 percent. For the rest of the world (R.O.W.), deductions may be as high as 40 to 50 percent.

Record clubs. Who hasn't received those enticing notices from record clubs offering lots of CDs for the price of one? This is a good deal for the consumer, but not for the artist. In addition to having a term in your contract that allows your label to pay you for record club sales, a royalty rate of half of what you'd normally get, the label also gets to give away (such as when they offer a certain number of free CDs if you buy one) as many of your records for free as it sells. Hence, the bigger artists (those who are often chosen as the free product selections) help sell the lesser artists' (the CD you buy) music. Sell 50,000 and the label can give away 50,000. Good deal?

Singles. Singles used to be big movers until some labels decided to limit their releases so that fans would buy the album first—not a popular move with music buyers. If your label does release a single from your record, don't be surprised if your royalty rate is cut in half.

Free product. In the record business, every record a record company sells is discounted. The size of the discount depends on the merchant. Record labels can offer retailers free product as an incentive to carry more of that label's artists. They might give free product to a new retailer with whom they're seeking to establish a relationship. They can use free product as an incentive/reward to retailers for selling x number of records. Retailers like free product because they can sell it at a discount without having to pay the record label a dime; this increases overall sales numbers and drives additional traffic into their stores. The record companies like it because they don't have to pay you royalties on free product sales and they keep their retailers smiling. However, you're probably not smiling about the 10 to 20 percent (15 percent is about average) that is automatically taken off the top for free product that you'll never get paid for.

New technology. Many label contracts have provisions that allow them to reduce your royalty rate by up to 50 percent should they use a "new technology" (i.e., one they theoretically might have to invest R&D money in, such as digital delivery) to get your music to consumers. However, while record companies will fight to keep this clause in, it can be negotiated. One way is by having the label reduce the deducted amount slightly during the first few years of the exploitation of the new technology, with the proviso that the full new technology royalty rate deduction will not kick in until at least 50 percent of your sales are made as a direct result of that new technology.

Promotion. Any promotional expense (e.g. independent radio promotions, music videos, television and radio campaigns, record store appearances, etc.) can be fully recouped by your label from your sales. Not only that, if you're doing a television promotional tour, the label can reduce your royalty during the 6-month period that your promotional tour takes place by as much as 50 percent.

Tour support. Sending you and the band on the road is expensive, especially if you need to buy music equipment. And while your label has a vested interest in seeing you build a fan base (read: potential record buyers), all this comes at a price—to you. Some labels split some of the costs with you, thereby reducing the amount you'll have to pay back to them. Others will pay the up-front costs only if 100 percent of those expenses are recoupable.

Packaging. Who doesn't enjoy seeing great CD covers and reading all the cool little tidbits in the liner notes? The labels know this and they make you, the artist, pay big time for it. How much? You would think it wouldn't be too much, since CD jewel cases are fairly inexpensive (especially if you're buying them in the quantity the label does). And for goodness sakes, cover art and design can't cost that much, can they? The record labels think so, and they have happily put a clause in contracts for a packaging deduction, typically 20 to 25 percent, which is subtracted from your record's agreed-upon selling price regardless of whether it's wholesale or retail. On your $12.98 retail-priced record, you've just lost anywhere from $2.60 to $3.25.

Other deductions. There are too many other possible deductions to list here. For more on this, I highly recommend Peter M. Thall's book *What They'll Never Tell You About the Music Business: The Myths, the Secrets, the Lies (& a Few Truths)*.

What's Left?

Okay, now let's do a little math to see what you're left with after calculating only some of the deductions I've just mentioned.

First, let's recap the price of your CD, your royalty rate, and the first deduction, producer points.

You have a record that has a $12.98 retail price.

You have a record deal that pays you a 13 percent royalty on the retail price of your record.

You must pay 2 percent in producer points, which is deducted from your 13 percent royalty rate up front, giving you a royalty rate of 11 percent. Now let's start with the $12.98 retail price and figure in the free product, packaging, breakage, and new technology deductions.

$12.98 × 85% = $11.03 (what's left after subtracting the free product deduction.

$11.03 × 75% = $8.27 (what's left after subtracting the packaging deduction.

$8.27 × 90% = $7.44 (what's left after including the breakage deduction.

$7.44 \times 75\% = \$5.58$ (what's left after taking the technology deduction.

You might be thinking "Geez, that's a bunch taken off, but I can live with $5.58 per record." But, hold on! I don't recall saying we were finished yet. Now it's time to calculate what percentage of that $5.58 you will actually get. Remember, your royalty rate is 11 percent. At that rate you get a whopping $5.58 × 11 percent = $0.61 cents for every record you sell after all costs are recouped by your label. And let's not forget that the label credits your account (to pay them back) at your royalty rate, not from the total monies it receives.

So how much has your label made on all this? Well, if the label sells your record to retailers at $9.00, it receives $900,000 if all 100,000 records were paid for. Even if you're recouped (all debts paid off) and the label now owes you royalty money, after all the deductions you only get paid on 25,000 of the 100,000 records sold. (Remember, all the deductions total up to 75 percent, leaving you 25 percent.) Multiply 25,000 times $0.61, and you get $15,250 for selling 100,000 records. Yippee! Factor in all the time you've invested and all the money you've spent to get yourself this far, and you're losing money big time.

If that doesn't have you reeling, then perhaps this might. Of the $0.61 per record you're now getting (I'm being generous here and not deducting everything that could be deducted), you still have to pay your attorney (if he or she gets a cut of what you make), your manager (if he or she gets a cut of what you make), and your agent (if he or she gets a cut of what you make). After those fine folks get paid, you might be left with little more than $0.50 per record sold. Fifty cents!

Now, factor in how much your time is worth. Do you know? You should, because when you include all the hours, days, months, and perhaps years you've put in to becoming a professional musician and to getting a label deal, plus the time you put into making your record and all the touring and promotional appearances you did to sell it, plus the amount of time you've had to wait to collect your measly $0.50 per record, and then add to your expenses all the taxes you'll have to pay whatever the total turns out to be, the reality is, you're working for free. Sure hope you really love the record business.

And that scenario, ugly as it is, can only happen if the record label decides to actually release your record. They don't have to do that, you know. Even if you've got a major label deal, the record company isn't obligated to release your recording. Let me explain.

Now Consider an Even Worse Scenario

Record labels have clauses in their contracts that give them the option, if they so choose, to release your recording. You'd think that if they've gone to all the trouble of signing you and perhaps paying you a little signing advance, they'd be in a hurry to get your music out and sold. But that's not always the case.

If a new act or singer comes along (after you've been signed) and the label believes that they are, as they say, "the bomb," then guess where those limited new artist development dollars are now going? You guessed it, and so sorry to break the news to you, but you've been officially put on hold (Aimee Mann can speak from experience about this).

With few exceptions, this is not a good move for your career. The record business is such that listeners want the newest and hippest sounds (and this changes quickly), and labels are focused on how this artist or the next one can increase next quarter's profits. The days of slowly building and breaking an artist's career over multiple years and albums are pretty much over. For you, the signed major label artist, whose career and life have now been put on hold, that can mean huge frustration and seeing your window of opportunity to make it in the music business slam shut.

You see, when you signed that record deal, you also signed away your option to quickly terminate your agreement if the label didn't release your record within a specified time (unless you had your attorney put in a weasel-out clause that allows you to terminate the agreement without penalty). The record company is likely to have language in their agreement that basically says that, at their discretion, they have the option to record and release your recording within the next 12, 18, 24, or 36 months, and if they don't, then your agreement with them can be terminated.

However, keep in mind that during those 1 to 3 years that they haven't recorded or released anything on you, you are still exclusively bound to them. You read it right. You're exclusively theirs, and they don't need to do anything more with you if they don't want to. Meanwhile, as you're waiting, and with each passing day you're not on radio, the Internet, or in record stores, your career, and the audience for your music, are going bye-bye.

Let's change all that.

Welcome to the New Reality: New School vs. Old School

The new music business says it's time for you to be in charge of your musical destiny and life. The new music business says those who embrace change and technology and ride its wave will be greatly rewarded. The new music business says no one can write, record, perform, and promote your music better than you. The new music business says the more time you spend playing other people's music, the less time you'll have to create your own. And the new music business says you don't need to pay people who simply see you as another number that exists only to generate profit for them.

I've often wondered why some major label stars don't do more things on their own. With all the money they've made, with all the great contacts and millions of fans they have, they no longer need the power of major label dollars to jump-start a beginning career or carry on a successful one.

What if they realized how much freedom and financial reward they could gain by having their own label and doing music on their own terms, without having a company tell them what kind of music they can record and when they can release it? What a different world they would experience. Yes, all of them—creators, owners, and visionaries in a world called the new music business.

To them, and to you, I say, Welcome to the new reality.

Your decisions vs. corporate structures. In the old school corporate record world, decisions are often made by committees and can take weeks; this is quickly apparent when you're the party on the other end of the line or e-mail who's been waiting for a response. Now throw in office politics, be it people constantly jockeying for position over one another, or supposed deal makers not going after an artist because they don't want to take the risk of losing whatever power and position they currently have. The fact is, when you deal with an old school label, you are dealing with a hierarchy and structure (often with a limited creative vision) that must operate within the walls, dictates, and beliefs of "the company."

In complete contrast, as an owner in the new music business, you have free rein—in wide-open fields with no fences—to be both maverick and visionary. The only limit to your dreams and decisions about your music is what you believe about them. As Master P, independent hip-hop record mogul and impresario, always believed about his dreams, there are no limits and he named his company and empire just that, No Limit Records. His attitude and belief were that he was going to grow something. He did, others wanted to help grow it with him, and his phenomenal success is proof you can do it, too.

Master P started out on his own; he owned his masters and copyrights, and used the major labels only to distribute his records. Yes, the labels may have made a little money, but P made an empire. He promoted his artists anywhere and everywhere. He personally financed each record and video. And he always controlled the bank. His bank. More than four hundred million dollars later, he hasn't done too badly for a guy from the projects in Louisiana who started with $10,000 and sold records out of the trunk of his car.

The major labels aren't going away anytime soon. Perhaps the old business model they've used for so long will change, but there will always be some type of major record label. Learn from them. Study what you think they do right and wrong. Continuously adjust your label and new music business model so you can capitalize on what's good about today's music business, but never stop thinking ahead about what tomorrow's hits will sound like—and then create them. And use the distribution services of a major label as one of the many ways that will help you distribute them. That's having your cake and eating it, too. That's the new music business.

Home studio vs. big studio. The new music business has seen a paradigm shift from large studios to home studio recording. The old school belief was that if you wanted major label/hit radio sound and quality, you needed to record your music in a big studio, an undertaking that often required weeks and months of planning financing equivalent to taking out a second mortgage on your home.

The digital revolution and new music business have changed all that. Never again do you have to put your inspiration on hold until a studio has an open calendar.

As muses in the arts go, music is a quirky one whose inspiration and creative ideas can come to you in the strangest of places and at the oddest times— often in the middle of the night. In the new music business, that's plenty of time for you to turn on the computer and begin recording.

And that's the beauty of today's technology. You buy it once, use it however long or often you want, and most likely that's the biggest expense you'll have. Old school big recording studios charge you by the hour, day, week, or month. You must turn on your creative juices according to their schedules. And there's also the time and expense of travel, meals, lodging (if you don't live near the studio), lugging equipment and setting it up, and the discomfort of being in a strange place, with people you don't know staring at you through the control room glass as you "perform." This is not the greatest environment for the artist who needs to go at his or her own pace, not force the flow, and experiment with the infinite palette of sounds and textures that can produce an amazing piece of work.

Your business in the new music business allows you that expression and that freedom, and so much more. Just as the major labels won't all disappear, there'll always be big studios and they'll have their purpose and place. But in your new music world, the most important place will be yours. And the beauty of it is, with the digital revolution your recording studio will be any place you want it to be.

Internet radio vs. traditional radio. Old school says traditional radio will always be important in breaking and promoting artists and music. New school says Internet radio can be used for a fraction of the entry fee you'd need to sit at the "good ol' boys" poker table because you don't need the chips to wager big dollars on old school's traditional, and risky, radio bets.

Old school says that radio is so powerful because it's a passive medium. You don't need to do anything but listen to it once you've turned it on. Not entirely true, because you still need to change the stations and hit the buttons if don't like what they're playing. New school says that's about to change.

Streaming audio is one of the Internet's terrific technologies; it allows you to listen to your favorite Internet radio station(s) while you're busy surfing, researching, e-mailing, or doing anything else on the Web, be it on your home computer, laptop and Wi-Fi, or even smartphone. And with DSL or cable that always keeps you connected to the Internet, you don't even need to be in front of your computer screen to have Internet radio playing 24/7 throughout the house. All you have to do, just like old school radio, is simply turn it on and listen. With Internet radio scanning technology, you can have the same features of traditional radio (i.e., like scanning until you find the right music station and clicking your mouse to select the station to stop scanning) all with the click of your mouse.

The key to making new school Internet radio work is how you promote it. Like old school radio, promotions drive artist, music, and station popularity. Old school radio likes contests, remotes, and giveaways. New school Internet radio can do the same, and from anywhere you choose to do your remote/on-location broadcast. Traditional radio is limited to what they say, what they play, and how long they can say and play it. You are not.

The Internet is one of the last bastions of interstate communications freedom because its content is not regulated by the FCC (Federal Communication Commission) in the same way that old school radio is, and you don't have to play by old school radio rules to achieve new music business rewards. Your creative potential is unlimited, and so can be your possibilities for success in the new school Internet radio world, that is, if you give listeners the music and entertainment content they can't get anywhere else. Always think in terms of "what kind of experience would this be for me?" If it's one that excites you, chances are, it's going to do the same for all those people out there who are your potential listeners.

Your label vs. their label. Old school says you need a major record label to make major things happen with your music. New school says, not so fast. New school says, let's make it that you need your label.

The old and new reality is, and will be, regardless of who owns the label, the artist needs to be unique and have the sound and the song that'll translate to hit quality and potential. If you can provide that, major labels will be interested. And that's what you want—interest. You want them to make money by helping you distribute your dreams, but in the new music business, you want the Wells Fargo truck pulling up to your door and not theirs. You don't want them to own you.

Despite what they say, major labels like distribution deals. And they also like new artist deals where the new artist comes to the table with something of value besides their talent.

Yes, money.

There are a number of major Grammy-winning and million selling recording artists on major labels right now, who first came to the major label with financial backing to get their recording and career off the ground.

Instead of doing the same old, doesn't-work-like-it-used-to approach of just going to a major label with a look, a song, and a voice and hoping someone at the label will like them enough to maybe give them a development deal, the savvy artists got investors and financial backers (think family, friends, and fans who love your stuff) and went to the label as equity partners in the deal.

From a business perspective, it makes sense and cents.

Each is putting up time, resources, capital, and risk; but because each is contributing things of significance, that risk is spread out and minimized and the potential for rewards is upsized.

And even if it's a distribution deal, labels like them.

Think about it: They don't have to go to all the "expense" of finding, developing, and recording a new artist (read: throwing huge major label money out for projects), and since they already have their well-oiled and constantly flowing distribution pipeline in place, it's easy to add another CD/artist to the mix. And for just saying yes to distributing your music or artist on your label, they get a cut of the profits and they're not out a dime.

Ah, but new school says, you don't stop there. If your label's music and talent are strong enough with huge upside potential, you can cut a deal with the major label whereby they agree to help promote the music, too. Shoot for the best deal you can, but focus on at least a 75/25 split, with your label receiving the 75 percent. Depending on what kinds of things old school label will kick into the pot, new school label may decide to give up a little more; but for doing so, it could realize a lot more on the back end. End result: old school helps new school and both are smiling.

Start thinking of the many ways you can bring value to the table, and then watch the doors start opening.

Your marketing vs. their marketing. The new music business says take a look at the kinds of music marketing that's been done in the past to determine the kinds of new marketing to do for the future. Old school likes to dole out dollars for things that cost lots of them. Radio promotion and concert tours (all that you, as an old school artist, pay for) are high on the list. But new school asks why so much emphasis there and not in other, often-neglected avenues?

Take, for example, school promotions. The biggest audience of record buyers remains those who are school age—from elementary school through college. The amazing success of the movie *The Blair Witch Project* proves that a low-budget project can make major studio dollars when the power of buzz is added to the mystique of an underground movement that's promoted by word of mouth. The same can happen with your music.

College radio is and will continue to be one of the best oases for artists who don't fit the old school corporate label and playlist rosters. Yes, it's regulated by the FCC. Yes, many of the FM college stations are in big cities and are 100,000-watt full-power stations (just like the commercial ones). But no, they don't accept independent promotional "consideration" (if you know what I mean) and they aren't influenced by the corporate owners and higher-ups who tell them which artists and songs to play. The students decide, and if you've got a great song you think they'll like, the next song they play could be yours.

The Internet has made it easy to locate directories, addresses, and contacts of all the high schools and colleges that have radio stations, so finding the right people and places to send your CD and promo package to has never been easier. Old school believes there are only a limited number of promotional avenues for music that can recoup their huge investments quickly. New school says it likes building an audience in places where old school pays little attention, for little money, and watching the power of word of mouth create behind-the-scenes momentum that builds an audience base that can sustain an empire—a new music business empire.

Your profits vs. their profits. Old school believes that even though you create and perform the songs, the label should make the majority of the money. Old school knows the power and attraction of being able to say, "I've just been signed to a major label." Old school knows that once their artists learn how the game is played, many will wish they could "resign" from the major label. But they also know that by then it'll be too late.

New school asks what will a major label do for me that I can't do on my own? Do I need to pay inflated recording costs when, thanks to the digital revolution, I can get hit quality music for a fraction of the price? Do I need to pay for radio promotion at a major label price when I can get both traditional and Internet radio promotion for a fraction of the price? Can a label that doesn't know me or my music promote me better than I can promote myself?

And new school also asks, Why am I giving away roughly $0.90 of every dollar in profit my music makes to an old school label, when that label is basically a lending institution, advancing me money I'm contractually bound to pay back but keeping almost 100 percent of everything I make?

Your control vs. their control. Old school likes structure and control. New school likes freedom and unlimited opportunity. Old school has rules that anyone who enters its doors (i.e., signs a contract) must play by or they're either ostracized, neglected, or forgotten. New school says I make my own rules and even those rules are made to be broken—by me!

Old school has a catalog and roster of artists and dates for release that are followed slavishly. Old school constantly seeks new artists to create magic, while old artists are given one more chance to spin the profit wheel. Old school label decision makers decide which new album cuts will get released and which ones won't. And when it comes to artists and their music, old school decides when, where, and how they'll be released.

The new music business says it's time to change that. New school knows that many times an artist's best work is passed on by the old school decision committee that believes it knows the artist's music and fans better than the artist. Old school will often chose unflattering album covers and photos and fill those CDs with one, maybe two strong songs, with the rest being filler. They'll then overprice the CD, do little, if any, promotion for a few weeks, and then blame the artist for the lack of sales.

The new music business says that's a failing business model and one we will not follow. In the new music business, the artist picks his or her own songs and decides which ones should be on that life work called their album. The artist is the one who says "Let's give listeners a CD full of my best work, let's give them more tracks than they'll get from CDs from old school, and let's price our CD below all the others." The new school dictum is "Let's give 'em more than they paid for and let's make it better than they ever expected." Follow that model, and in the new music business you will succeed.

Lesson 2
Radio and Records: How to Play the Game

D uring the California Gold Rush of the late 1800s, people had dreams of a new life and new prosperity and a desire to follow their adventurous spirit to virgin territory where untold opportunities and possibilities awaited. It was a heady time when folks like you and me could strike it rich overnight. All one needed was an opportunity and a willingness to try.

Radio in its infancy was much like that. And back in the '40s, '50s, and '60s, radio was the first place that people who sang or played music went to for their big break. Disc jockeys were mavericks, and stations were often mom-and-pop operations that got just as much of a kick discovering new artists as the DJs who played their records.

Then it all changed. Not suddenly, mind you, but station by station, and under the radar. Corporations began buying up radio stations ("business units" as they call them), and each time they gobbled up a station, another piece of the great American dream was taken away. Untold numbers of artists and their music were silenced—many before anyone had the opportunity to hear their first note.

The business of radio has a long, checkered past, from the famous payola scandal of 1960, when disc jockeys like Alan Freed actually admitted taking money from record companies to play their artists, to today, where many say it's still done, only now through the back door. It may have a new spin, a new name, and a new set of players, but if you're an artist, you'd better have a lot of money if you want to get your song heard on the airwaves.

The Radio/Record Company Dance

I have many friends who work in radio, and they and many others in the music business completely agree on one thing: Radio is the ruler and the record companies are the servants. Let me give you an example. Did you know that, depending on the station and the market, a radio station only plays 15 to 30 different songs a day? Which songs do you think they keep recycling throughout each 24-hour period? You guessed it: the songs performed by stars on major record labels. When it comes to radio, however, things aren't all a bed of roses, even for the stars. A music industry insider revealed to me the little-known (and even less admitted-to) practice involving what is known as the "26-week cycle." Twenty-six weeks is the time it usually takes for a record label or independent promoter to get a new single pitched, placed on stations, and played regularly. Once placed on the rotation, the song will be played until the promotional money dwindles and/or the song loses chart position. Once either of those things happens, the song will be replaced on the station's playlist by the next potential hit. The typical cycle usually ends up taking about 26 weeks. The only way to keep a song on the playlist beyond that 26 weeks is to spend big-time promotional dollars.

Let's call our artist Superstar. Radio networks (i.e., companies and stations) tell Superstar's record company that they expect the label to commit major marketing dollars to promote Superstar's single. The more money Superstar's record company is willing to spend, the more buzz and enthusiasm for Superstar's record it'll likely create. The more buzz and enthusiasm that's created, the more people will listen to the song and request it on radio. The more people who listen to that station, the more money the station can charge per 30- or 60-second spot for advertising. (Never forget: Radio, like television, is in business to sell ads. Ads pay the bills and generate hefty profits for owners and shareholders. Music or talk is simply the product the companies use to sell ads.) Ah, but woe to the artist whose record company won't commit major marketing dollars to a new recording. Unless radio gets the dollar commitment it wants from Superstar's record label, Superstar's new single won't get much airplay. Of course, according to radio, the lack of airplay has nothing to do with the movement of promotional dollars from record label to radio. It's because focus group feedback and nonexistent call-in response have made it clear that audience interest is falling off. Get it?

And what happens if radio decides early on to stop playing Superstar's new single? Do you remember that "26-week cycle" I mentioned? Well, two of those 26-week periods equals one year (52 weeks), and it doesn't take a college degree to figure out that Superstar could very well have to wait until the next "26-week cycle" before radio is willing to consider his or her next single.

When I first heard people talk about this, I was shocked. Obviously it's inherently unfair to an artist whose song deserves a shot at being successful. But what's more, even for those who have sold gold or platinum and have come out with a new album filled with great songs, under this system, few Superstars will get the opportunity to have more than two or three hits a year.

One of my friends, a top-rated disc jockey in a major East Coast market, has said to me, "I can't even begin to tell you how much I want to play new songs, but I can't. I get new songs sent to me all the time from unknown artists. I hear great new songs (that never get played) from known artists, but it does little good, because I'm told what to play and what to say."

At the same time that the mechanics of how network radio operates have stayed the same—that is, they work to limit the opportunities for new artists as well as superstars with new releases to get their music heard—the business of radio has changed. The majority of all the radio stations in this country are owned by only a small number of corporations, and these companies all operate very much the same way.

Many big city stations owned by one of these corporations are run by computer-automated systems. Many of them use something called "voice tracking." Suppose you're listening to WWWW, Your City. You might hear the announcer say, "You're listening to the best of the '80s, '90s, and today on WWWW." However, there's a good chance that what you've just heard is a taped loop, and the announcer doesn't even live in Your City. Listeners in numerous cities and states may be listening to the same announcer at the same time you are! Everything you've heard has been planned, programmed, and produced in a city and state many miles away. Ever wonder why you don't hear those listener request lines anymore?

These corporations have program directors (PDs) who do lots of research. Some stations and markets do research and focus group testing locally; others do it nationally, and the results can impact the corporation's other stations in other cities, depending on station format. The radio corporations brag that decisions on what to play are not made at the top, and that the corporate office regularly has conference calls with its PDs across the country who tell them who's hot and who's not. But industry insiders tell me not to put too much stock in that. The big decisions—on what to play and when to play it—continue to be made at the top by the Chiefs, with the Indians, as always, simply following orders.

According to music industry insiders I've spoken with, the stations do too much research. Based on their "research," stations choose the playlists for their formats. Unless an artist is well known, with a sound that fits ideally into the demographic of their audience, his or her music will not be heard on these stations.

And good luck trying to break in a new artist. Even if you're a big name producer, you're all too likely to be told something like this: "Sorry, Mr. Famous Producer. Unless your new artist is male, has this type of sound and look, and can appeal to women in the 28 to 34 age group, we're not interested."

Radio stations speak of their research and audience feedback in terms of such things as "percentage of burn." One hundred percent burn, for example, would mean that 100 percent of listeners are tired of hearing a particular song. If Superstar's record test results in a 20, 25, or even 33 percent burn, that means that one-fifth to one-third of that station's listeners are not interested in hearing the song anymore. And not surprisingly, the station soon pulls the song off the playlist. Often this happens very quickly, certainly way before the artist and song have enough time to create significant listening impressions and get any "traction."

With ad rates skyrocketing beyond what many markets will bear, and with radio's corporate owners wanting more and more stations, all in the belief it'll create more revenue and save a business facing diminishing listeners and revenue, they don't see that the solution to their problems is staring them right in the face. To see this, they'd have to spend less time being bean counters and focus on the answer to the age-old marketing paradox question, "Are your actions dictated by what the numbers do, or do your actions dictate what the numbers do?"

Much like the magazine business, radio and record companies give listeners what they—a handful of people—"think" listeners want. Having few options to choose from, listeners can only pick the best of what they're given. And you'd better believe that radio and record labels support their actions by telling us, "See. We know what our listeners want. We've tested and these are the numbers that prove it." Duh.

What many listeners want radio and record companies to understand is that, given a broader choice of artists and music, they would be very likely not to choose those same old 15 to 30 songs that air each day. Could it be that capturing a larger audience of listeners is not as complicated as radio and record businesses say? Maybe it's as simple as this: By giving listeners more variety, you broaden your market and appeal, and by broadening your appeal, you increase your audience, which brings you more sales, and—this will get 'em listening—more profits?

I remember when I worked for a major FM radio station in Nashville. One day I was having a conversation with an artist whose independent label had invested over $250,000 in him (in recording and promotion costs) and was trying to get him a major record label deal. This artist had a terrific voice, good looks, and the right attitude, and his single had reached the 30s on the Billboard Country charts. Not too shabby for an independent release. When the artist's indy label pitched his package to a major label, one of the major label execs told them, "There's no audience on radio for this guy, and if there is I seriously question their taste." The indy label was shocked. However, the major record label exec knew how the radio game was played, and Mr. "I Cracked the *Billboard* Top 50" didn't fit into the pigeonhole. "Next."

Let's talk money. Don't worry. With this book, you're not going to need a fraction of the numbers I'm about to give you.

In today's radio, with few exceptions, it takes big money for the opportunity to get big results. How does $1 million to promote that new album grab you? But maybe you only have a single you want to get on the air. You better figure on setting aside about $200,000—per record you want played—just to get access to the airwaves. Here's how you get that access. You're going to hire an independent promoter.

The cost? Well, a good independent promoter's time and access channels don't come cheap. Some records cost less and some cost more, but the $200,000 number should put you in the ballpark. But before I hear you say, "OK, let's play ball," wait.

Like radio station corporations, there are only a handful of independent promoters who do the majority of the work. Their job is to get you access to the radio stations, provided that you have the look, the sound, and the demographic audience appeal the radio stations want. Independent promoters have great contacts with the stations and program directors throughout the country, and when you hire them, you're essentially buying the use of their Rolodex and time. Here's how they do it.

Years ago, the record companies created the independent record promotion business not only to free up their in-house staff from doing that work, but to circumvent the federal payola law which essentially states that it's illegal for radio station personnel to accept money for playing a song if that station does not tell its listeners it has accepted some sort of financial compensation to do so. It's the "independent promotions person," not the station, who gets paid by the label to promote its music on each radio station. And note the word "promote." It's by promoting the label's music, and not any specific song or artist, that the independent—and thereby the label and the radio station—get around the letter of the payola law.

Think of the independent record promoter as an exclusive gatekeeper without whom you can't enter radio's doors. The independent pays radio stations (fees can range from $50,000 for a smaller station to more than $350,000 for a major station in a big city) to be the exclusive facilitator between a record label and a radio station. The independent then becomes the one and only person the record label deals with to get its new songs and artists on the radio stations the independent has access to.

Whenever the independent promoter gets a song added to a radio station's playlist, depending on the size of market, an invoice is sent to the label for $500 or more. If a station picks up 100 new songs a year (a very conservative number), the independent promoter has made at least $50,000, and that's just for one station out of many that he or she may have on the roster. Add to that the extra money that the independent promoter makes by billing the label for "spins" (extra plays of a song), and "adds" (having a song added to a station's playlist), and you can see that the amounts paid out by labels are enormous.

One estimate puts the money paid to independent promoters at more than $100 million a year—that's roughly $2 million a week.

Depending on how big a radio breakout the label has planned for an artist's new record, it can conservatively pay independent promoters from $150,000 to over a million dollars—per single—just to get it on the air. And keep in mind that the money the labels pay to independent promoters comes with a no money back/no results (read: even if I don't get results, you don't get your money back) guarantee. Sound like a good investment to you? If you're signed to a major label, you might not think so, since the independent promoter's cost (or at least 50 percent of it) comes out of your pocket (i.e., your royalty) and is recouped by the label.

The music industry sources I've talked to know that the independent promoter/record label relationship is not a good deal for them, but say they have little choice. The promoters have just become too powerful to avoid dealing with. The radio stations have gotten too accustomed to receiving all these wonderful windfall payments, which they say they use to buy much-needed station equipment like promo remote broadcast vans and the like. (Sure they do.) The result is a system that's broken and needs a major fix—in a hurry.

Making Radio Work for You

I'm going to show you a strategy that'll let you use radio—even old-school radio—to your own advantage—and you'll be spending a lot less than $200,000 per song.

The key to making your music any sort of commercial success is to get it out there and into people's laptops, iPads, cars, stereos, smartphones and other digital storage players. Music fans need to hear you. One of the biggest obstacles for any new artist attempting to get a record deal is generating enough interest, or buzz. Buzz is the feedback that gives record companies the confidence that there is an audience for your music that will pay money for it.

The more buzz you have, the safer the record label feels in taking a chance on being able to recoup its investment in you.

So, how can you create that buzz and, perhaps, even get your music played on radio without a record deal? Let's begin by reviewing what makes radio work. Radio stations make money by selling airtime to advertisers. But radio stations can't get and keep listeners, or stay in business, if all they broadcast are commercials, so they have two products that they use to fill the time between commercials: talk and music. The more listeners a radio station attracts, the more money it can charge advertisers for airtime, and thus the more money it makes.

Now let's see what action you can take to make radio work for you.

Pay-for-Play

No radio station is able to sell every commercial time slot that it has available in a day. Airtime is like hotel rooms. Rarely does any hotel sell out every night of the week, and on any given night, the empty rooms represent potential profits the hotel has missed for that night. In radio, empty time slots that are not filled with an ad to play represent missed profits.

Keep that in mind as we talk about how to get your song played on the radio without your label—or you—paying $200,000 to an independent promoter who might succeed in getting you airtime if you had a record deal and if you fit all those guidelines that the record labels, independent promoters, and radio stations have.

But what if you bought your own airtime? That's right. What if you became an advertiser? What if you were to buy a 30-second or 60-second spot on a radio station, and the product that you were selling was you and your music? Can you do it? You bet you can, and it's cheaper and easier than you think.

Remember years ago when infomercials hit cable television? First there were just a handful that you'd see over and over again late at night. It was perfect for the cable companies, since they had all of this unused airtime to sell and they could generate some profit where there wasn't any before. For the infomercial product company, it was perfect, too, since it had access to a potentially huge market and was able to buy airtime to reach that huge audience dirt cheap. As the number of infomercials proliferated, the time slots that the stations allotted to infomercial broadcasting expanded, and now you see them all hours of the day and night, on hundreds of channels, selling everything from computers to exercise equipment. By the way, they also sell music.

Using the same strategy, we're going to have you putting together your product commercial and buying select airtime on the radio station to play your ads. Here are some basic ground rules.

Figure out what you can comfortably afford and stay within your budget.

The rates for a 30- or 60-second spot vary with the station and time of day it airs, so while we'd like to get on the top station in your city at the best time slot, for now let's start generating some buzz (and money for you) by hooking you up with one of the stations that plays music similar to yours and sells spots at a price you can afford.

The late night/early morning time slots are cheapest, so to begin, you'll probably want to buy ads that air during those time slots. When I was selling airtime for a major FM station on Music Row in Nashville, I was able to sell some ads for as little as $10 per 30-second spot (late nights and weekends) as an incentive to get advertisers to buy a block of ads or a package.

Stations will give you a better deal if you buy a block of time rather than just buying one ad every one or two weeks. Besides, people need to hear your music repeatedly before any kind of impression can be made.

Stations traditionally give a 10 to 20 percent discount off their normal book rate to agencies that buy airtime for their clients. So before you negotiate with a station, think up a name for your agency and ask the station to give you the agency rate. They will if you ask, but they won't if you don't.

Next comes deciding what music you're going to use. If you have a new CD, choose "stingers" (a few seconds of music—the "hooks") from two to three of your songs with the most commercial appeal. Get opinions from friends and associates as to which songs you should use. Many times we think we know which songs other people will like best, but in the end they choose something completely different.

Be sure to create your ad to fit the station's policies as to content and what you can and cannot say or sell.

Basic Calls to Action

Once you've picked out a station and a time slot, negotiated a rate, and know what you're going to use, you need to decide what you want people to do who hear your commercial. Paying for airtime to get your song on the radio is a start, but it doesn't put money in your pocket or build the business of You, Inc. It's also not what a smart businessperson does. You need to figure out a call to action, an end result that you want to achieve.

Here are two simple calls to action.

- Have a toll-free 800 number in your ad that listeners can call to order your CD.

- Ask listeners to request your CD at their favorite record store. Even if a store has turned down your CDs in the past, if people start asking for them—and they will when they hear your radio ads—it will be calling you to supply the store.

Here's what this strategy—buying airtime plus having a call to action—does for you. It:

- Immediately starts creating buzz, because now you're on the air and being heard by lots of people.

- Begins building an audience, and that audience can only grow the more your music is heard.

- Puts you in control of your music and your message. You created your music, and you can create any message that you want to help promote you and your music to the world.

- Gives you a major calling card to an open-ended number of radio stations that might have been reluctant in the past to air your ads, because now you're being heard, you're a paying advertiser, and you have an audience, and that audience will follow you to whatever station plays your music. Remember what I told you: The more listeners a station gets, the higher their ratings, and the higher the ad rates they can charge for airtime.

- Provides you with a major calling card to the record labels—should you ever decide you need one—since now you will have created the buzz they want. You have an audience, a fan base, and a following, representing big numbers and profits if the company decided to put major label marketing money behind you (which they would of course always recoup).

Another Call to Action: The "Power of 200" Letter and Request

Have you ever wondered how some special interest groups—people who vocally and physically rally behind a cause—manage to create such a stir and get so much attention when the silent majority is just sitting on their hands and watching? The fact is that successful special interest groups know that the silent majority is watching, and they give them something to watch. They know that public actions produce results, and they use such things as the media, protest demonstrations, public meetings, phone calls, and letters to achieve the results they want. Since this strategy is so effective, why don't we use it to generate even more buzz for you? Here's how.

It's all about impressions—having people hear your music and message enough times that they remember it. The road to making an impression that gets results goes like this:

Stage 1: No interest
Stage 2: Some interest
Stage 3: Acceptance
Stage 4: Embracing
Stage 5: Desire

Each time your ad is heard, your music and message move one step closer to Stage 5, people's desire to hear them. Once you've reached Stage 5, then you've made a powerful impression, and it's that type of impression that will get people calling a station. If enough people call, believe me, the station will listen.

How many calls are enough? You'd be surprised. Radio industry people tell me that if a station gets a few calls a day requesting a song, it takes notice. And when people keep calling, if the local program director doesn't have the power to insert a new song that's generating local buzz, he or she passes the word to the corporate programming director(s) who does have that power. It all goes back to understanding how the radio game is played. Radio's audience is listeners, and those listeners buy advertisers' products. If those listeners and advertisers don't get what they want, they get upset.

Now it takes only a few listeners to write letters and make phone calls to complain to the advertisers on that station that the station is not playing what they—the listeners (read: potential customers) want to hear. When listeners complain, advertisers become unhappy, not only because of the negative feedback they're receiving from customers (listeners), but from the lack of positive results they're getting from the money they're spending on ads on that radio station. When advertisers become unhappy, they let the station know. People are given new directives, and things are changed. And it doesn't take much to accomplish this. Both Senator Orrin Hatch (R–Utah) and former House Minority leader Richard Gephardt (D–Missouri) have told me that the power that letters from constituents have in influencing laws and actions in this country is significant. They also said that although it's amazing how few people actually take the time to write those letters, those who do, however, get listened to. Advertisers listen, too, especially if you put everything I've told you behind the Power of 200.

It's been said that when we add up our friends, their friends, and the friends of their friends, etc., each of us has potential access to roughly 200 people, give or take a few either way. It's also been said that if someone is happy with a service, they'll tell two people, but if they're unhappy, they'll tell ten.

I'm going to teach a strategy that can help you get your music heard on radio, and all you'll need is a few friends who will write letters and make calls to radio stations in your city requesting that your music be played. It's called the Letter and Request Strategy, and you'll be amazed at how little work it can take to get results. Just remember that few people write or call, and those that do, get listened to. It all begins with having the right commercial with your music, message, and call to action for people to hear.

Create the Right Ad and Start Small

If you're buying airtime at a radio station, one of the little-known services many of these stations will offer you, the advertiser, is to help you physically create and record your ad. When I worked in radio, I helped create and produce an ad with a business owner who had a single tire store. Hey, I don't know about you, but selling tires on the radio is not the most exciting kind of ad I want to hear. To top it off, this guy wasn't flashy or full of hype.

The tire-store owner had never recorded his own ad before, so I invited him into the radio station. I worked with him on an ad concept and script, but instead of using a professional announcer, I had him read his own ad, in his own voice, in his own way. He was 100 percent down to earth, laid back, and believable, and people loved him. The response he got was fantastic. People were not only buying his tires left and right, but also brakes, alignments, and other services he offered.

The bigger stations typically reserve their ad production service for their best-paying clients, so you may have to get help on your first ad at a smaller station. But that's okay, too, since once you get a great ad recorded—and all it takes is one—you can take that ad to any station, anywhere you want, and have them play it whenever you decide you want to buy more airtime.

The strategy here is to start off small, get on the air, and see what kind of response you get. Buy a few ads during the cheapest times in a station's schedule. (Along with "the agency rate," always ask for their "best package deal.") It may take a few weeks of people hearing your ad and music at, say, every Saturday night at 1:30 a.m., but they will respond. And each time they hear your ad, you'll make an impression, and the more impressions you make, the greater the probability they will act.

But don't stop there. Keep the momentum going, because as tough as it is to get started, once you do, it only takes a little action to keep it flowing. It's a lot like priming the pump. It takes a lot of pumping the well handle up and down to get anything to come out of the spout, but once it starts flowing, then all it takes is a little pump every now and then to keep it flowing.

Once the money starts coming in from people buying your product, I want you to earmark a portion of that money (10 to 30 percent) to buy airtime on another station in town. Go a step up in station rank and audience size. The ads will most likely cost more, but you'll be hitting a bigger audience for those higher dollars, with the potential for bigger results. I also want you to use a portion of that money to buy ads on the station you started with, but in earlier time slots and on different days and watch what happens.

Once you've done this, I want you to test your ad, music, and message (the "call to action") by looking at how many responses you received for the number of ad(s) and the time periods they played. If listeners have ordered CDs from your 800 number, how many did they order, and how many ads did they need to hear before they bought? If one of your ads asked them to request your CD at ABC record store (the "call to action"), how many ads had to play before ABC contacted you to order product? Always know how many ads need to be aired before action is taken, what the best times for them to play are, and what stations produce the best results for the money.

Do sequential tests, with clearly defined, simple parameters. For example, try looking at one month of ads playing on just one station at one time period. Then look at another month on that same station but in a different time period or perhaps a combination of time periods. If you find that a particular time period or combination of time periods is getting good results, stick with it until it stops getting results. When it does, you can either change your ad or try a different station. Start off slowly and find out what works and what doesn't. Refine your marketing plan using the tips I just gave you, and you'll be amazed at how quickly you and your music take off.

Stop and think about what you've done by using this strategy. In buying airtime on that first station, you instantly had access to the same station and the same potential audience that Superstar and his or her record label paid dearly for (did you write that $200,000 check yet?), and you've done it for a fraction of the cost.

To repeat: Always know your market and spend only the amount necessary to give you the results you want. Be smart. Be wise. Treat people right. Be a person of your word. Stay in control of your market, your image, and your music, and the rest will take care of itself.

Lesson 3
The Illusion of Needing a Record Deal:
Courtney Love's Real-World Wake-up Call

If you ever thought you needed to have a record deal in place before being able to make your mark in the music business, you need to think again. The media love to regale us with stories about how much money this artist or that artist has made. Yet what we're not told is how few musicians make it to the level of financial success, or who actually keeps the majority of Mr. or Ms. Superstar's hard-earned money. In case you've been on vacation, it's the record company.

Courtney Love may be known as an actor, a singer, a songwriter, and perhaps a bit of a lightning rod for controversy, but no one can ever say she doesn't tell it like it is. Especially when it comes to the record business and where all the money goes. The musical lineage of Courtney Love is one that brought her fame in her first group, the Minneapolis-based all-female punk band Babes in Toyland, and ultimately the recognition of being one of the most famous people in alternative rock.

Love, the singer and guitarist, started the band Hole in 1989, and in 1991 the band released its debut album, *Pretty on the Inside*. Its follow-up *Live Through This* hit platinum. However, things suddenly changed. Tragedy struck when the band's bassist Kristen Pfaff died from a heroin overdose.

Perhaps most people know Courtney Love for her now-famous relationship and marriage to the late Nirvana singer/songwriter/guitarist Kurt Cobain. Despite the downs of losing husband Kurt (who committed suicide) and bassist Pfaff, Love has always emerged as a fighter and has been able to reinvent herself (her image and appearance) whenever the situation called for it.

To this day, rumors about her drug use and her relationship with Cobain continue to swirl in gossip circles, but one thing is indisputable: Love's talent. Her first movie, *Sid & Nancy* (the story of Sex Pistols bassist Sid Vicious and lover Nancy Spungen), wasn't a big box office success, nor was her other film *Straight to Hell*, which was more like straight to video. But things would soon change.

Courtney received critical praise for her roles in such movies as *Man on the Moon* with Jim Carrey and *Feeling Minnesota* with Keanu Reeves and Cameron Diaz, and in 1999 she was nominated for a Golden Globe for her performance in the movie *The People vs. Larry Flynt*. Since then, she's continued to be outspoken in her support for the causes she believes in, and the rights of artists in the music business is one of the causes she believes in most deeply.

In May 2000, at the Digital Hollywood Online Entertainment Conference, an annual conference that brings together many of the biggest stars and players in entertainment, Love gave a speech that was quickly recognized as a devastating expose of the record business, Napster, and the Record Industry Association of America (RIAA). It was a time of huge popularity for Napster, unlimited downloads, and a music business desperately looking for a new way to do business. The speech pulled no punches. What Courtney Love had to say is about to open your eyes to the real world of the music business and how the math is done. What follows is an unedited transcript of Love's speech, reprinted with the permission of *Salon.com*.

Courtney Does the Math on Record Contracts

Today I want to talk about piracy and music. What is piracy? Piracy is the act of stealing an artist's work without any intention of paying for it. I'm not talking about Napster-type software. I'm talking about major label recording contracts.

I want to start with a story about rock bands and record companies, and do some recording-contract math: This story is about a bidding-war band that gets a huge deal with a 20 percent royalty rate and a million-dollar advance. (No bidding-war band ever got a 20 percent royalty, but whatever.)

This is my "funny" math based on some reality and I just want to qualify it by saying I'm positive it's better math than what Edgar Bronfman Jr. [president and CEO of Seagram, which owns Polygram] would provide. What happens to that million dollars?

They spend half a million to record their album. That leaves the band with $500,000. They pay $100,000 to their manager for 20 percent commission. They pay $25,000 each to their lawyer and business manager. That leaves $350,000 for the four band members to split. After $170,000 in taxes, there's $180,000 left. That comes out to $45,000 per person. That's $45,000 to live on for a year until the record gets released.

The record is a big hit and sells a million copies. (How a bidding-war band sells a million copies of its debut record is another rant entirely, but it's based on any basic civics-class knowledge that any of us have about cartels. Put simply, the antitrust laws in this country are basically a joke, protecting us just enough to not have to re-name our park service the Phillip Morris National Park Service.)

So, this band releases two singles and makes two videos. The two videos cost a million dollars to make and 50 percent of the video production costs are recouped out of the band's royalties. The band gets $200,000 in tour support, which is 100 percent recoupable. The record company spends $300,000 on independent radio promotion. You have to pay independent promotion to get your song on the radio; independent promotion is a system where the record companies use middlemen so they can pretend not to know that radio stations—the unified broadcast system—are getting paid to play their records. All of those independent promotion costs are charged to the band.

Since the original million-dollar advance is also recoupable, the band owes $2 million to the record company. If all of the million records are sold at full price with no discounts or record clubs, the band earns $2 million in royalties, since their 20 percent royalty works out to $2 a record. Two million dollars in royalties minus $2 million in recoupable expenses equals... zero! How much does the record company make? They grossed $11 million.

It costs $500,000 to manufacture the CDs and they advanced the band $1 million. Plus there were $1 million in video costs, $300,000 in radio promotion, and $200,000 in tour support. The company also paid $750,000 in music publishing royalties. They spent $2.2 million on marketing. That's mostly retail advertising, but marketing also pays for those huge posters of Marilyn Manson in Times Square and the street scouts who drive around in vans handing out black Korn T-shirts and backwards baseball caps. Not to mention trips to Scores and cash for tips for all and sundry. Add it up and the record company has spent about $4.4 million. So their profit is $6.6 million; the band may as well be working at a 7-Eleven.

Of course, they had fun. Hearing yourself on the radio, selling records, getting new fans, and being on TV is great, but now the band doesn't have enough money to pay the rent and nobody has any credit. Worst of all, after all this, the band owns none of its work. They can pay the mortgage forever, but they'll never own the house.

Like I said: Sharecropping. Our media says, "Boo hoo, poor pop stars, they had a nice ride. Fuck them for speaking up"; but I say this dialogue is imperative. And cynical media people, who are more fascinated with celebrity than most celebrities, need to reacquaint themselves with their value systems.

When you look at the legal line on a CD, it says copyright 1976 Atlantic Records or copyright 1996 RCA Records. When you look at a book, though, it'll say something like copyright 1999 Susan Faludi, or David Foster Wallace. Authors own their books and license them to publishers. When the contract runs out, writers get their books back. But record companies own our copyrights forever. The system's set up so almost nobody gets paid.

Artists, Copyright Law, and the RIAA

A Congressional aide named Mitch Glazier, with the support of the RIAA, added a "technical amendment" to a bill that defined recorded music as "works for hire" under the 1978 Copyright Act.

He did this after all the hearings on the bill were over. By the time artists found out about the change, it was too late. The bill was on its way to the White House for the President's signature. That subtle change in copyright law will add billions of dollars to record company bank accounts over the next few years—billions of dollars that rightfully should have been paid to artists. A work for hire is now owned in perpetuity by the record company.

Under the 1978 Copyright Act, artists could reclaim the copyrights on their work after 35 years. If you wrote and recorded "Everybody Hurts," you at least got it back as a family legacy after 35 years. But now, because of this corrupt little pisher, "Everybody Hurts" never gets returned to your family, and can now be sold to the highest bidder.

Over the years, record companies have tried to put work-for-hire provisions in their contracts, and Mr. Glazier claims that the "work for hire" only "codified" a standard industry practice. But copyright laws didn't identify sound recordings as being eligible to be called works for hire, so those contracts didn't mean anything. Until now.

Writing and recording "Hey Jude" is now the same thing as writing an English textbook, writing standardized tests, translating a novel from one language to another, or making a map. These are the types of things addressed in the work-for-hire act. And writing a standardized test is a work for hire. Not making a record.

So an assistant substantially altered a major law when he only had the authority to make spelling corrections. That's not what I learned about how government works in my high school civics class. Three months later, the RIAA hired Mr. Glazier to become its top lobbyist at a salary that was obviously much greater than the one he had as the spelling corrector guy.

The RIAA tries to argue that this change was necessary because of a provision in the bill that musicians supported. That provision prevents anyone from registering a famous person's name as a Web address without that person's permission. That's great. I own my name, and should be able to do what I want with my name.

But the bill also created an exception that allows a company to take a person's name for a Web address if they create a work for hire. Which means a record company would be allowed to own your website when you record your work-for-hire album. Like I said: Sharecropping.

Although I've never met anyone at a record company who "believed in the Internet," they've all been trying to cover their asses by securing everyone's digital rights. Not that they know what to do with them. Go to a major-label–owned band site. Give me a dollar for every time you see an annoying "under construction" sign. I used to pester Geffen (when it was a label) to do a better job. I was totally ignored for two years, until I got my band name back. The Goo Goo Dolls are struggling to gain control of their domain name from Warner Bros., who claim they own the name because they set up a shitty promotional website for the band.

Orrin Hatch, songwriter and Republican senator from Utah, seems to be the only person in Washington with a progressive view of copyright law. One lobbyist says that there's no one in the House with a similar view and that "this would have never happened if Sonny Bono was still alive."

By the way, which bill do you think the recording industry used for this amendment? The Record Company Redefinition Act? No. The Music Copyright Act? No. The Work for Hire Authorship Act? No. How about the Satellite Home Viewing Act of 1999? Stealing our copyright reversions in the dead of night while no one was looking, and with no hearings held, is piracy.

It's piracy when the RIAA lobbies to change the bankruptcy law to make it more difficult for musicians to declare bankruptcy. Some musicians have declared bankruptcy to free themselves from truly evil contracts. TLC declared bankruptcy after they received less than 2 percent of the $175 million earned by their CD sales. That was about 40 times less than the profit that was divided among their management, production, and record companies.

Toni Braxton also declared bankruptcy in 1998. She sold $188 million worth of CDs, but she was broke because of a terrible recording contract that paid her less than 35 cents per album. Bankruptcy can be an artist's only defense against a truly horrible deal and the RIAA wants to take it away.

Artists want to believe that we can make lots of money if we're successful. But there are hundreds of stories about artists in their sixties and seventies who are broke because they never made a dime from their hit records. And real success is still a long shot for a new artist today. Of the 32,000 new releases each year, only 250 sell more than 10,000 copies. And less than 30 go platinum.

The four major record corporations fund the RIAA. These companies are rich and obviously well-represented. Recording artists and musicians don't really have the money to compete. The 273,000 working musicians in America make about $30,000 a year. Only 15 percent of American Federation of Musicians members work steadily in music.

But the music industry is a $40-billion-a-year business. One-third of that revenue comes from the United States. The annual sales of cassettes, CDs, and video are larger than the gross national product of 80 countries. Americans have more CD players, radios, and VCRs than we have bathtubs.

Story after story gets told about artists—some of them in their sixties and seventies, some of them authors of huge successful songs that we all enjoy, use, and sing—living in total poverty, never having been paid anything. Not even having access to a union or to basic health care. Artists who have generated billions of dollars for an industry die broke and un-cared for. And they're not actors or participators. They're the rightful owners, originators, and perform-ers of original compositions. This is piracy.

Technology Is Not Piracy

This opinion is one I really haven't formed yet, so as I speak about Napster now, please understand that I'm not totally informed. I will be the first in line to file a class action suit to protect my copyrights if Napster or even the far more advanced Gnutella doesn't work with us to protect us. I'm on [Metallica drum-mer] Lars Ulrich's side, in other words, and I feel really badly for him that he doesn't know how to condense his case down to a sound-bite that sounds more reasonable than the one I saw today.

I also think Metallica is being given too much grief. It's anti-artist, for one thing. An artist speaks up and the artist gets squashed: Sharecropping. Don't get above your station, kid. It's not piracy when kids swap music over the Internet using Napster or Gnutella or Freenet or iMesh or beaming their CDs into a My.MP3.com or MyPlay.com music locker. It's piracy when those guys that run those companies make side deals with the cartel lawyers and label heads so that they can be "the labels' friend," and not the artists'.

Recording artists have essentially been giving their music away for free under the old system, so new technology that exposes our music to a larger audience can only be a good thing. Why aren't these companies working with us to create some peace?

There were a billion music downloads last year [1999], but music sales are up. Where's the evidence that downloads hurt business? Downloads are creating more demand. Why aren't record companies embracing this great opportunity? Why aren't they trying to talk to the kids passing compilations around to learn what they like? Why is the RIAA suing the companies that are stimulating this new demand? What's the point of going after people swapping cruddy-sounding MP3s? Cash! Cash they have no intention of passing on to us, the writers of their profits.

At this point the "record collector" geniuses who use Napster don't have the coolest, most arcane selection anyway, unless you're into techno. Hardly any pre-1982 REM fans, no '60s punk, even the Alan Parsons Project was underrepresented when I tried to find some Napster buddies. For the most part, it was college boy rawk without a lot of imagination. Maybe that's the demographic that cares—and in that case, My Bloody Valentine and Bert Jansch aren't going to get screwed just yet. There's still time to negotiate.

Somewhere along the way, record companies figured out that it's a lot more profitable to control the distribution system than it is to nurture artists. And since the companies didn't have any real competition, artists had no other place to go. Record companies controlled the promotion and marketing; only they had the ability to get lots of radio play, and get records into all the big chain stores. That power put them above both the artists and the audience. They own the plantation.

Being the gatekeeper was the most profitable place to be, but now we're in a world half without gates. The Internet allows artists to communicate directly with their audiences; we don't have to depend solely on an inefficient system where the record company promotes our records to radio, press, or retail and then sits back and hopes fans find out about our music.

Record companies don't understand the intimacy between artists and their fans. They put records on the radio and buy some advertising and hope for the best. Digital distribution gives everyone worldwide, instant access to music.

And filters are replacing gatekeepers. In a world where we can get anything we want, whenever we want it, how does a company create value? By filtering. In a world without friction, the only friction people value is editing.

A filter is valuable when it understands the needs of both artists and the public. New companies should be conduits between musicians and their fans.

Right now the only way you can get music is by shelling out $17. In a world where music costs a nickel, an artist can "sell" 100 million copies instead of just a million. The present system keeps artists from finding an audience because it has too many artificial scarcities: limited radio promotion, limited bin space in stores, and a limited number of spots on the record company roster. The digital world has no scarcities. There are countless ways to reach an audience. Radio is no longer the only place to hear a new song. And tiny mall record stores aren't the only place to buy a new CD.

Artists Have Options

Now artists have options. We don't have to work with major labels anymore, because the digital economy is creating new ways to distribute and market music. And the free ones amongst us aren't going to. That means the slave class, which I represent, has to find ways to get out of our deals. This didn't really matter before, and that's why we all stayed.

I want my 7-year contract law California labor code case to mean something to other artists. (Universal Records sues me because I leave because my employment is up, but they say a recording contract is not a personal contract; because the recording industry—who, we have established, are excellent lobbyists, getting, as they did, a clerk to disallow Don Henley or Tom Petty the right to give their copyrights to their families—in California, in 1987, lobbied to pass an amendment that nullified recording contracts as personal contracts, sort of. Maybe. Kind of. A little bit. And again, in the dead of night, succeeded.)

That's why I'm willing to do it with a sword in my teeth. I expect I'll be ignored or ostracized following this lawsuit. I expect that the treatment you're seeing Lars Ulrich get now will quadruple for me. Cool. At least I'll serve a purpose. I'm an artist, and a good artist, I think, but I'm not that artist that has to play all the time, and thus has to get fucked. Maybe my laziness and self-destructive streak will finally pay off and serve a community desperately in need of it. They can't torture me like they could Lucinda Williams.

I want to work with people who believe in music and art and passion. And I'm just the tip of the iceberg. I'm leaving the major label system, and there are hundreds of artists who are going to follow me. There's an unbelievable opportunity for new companies that dare to get it right.

How can anyone defend the current system when it fails to deliver music to so many potential fans? That only expects of itself a "5 percent success rate" a year? The status quo gives us a boring culture. In a society of over 300 million people, only 30 new artists a year sell a million records. By any measure, that's a huge failure.

Maybe each fan will spend less money, but maybe each artist will have a better chance of making a living. Maybe our culture will get more interesting than the one currently owned by Time-Warner. I'm not crazy. Ask yourself, are any of you somehow connected to Time-Warner media? I think there are a lot of yes's to that, and I'd have to say that in that case President McKinley truly failed to bust any trusts. Maybe we can remedy that now.

Artists will make that compromise if it means we can connect with hundreds of millions of fans instead of the hundreds of thousands that we have now. Especially if we lose all the crap that goes with success under the current system. I'm willing, right now, to leave half of these trappings—fuck it, all these trappings—at the door to have a pure artist experience. They cosset us with trappings to shut us up. That way when we say "sharecropper!" you can point to my free suit and say "Shut up, pop star."

Here, take my Prada pants. Fuck it. Let us do our real jobs. And those of us addicted to celebrity because we have nothing else to give will fade away. And those of us addicted to celebrity because it was there will find a better, purer way to live.

Since I've basically been giving my music away for free under the old system, I'm not afraid of wireless, MP3 files, or any of the other threats to my copyrights. Anything that makes my music more available to more people is great. MP3 files sound cruddy, but a well-made album sounds great. And I don't care what anyone says about digital recordings. At this point they are good for dance music, but try listening to a warm guitar tone on them. They suck for what I do.

Record companies are terrified of anything that challenges their control of distribution. This is the business that insisted that CDs be sold in incredibly wasteful 6-by-12 inch long boxes just because no one thought you could change the bins in a record store.

Let's not call the major labels "labels." Let's call them by their real names: They are the distributors. They're the only distributors and they exist because of scarcity. Artists pay 95 percent of whatever we make to gatekeepers because we used to need gatekeepers to get our music heard. Because they have a system, and when they decide to spend enough money—all of it recoupable, all of it owed by me—they can occasionally shove things through this system, depending on a lot of arbitrary factors.

The corporate filtering system, which is the system that brought you (in my humble opinion) a piece of crap like "Mambo No. 5" and didn't let you hear the brilliant Cat Power record or the amazing new Sleater Kinney record, obviously doesn't have good taste anyway. But we've never paid major label/distributors for their good taste. They've never been like Yahoo and provided a filter service.

There were a lot of factors that made a distributor decide to push a recording through the system:

How powerful is management?

Who owes whom a favor?

What independent promoter's cousin is the drummer?

What part of the fiscal year is the company putting out the record?

Is the royalty rate for the artist so obscenely bad that it's almost 100 percent profit instead of just 95 percent so that if the record sells, it's literally a steal?

How much bin space is left over this year?

Was the record already a hit in Europe so that there's corporate pressure to make it work?

Will the band screw up its live career to play free shows for radio stations?

Does the artist's song sound enough like someone else that radio stations will play it because it fits the sound of the month?

Did the artist get the song on a film soundtrack so that the movie studio will pay for the video?

These factors affect the decisions that go into the system. Not public taste. All these things are becoming eradicated now. They are gone or on their way out. We don't need the gatekeepers anymore. We just don't need them.

And if they aren't going to do for me what I can do for myself with my 19-year-old Webmistress on my own website, then they need to get the hell out of my way. [I will] allow millions of people to get my music for nothing if they want and hopefully they'll be kind enough to leave a tip if they like it.

I still need the old stuff. I still need a producer in the creation of a recording, I still need to get on the radio (which costs a lot of money), I still need bin space for hardware CDs, I still need to provide an opportunity for people without computers to buy the hardware that I make. I still need a lot of this stuff, but I can get these things from a joint venture with a company that serves as a conduit and knows its place. Serving the artist and serving the public: That's its place.

Equity for Artists

A new company that gives artists true equity in their work can take over the world, kick ass, and make a lot of money. We're inspired by how people get paid in the new economy. Many visual artists and software and hardware designers have real ownership of their work.

I have a 14-year-old niece. She used to want to be a rock star. Before that she wanted to be an actress. As of 6 months ago, what do you think she wants to be when she grows up? What's the glamorous, emancipating career of choice? Of course, she wants to be a Web designer. It's such a glamorous business!

When you people do business with artists, you have to take a different view of things. We want to be treated with the respect that now goes to Web designers. We're not Dockers-wearing Intel workers from Portland who know how to "manage our stress." We don't understand or want to understand corporate culture.

I feel this obscene gold rush greed…greed…greed… vibe that bothers me a lot when I talk to dot-com people about all this. You guys can't hustle artists that well. At least slick A&R guys know the buzzwords. Don't try to compete with them. I just laugh at you when you do! Maybe you could a year ago when anything dot-com sounded smarter than the rest of us, but the scam has been uncovered.

The celebrity-for-sale business is about to crash, I hope, and the idea of a sucker VC gifting some company with four floors just because they can "do" "chats" with "Christina" once or twice is ridiculous. I did a chat today, twice.

Big damn deal. 200 bucks for the software and some elbow grease and a good back-end coder. Wow. That's not worth 150 million bucks.

I mean, yeah, sure it is if you'd like to give it to me.

Music Is a Service to Its Customers

I know my place. I'm a waiter. I'm in the service industry. I live on tips. Occasionally, I'm going to get stiffed, but that's OK. If I work hard and I'm doing good work, I believe that the people who enjoy it are going to want to come directly to me and get my music because it sounds better, since it's mastered and packaged by me personally. I'm providing an honest, real experience. Period.

When people buy the bootleg T-shirt in the concert parking lot and not the more expensive T-shirt inside the venue, it isn't to save money. The T-shirt in the parking lot is cheap and badly made, but it's easier to buy. The bootleggers have a better distribution system. There's no waiting in line and it only takes 2 minutes to buy one.

I know that if I can provide my own T-shirt that I designed, that I made, and provide it as quickly or quicker than the bootleggers, people who've enjoyed the experience I've provided will be happy to shell out a little more money to cover my costs. Especially if they understand this context, and aren't being shoveled a load of shit about "uppity" artists.

It's exactly the same with recorded music. The real thing to fear from Napster is its simple and excellent distribution system. No one really prefers a cruddy-sounding Napster MP3 file to the real thing. But it's really easy to get an MP3 file; and in the middle of Kansas you may never see my record because major distribution is really bad if your record's not in the charts this week, and even then it takes a couple of weeks to restock the one copy they usually keep on hand.

I also know how many times I have heard a song on the radio that I loved only to buy the record and have the album be a piece of crap. If you're afraid of your own filler, then I bet you're afraid of Napster. I'm afraid of Napster because I think the major label cartel will get to them before I do.

I've made three records. I like them all. I haven't made filler and they're all committed pieces of work. I'm not scared of you previewing my record. If you like it enough to have it be a part of your life, I know you'll come to me to get it, as long as I show you how to get to me, and as long as you know that it's out.

Most people don't go into restaurants and stiff waiters, but record labels represent the restaurant that forces the waiters to live on, and sometimes pool, their tips. And they even fight for a bit of their tips. Music is a service to its consumers, not a product. I live on tips. Giving music away for free is what artists have been doing naturally all their lives.

New Models for the Record Business

Record companies stand between artists and their fans. We signed terrible deals with them because they controlled our access to the public. But in a world of total connectivity, record companies lose that control. With unlimited bin space and intelligent search engines, fans will have no trouble finding the music they know they want. They have to know they want it, and that needs to be a marketing business that takes a fee.

If a record company has a reason to exist, it has to bring an artist's music to more fans and it has to deliver more and better music to the audience. You bring me a bigger audience or a better relationship with my audience or get the fuck out of my way. Next time I release a record, I'll be able to go directly to my fans and let them hear it before anyone else.

We'll still have to use radio and traditional CD distribution. Record stores aren't going away any time soon and radio is still the most important part of record promotion. Major labels are freaking out because they have no control in this new world. Artists can sell CDs directly to fans. We can make direct deals with thousands of other websites and promote our music to millions of people that old record companies never touch. We're about to have lots of new ways to sell our music: downloads, hardware bundles, memory sticks, live Webcasts, and lots of other things that aren't even invented yet.

An Open Letter to Steve Case

But there's something you guys have to figure out. Here's my open letter to Steve Case:

> Avatars don't talk back! But what are you going to do with real live artists? Artists aren't like you. We go through a creative process that's demented and crazy. There's a lot of soul-searching and turning ourselves inside-out and all kinds of gross stuff that ends up on Behind the Music.
>
> A lot of people who haven't been around artists very much get really weird when they sit down to lunch with us. So I want to give you some advice: Learn to speak our language. Talk about songs and melody and hooks and art and beauty and soul. Not sleazy record-guy crap, where you're in a cashmere sweater murmuring that the perfect deal really is perfect, Courtney. Yuck. Honestly hire honestly committed people. We're in a "new economy," right? You can afford to do that. But don't talk to me about "content."
>
> I get really freaked out when I meet someone and they start telling me that I should record 34 songs in the next 6 months so that we have enough content for my site. Defining artistic expression as content is anathema to me.

What the hell is content? Nobody buys content. Real people pay money for music because it means something to them. A great song is not just something to take up space on a website next to stock market quotes and baseball scores. DEN tried to build a site with artist-free content and I'm not sorry to see it fail.

The DEN shows look like art if you're not paying attention, but they forgot to hire anyone to be creative. So they ended up with a lot of content nobody wants to see because they thought they could avoid dealing with defiant and moody personalities. Because they were arrogant. And because they were conformists. Artists have to deal with businesspeople and businesspeople have to deal with artists. We hate each other. Let's create companies of mediators.

Every single artist who makes records believes and hopes that they give you something that will transform your life. If you're really just interested in data mining or selling banner ads, stick with those "artists" willing to call themselves content providers.

I don't know if an artist can last by meeting the current public taste, the taste from the last quarterly report. I don't think you can last by following demographics and carefully meeting expectations. I don't know many lasting works of art that are condescending or deliberately stupid or were created as content.

Don't tell me I'm a brand. I'm famous and people recognize me, but I can't look in the mirror and see my brand identity. Keep talking about brands and you know what you'll get? Bad clothes. Bad hair. Bad books. Bad movies. And bad records. And bankrupt businesses. Rides that were fun for a year with no employee loyalty but everyone got rich fucking you. Who wants that? The answer is purity. We can afford it. Let's go find it again while we can.

I also feel filthy trying to call my music a product. It's not a thing that I test-market like toothpaste or a new car. Music is personal and mysterious. Being a "content provider" is prostitution work that devalues our art and doesn't satisfy our spirits. Artistic expression has to be provocative. The problem with artists and the Internet: Once their art is reduced to content, they may never have the opportunity to retrieve their souls. When you form your business for creative people, with creative people, come at us with some thought. Everybody's process is different. And remember that it's art. We're not craftspeople.

Corporate Sponsorships

I don't know what a good sponsorship would be for me or for other artists I respect. People bring up sponsorships a lot as a way for artists to get our music paid for upfront and for us to earn a fee. I've dealt with large corporations for long enough to know that any alliance where I'm an owned service is going to be doomed.

When I agreed to allow a large cola company to promote a live show, I couldn't have been more miserable. They screwed up every single thing imaginable. The venue was empty but sold out. There were thousands of people outside who wanted to be there, trying to get tickets. And there were the empty seats the company had purchased for a lump sum and failed to market because they were clueless about music. It was really dumb. You had to buy the cola. You had to dial a number. You had to press a bunch of buttons. You had to do all this crap that nobody wanted to do. Why not just bring a can to the door?

On top of all this, I felt embarrassed to be an advertising agent for a product that I'd never let my daughter use. Plus they were a condescending bunch of little guys. They treated me like I was an ungrateful little bitch who should be groveling for the experience to play for their damn soda. I ended up playing without my shirt on and ordering a six-pack of the rival cola onstage. Also lots of unwholesome cursing and nudity occurred. This way I knew that no matter how tempting the cash was, they'd never do business with me again.

If you want some little obedient slave content provider, then fine. But I think most musicians don't want to be responsible for your clean-cut, wholesome, all-American, sugar-corrosive, all-white-people, no-women-allowed sodapop images.

Nor, on the converse, do we want to be responsible for your vice-inducing, liver-rotting, child-labor-law-violating, all-white-people, no-women-allowed booze images. So as a defiant moody artist worth my salt, I've got to think of something else. Tampax, maybe.

Money as Incentive

As a user, I love Napster. It carries some risk. I hear idealistic business people talk about how people that are musicians would be musicians no matter what and that we're already doing it for free, so what about copyright?

Please. It's incredibly easy not to be a musician. It's always a struggle and a dangerous career choice. We are motivated by passion and by money. That's not a dirty little secret. It's a fact. Take away the incentive for major or minor financial reward and you dilute the pool of musicians. I am not saying that only pure artists will survive. Like a few of the more utopian people who discuss this, I don't want just pure artists to survive.

Where would we all be without the trash? We need the trash to cover up our national depression. The utopians also say that because in their minds "pure" artists are all Ani DiFranco and don't demand a lot of money. Why are the utopians all entertainment lawyers and major label workers anyway?

I demand a lot of money if I do a big huge worthwhile job and millions of people like it, don't kid yourself. In economic terms, you've got an industry that's loathsome and outmoded, but when it works it creates some incentive and some efficiency even though absolutely no one gets paid. We suffer as a society and a culture when we don't pay the true value of goods and services delivered. We create a lack of production. Less good music is recorded if we remove the incentive to create it.

Music is intellectual property with full cash and opportunity costs required to create, polish, and record a finished product. If I invest money and time into my business, I should be reasonably protected from the theft of my goods and services. When the judgment came against MP3.com, the RIAA sought damages of $150,000 for each major–label–"owned" musical track in MP3's database. Multiply by 80,000 CDs, and MP3.com could owe the gatekeepers $120 billion.

But what about the Plimsouls? Why can't MP3.com pay each artist a fixed amount based on the number of their downloads? Why on earth should MP3. com pay $120 billion to four distribution companies, who in most cases won't have to pay a nickel to the artists whose copyrights they've stolen through their system of organized theft?

It's a ridiculous judgment. I believe if evidence had been entered that ultimately it's just shuffling big cash around two or three corporations, I can only pray that the judge in the MP3.com case would have seen the RIAA's case for the joke that it was.

I'd rather work out a deal with MP3.com myself, and force them to be artist-friendly, instead of being laughed at and having my money hidden by a major label as they sell my records out the back door, behind everyone's back.

How dare they behave in such a horrified manner in regards to copyright law when their entire industry is based on piracy? When Mister Label Head Guy, whom my lawyer yelled at me not to name, got caught last year selling millions of "cleans" out the back door, "cleans" being the records that aren't for marketing but are to be sold. Who the fuck is this guy? He wants to save a little cash so he fucks the artist and goes home? Do they fire him? Does Chuck

Phillips of the *LA Times* say anything? No way! This guy's a source! He throws awesome dinner parties! Why fuck with the status quo? Let's pick on Lars Ulrich instead because he brought up an interesting point!

In Conclusion

I'm looking for people to help connect me to more fans, because I believe fans will leave a tip based on the enjoyment and service I provide. I'm not scared of them getting a preview. It really is going to be a global village where a billion people have access to one artist and a billion people can leave a tip if they want to.

It's a radical democratization. Every artist has access to every fan and every fan has access to every artist and to the people who direct fans to those artists. People that give advice and technical value are the people we need. People crowding the distribution pipe and trying to ignore fans and artists have no value. This is a perfect system.

If you're going to start a company that deals with musicians, please do it because you like music. Offer some control and equity to the artists and try to give us some creative guidance. If music and art and passion are important to you, there are hundreds of artists who are ready to rewrite the rules.

In the last few years, business pulled our culture away from the idea that music is important and emotional and sacred. But new technology has brought a real opportunity for change; we can break down the old system and give musicians real freedom and choice.

A great writer named Neal Stephenson said that America does four things better than any other country in the world: rock music, movies, software, and high-speed pizza delivery. All of these are sacred American art forms. Let's return to our purity and our idealism while we have this shot. Warren Beatty once said: "The greatest gift God gives us is to enjoy the sound of our own voice. And the second greatest gift is to get somebody to listen to it." And for that, I humbly thank you.

Lesson 4
A View from Both Sides of the Fence: Steve Lukather on What's Right and What's Wrong with the Music Business

Steve Lukather. Where do I begin to tell you about this guy? As a guitar player, there's no denying the inspiration and soul that pours from his fingers to the six strings of his instrument. His playing has influenced and will go on influencing untold numbers of people all over the world. Yet, if you ask Luke, as friends call him, he'll tell you he's not that good and he's one lucky mutha to earn a living—albeit a good one—at playing the guitar for people.

Luke, of course, is a cofounding member of the band Toto, which sold over 27 million records. As a solo artist, he's sold many more records on his own.

Then there's that little thing he did in his life called doing sessions. In the course of Luke's studio journeys, he's played on over 1,000 records, including hits by almost every major musical artist in the last 30 years. He's been nominated for a Grammy 12 times, and has won 5 of those little prized statues.

But all of this means little to a man who values family and friends above all, is thankful every day for the Gift of Life, and whose philosophy encompasses such feelings as "Live for today," "Enjoy every moment," "Deny yourself nothing," "Have a great time," "Try to be nice to people," and always "Try to leave a little love behind."

Luke is a guy who's been around the block a time or two. He also has a unique perspective on the music business, since he has been a successful recording artist on both sides of the fence, winning Grammys both as an independent and as a major label artist. He also knows how to put things in perspective on how the old music business works—or doesn't—why music is where it is today, and, most importantly, why you need to be thinking and doing things differently in today's new music business.

As Luke likes to say, "I'm old school," and it's his old school education that's about to teach you some new school lessons on becoming the success you were meant to be.

Lukather on the Music Business, Yesterday and Today

When I was first starting to play music, it used to be that people practiced and tried to get really good at whatever instrument they played. Nowadays, it seems most people could give a rat's ass. All my peers—Van Halen, Satriani, Vai, Landau, all the A-level cats—practiced their asses off to get really good, and today, hardly anyone cares about being a great musician anymore. I wish someone would've told me this 25 years ago so I could've stopped all the hours of practice and had more fun [laughs].

Right now, I still get up and practice every day because I still care and it's because I love playing the guitar and what I do. I mean, I do it because first and foremost I care about it for myself. I don't care how many years I'll play the guitar, I'll never have it all figured out. Not even close. And that's what I like about it because it's always a challenge to see if I can become just a little better today than yesterday. God gave me whatever talent I have—and thank God it was playing the guitar because I ain't the prettiest mutha you've ever seen—and I try each day to make the most of it.

I have a recording studio where major record producers work, and would you believe that the most important person on the gig is not the musicians? It's the Pro Tools guy. These young muthas come into the studio with the attitude that "I'm all this or that" and yet they can't play four bars in time. And when it ain't working on the session, they'll say, "Screw it. Go ahead and Pro Tool it and it'll be cool." That's their excuse for not becoming a good player.

When I was a kid, I spent 10 hours a day trying to get my shit together just so I could be good enough to get asked to play on one record, which maybe might get me a second record. And now, people who practice, people who truly care about the music and less about technology, are considered a bunch of old assholes.

Let me tell you something. I was in Toronto jamming with an old pal named Jeff Healy and I got invited to a Rolling Stones rehearsal. These 60-year-old players started their rehearsal at midnight and there I was sitting there watching them like a kid with cotton candy and a hard-on [laughs]. When I heard them play "Satisfaction" and "Start Me Up," those 60-year-old guys sounded better than anything I've heard in the last 20 years. They had the fire, they had the attitude, they were laughing, they were partying, they were just groovin'.

Say what you will about my man Keith, but he was playing his ass off. And when Mick sang, I actually called my home answering machine and held up my cell phone to record how great they sounded, to have a memory of being there and inspired.

I've been doing sessions since I was 17 years old. Back in the old days, they didn't have machines that did everything, like they do today, and you actually had demo sessions. There'd be singers, songwriters, piano players, acoustic guitar players who were trying to get record deals, and there were lots of demos going on. I was making 25 dollars a tune and that was great money then.

That was where we all got our practical knowledge about how you play on sessions, how you get your sound, and all that good stuff. There was a wealth of work back in those days from 1975 to 1985. During that 10-year period, I played on over 1,000 records.

When I was doing sessions, each day that I'd come into the studio was always a surprise. I'd ask, "So who's playing on the record today? Steve Gadd is playing drums. Awesome! Anthony Jackson on bass. Who's on keyboards? David Paich. David Foster. Incredible. Lenny Castro is playing percussion and me and Ray Parker or Dean Parks or Jay Graydon or Larry Carlton is playing guitar? Excellent." The exciting question each day I walked into any studio was always, "Who am I playing with today?"

And it was fantastic, as many, many times, we'd immediately begin writing this record for whoever singer/songwriter we were working with who came into the session with three chords on a piece of paper and no demo and we'd all write and rewrite the song just like that. We were arranging and rewriting this guy or gal's material every day. That was what we got hired to do. And even though being a studio musician was a thankless gig, it was still fun.

I played on records of every musical hero in my life, from the lamest singer/songwriters to Miles Davis to Paul McCartney and every major artist that's been on the music scene in the last 30 years. And you know how it all started? I began doing those 25-dollar-a-song demos and those led to a bigger gig which led to a bigger gig and it just sort of snowballed from there. It was word of mouth.

I was lucky enough to grow up with the Porcaro brothers, and Jeff Porcaro (the late legendary drummer) was doing Steely Dan sessions when I was in high school. Guys I grew up with and began playing gigs with, like David Paich's and Jeff Porcaro's fathers, were A-level studio musicians, and that was a powerful influence and inspiration. That inspired me to learn to read music and do whatever I needed to do so I could play on everybody's records.

I could go on and on about the incredible experiences I've had playing on records. I remember one record date with Elton John where Elton and I are sitting at the piano drinking cognac and there he was playing "Levon" for me. I was 20 years old and having the time of my life, and you know, I'm still having the time of my life playing music.

Early on, I got hooked up with some great people like Boz Scaggs, and did his world tour and all the records that followed. Of course, there were many times in the studio when we were tested when the unexpected happened. Like the time when we played on Michael Jackson's "Beat It" and Eddie Van Halen had come in and cut the tape and screwed up the whole SMPTE code and Jeff Porcaro and I had to put the whole record together without producer Quincy Jones (a guy I truly love working with) in the room, and would you believe, that record ended up winning record of the year.

I can't even begin to tell you how many times we pulled producers' asses out of the fire. So many times we were doing all this arranging—and not getting credit or money for it—while this or that friggin' producer was in the bathroom snortin' blow or taking Quaaludes or passed out on the studio couch.

Or... guys who will remain nameless—who were the head of record labels for the biggest record companies in the world—didn't even show up to their own sessions when they were producing. They'd walk into the studio when we were finished and say, "Wow, that sounds great. Where do you want to go for dinner?"

Many, many times they'd come into the session early or late and after one or two takes, they'd say, "Great, that sounds perfect... next" when in fact, we were just getting things started and could've given them far better takes. Meanwhile, they're up there on the stage accepting their Grammy awards with the attitude "I'd like to thank no one because I'm a genius."

These are the same people whose asses we'd pull out of the fire time and time again. Guys who never gave us any extra taste—i.e., money—or credit for what we did. I'm talking about guys who are heads of major record companies right now, that if you put a gun to their friggin' head and told them, "You play me a C scale right now or you're dead," you'd have a bunch of dead record company people, because they couldn't do it. And these are the people who are in charge of the music business and the music that gets made today, and we wonder why the record business is so screwed up.

Think of it: If you're the head of all the doctors in a hospital, chances are you're going to be one of the best doctors. You're the go-to guy. But if you're the head of a record label, chances are you're not only one lucky bastard, but you're also not the best guy for the job, you're also not a musician, you also don't have much of a musical background, and your typical plan of action is "Let's fire 5,000 people, so we can show shareholders great numbers and a profit and while we're at it, why don't we give ourselves millions of dollars as a bonus."

I'm old school. I mean I was crushed when I found out the Monkees didn't play on their own records. That's when I found out about studio guys like Tommy Tedesco and all the others who played on those records. Then I found out about the Motown guys. Do you know who played on all those records? Those Motown session guys and they got 25 bucks a tune!

I mean c'mon, where do you want to start with the Motown shit? There were 25 guys in the studio and everything was going down live. It was when music was real, instead of today of "Let's Pro Tools everything into oblivion."

You can hear Pro Tools on the radio today. I can hear the shit. I mean they auto-tune this or that to the point as soon as you hear some dude singing, you know that mutha couldn't sing "Happy Birthday" in tune if his friggin' life depended on it. What the hell is that all about?

I keep going back to the old school because that's where the inspiration and soul still is. Listen to The Beatles and The Rolling Stones. They're playing live. Those records are what happened when they pressed the red button and heard "One, two, three, four." Compare that to today. You go and see those artists on MTV live and few of them can play. I'm talking about "play" their instrument. My kids and their friends come back from these concerts and say, "Dad, it was weak."

Today, there is no session scene. It's dead, it's gone. Today, all you need is Pro Tools in your house and if you can't play it, no problem we'll fix it. We'll tune it. We'll make it in time and we'll cut and paste your parts so you don't have to play them again and possibly mess things up.

The day of the session player is gone. Bye-bye, nice talking to you. Unless you're doing TV and film, you can forget about all those big recording dates like we used to do not too many years ago. Even top call A-list players are not making a living being session players. They're taking high-paying road gigs.

People often ask me how has music changed and I tell them that it's no longer necessary to become a good musician anymore. Seems like some people who are making music today will accidentally trip and fall down on a sound, and if that sound turns into a hit record, then you're labeled a genius.

Whereas, with the people I grew up with, we actually sat in a room for hours at a time—with fingers numb and bleeding—as we took vinyl LPs and lifted the needle off the record to learn Eric Clapton solos from "Crossroads," all the while driving our parents crazy from lifting it (the needle) up and down just so we could learn every freakin' lick.

Today, people who do that kind of shit are considered pompous old pricks because the attitude of today's musicians is that all that shit really doesn't matter 'cause you don't need to do it to create a hit. Technology and not talent is their crutch and solution.

It is getting so hard to find good musicians anymore. It really is. Perhaps that's why I have more affinity for jazz musicians than I do rock musicians, even though I'm not a jazz musician because I'm not good enough. Call me a rock guy with jazz aspirations.

I look up to cats like Pat Metheny, Mike Stern, Scott Henderson, Michael Landau, and these kinds of great players who set the bar a little higher, but aren't household names because we live in an Eminem world. Jazz guys may not make a million dollars or sell a million records but they can inspire you. For jazz, it's always been the old joke, How do you make a million dollars playing jazz? Start with five million.

For years, people have believed that if only you could have a hit record, then life would be wonderful, but thinking like that is going to get you in big trouble. You see, it's not as hard as people think to have a one-hit record. But let me tell something, having a one-hit record is not going to make you a millionaire, and you're still going to be in debt to the record company. And even if your record hits gold (sale of 500,000 units), you're still in debt to the record company. Make that deep in debt.

To give you an idea of how things work, let's go back to "old school." Old school in my day is when they had big budgets for records. They'd give you half a million dollars to make a record. That's when we used to play on sessions and when they used to hire human beings to make music instead of computers to play on records.

We used to get double-scale rates to be in the studio and come up with ideas while the drummer took 2 or 3 days to get a great drum sound. It was a shameless display of wealth, the total opposite end of the spectrum, whereby there was too much money to make records. Nowadays, people do records in their house for one hundredth of the budget.

However, even though the way music is made has greatly changed and the pendulum has swung from excess money to do it, to now doing it on a budget in your house, what cats today are missing is the human element and soul in their music and creation.

That's what's going on right now. Record companies are dying and it's a dead scene. And you know what? They [the record labels] deserve to go out of business because they make too much friggin' money for doing friggin' nothing and promoting the mediocrity that we call "music" these days.

And the negative influence of many of the magazine music critics on promoting the music we have today isn't any better. I ask you, why does it seem that the magazine music critics seem to like the music of artists that they can play themselves, which is why they almost always critique the lyrics, as opposed to the musicality or musicianship of the records they review?

I can say this shit now, because I've been in the game close to 30 years and the critics already hate me for telling it like it is, so what am I going to do, piss them off? Who cares? If they'd be honest and tell things like they were, then you wouldn't be hearing me rant.

But it's not just me, some old school geezer, that knows the story. You should hear my teenage kids and their friends. They read so many of the bullshit magazine music reviews about this or that artist and where time and time again they say, "Man, that magazine and the artists they promote are so lame." They know the difference between who sounds good and who doesn't and they know the reality of what's happening in music right now, and let me tell you, it ain't pretty.

People today don't have an idea of how the music business works. All they see on TV is reality shows where people are turned into stars in weeks and given million-dollar recording deals if they win the show. They see other music stars display excesses of wealth and think the music business is the easy road to big money. My friend, it ain't true.

Let me give you an example. I love this MTV show called *Cribs*. Let me just say that I don't like MTV, as I think it's one of the big reasons for music's downfall, but the show *Cribs* is a powerful wake-up call for musicians who want to be stars.

First of all, I would bet you that half the people featured on *Cribs* rent the fabulous house for the day to show off their shameless grotesque show of wealth. Then, after the cameras are packed up and gone, these "stars" go back to their two-bedroom apartment and wonder why they aren't making any money from the record label.

And I'll go a step further. I'd also be willing to bet that most of those "stars" have yet to see the bank statement from the record label that says you're making money. For the handful of them that are making money, I've heard story after story of them living the good life for a few years and a few years later, they're friggin' broke, they're back in their little apartments and people saying, "Who the hell were you?"

Musicians and Their Craft

Let me give you a little advice: As soon as you have a little success, get ready for people to start bashing you and your music. It happens to anyone. But always stay true to your music and your art and you'll be fine. Over the years, the press hated our group, Toto. They'd make up stories about the band that weren't true and they were gunning for us.

Maybe it was the name, who knows? The reality is, between 1980-84, our band Toto was the house band that won the album, song, and producer of the year at the Grammys. We also played on more than 100 of the records that were nominated for Grammys within those 3 years. We were the go-to band to hate. I laugh at the shit now because even though people hated us, we were good enough to play with Paul McCartney, George Harrison, and Miles Davis and had a discography that people tell us is staggering.

And even with all the press and critic bashing, talk about musicians who loved their craft. Even all these years after his passing, there isn't a day that goes by that I don't think of my buddy, Jeff Porcaro.

Not only was his charisma so deep that people would call him "God's drummer," he would walk into the room and the room would light up and everything got better. He always had the coolest clothes, the coolest music, he was always the guy that found the newest shit to listen to.

His groove was so deep. He could take a piece of shit tune on a session and turn it into something you could really groove with. And he could turn something that was great into something that was really great. He was just special in that way.

Everyone looked to Jeff for the okay and direction. I mean the biggest friggin' record producers in the world would look to Jeff and ask, "Is that the take?" and he'd say, "Yeah, that's the one, man."

I'm telling you, we'd be on sessions playing some suck ass tune that wasn't going anywhere, with all of us just wanting to leave, and we'd look over at Jeff and he'd get a groove going and get that big smile on his face and wink at me and say, "We're out of here in like 10 minutes" and we'd know he would always find the right groove that everyone loved.

I've worked with a lot of really great famous people, yet I still get giddy like a kid when I see and hear greatness. I mean, I was once sitting next to Miles Davis and he was playing one of my songs and my weenie was so hard I could cut diamonds with it [laughs]. I was listening to greatness.

But today, thanks to the record labels and who they and radio promote, we have rock stars and wannabe rock stars, who, if they're lucky, will have 5 years of fame. Check back in 5 years, when there's a good chance you'll see them down at the club or bar, drinking to forget their problems and telling anyone who'll listen, "Yeah, my wife took all the money and I'm not really good enough to play with other musicians and I used to be a rock star, so screw you all." None of them are good enough to make a career as a musician, but they're rock stars.

Anyone can be a rock star. In one day, I taught my son how to play the guitar. Gave him a drop D tuning, plugged him into a little mini Marshall amp, gave him some distortion, showed him a few chords and one riff, and an hour later, he was playing everything he was listening to on MTV. He's a rock star I tell ya.

I gave a clinic at MIT [Musician's Institute of Technology] and I asked the people there, how many of you want to be rock stars? They all raised their hands. Then I asked them, how many of you want to be working musicians who do studio gigs, play Bar Mitzvahs, weddings, club dates, and everything else that blue-collar musicians play? Would you believe only two of them raised their hands?

I never wanted to be a rock star or some guitar guy that people put on a pedestal. All I ever wanted to be—and still want to be—is a working musician. I'll play on anybody's record. Call me up, pay me, I'm there.

Signing with a Major Label or an Independent

People often ask me what's the difference between being signed on a major label or doing the independent label thing? First of all, if you are signed to a major label, they will bleed you big time. If you sell 2 million records, you'll still be in debt to them for 3 million dollars, because you have to pay for the record, pay for the producer, pay for the rehearsal time, pay for the musicians, pay for the video, pay for tour support, and pay, pay, pay.

The testimony that Courtney Love gave about the record business [Lesson Three] is absolutely a fact, and she spoke for a lot of people. Hey, a platinum record [sales of 1 million units] means nothing. It's like a friggin' bowling trophy.

I know because I've lived it. I've sold over 27 million records in my life and the only thing I can say about that is "Show me the money! Where's all the friggin' money?" People think that by selling that many records I should be wiping my arse with hundred dollar bills, but I'm still waiting for that day to happen.

People mistakenly believe that if they can have a one-hit record and sell a million copies, then they're going to have money and the good life and I'm here to tell you, if you're playing the major label game, it ain't going to happen. It's a lie, and anybody that buys into that is a fool.

Don't tell me there's no payola out there when it costs you a million dollars to get on the radio. The record business is the most corrupt business—next to politics—in the world. C'mon, cats that are running the business can't play music, yet they think they know better than anyone else how to sell music!

They actually believe they know what's going on and they buy into their genius. Yet, look what all that genius has done to the record and music business. Guys that know nothing about the music business are getting promoted onward and upward. It's because of them that music sucks now, and the record business is in the shitter and my prediction is, in 5 years, the record business as we know it today will not be around.

Look at what happened with recording artist Robbie Williams, where they paid him in the neighborhood of 80 million dollars. His record label fired more than 1,000 people, yet the record executives gave themselves a bonus. Meanwhile, their quarterly profits are down and their losses are in the tens of millions of dollars.

The artists never see the money. Robbie Williams means nothing to them except over in Europe where he's a big name. They can't give the shit away in Asia and the United States, but that 80-million-dollar deal to sign him and fire all those people and have the company willing to go bankrupt because of this guy was deemed a good deal? Who made that decision? I want that guy to manage my career, that is, if I'm looking to quickly run it into the ground. The whole friggin' record business is smoke and mirrors.

Anyone who is signed to a major label right now is a fool. What you need to do right now is become independent. You make your record and then you license it to a major company who can help you get it into the stores. You will make 10 times the royalty rate doing it the independent way and you own it at the end of 7 years.

I was signed to Sony Records for 25 years, and I had a 1977 royalty rate when records cost 7 dollars. When record prices bumped up to 15 dollars, guess what? Our royalty rate didn't get bumped up. We were still making the 1977 royalty rate of 1 dollar 20 cents a record.

And we still owed money for all those videos the record company made us shoot and pay for that no one would ever see. All that shit still had to be recouped from any record sales. And we had to do it and we had to pay for it because the record company was afraid of not having a video they hoped MTV might play.

If you're a musician and you want control of your career and your life, then you need to make sure you own everything you do. You mark my words that 5 years from now, major record companies will not exist anymore. They will become major distribution outlets for independent music.

All these rap guys got it right a long time ago. Guys like Master P own their shit and they're making 5 bucks a record. They sell 100,000 units and they make $500,000. They make enough money so they'll have the money to promote themselves and their artists so that people you've never heard of can enter the charts at number one.

These guys are smart. My respect, my thumbs up, goes to all these cats, these rappers, who said, "Screw the white man and his record company games. Why is that mutha making more money than me?"

These guys figured it out and they took their music and message to the streets where they were telling everyone, "Hey, dig this new record." By the time the record hit the stores, all these people were already hip to it and were already playing it in their cars. These rappers gave the shit away just to get the word out. Now that's smart. They know how to promote. They know how to work it. They are the really smart ones and I have so much respect for them.

Keeping It Real

Whatever you do, however you want to create, record, and promote your music, always keep it real. I love the underdog story. Take Norah Jones. You gotta love this chick. A few years ago she was an unknown and she's still living in the same apartment, yet she's a real musician. Same with Diana Krall. She's great. She's a schooled musician who loves playing music.

I'm a Grammy-voting member and I left half the voting ballot blank this year because I never heard of some of these people. I mean, c'mon. Are the people who made the ballot list the best we've got? I wanna see real shit. Norah Jones. Real. Bruce Springsteen. Real. Arif Marden. Real. I've worked with him for years. He's real, he's a genius, and he's a guy that knows how to put it all together.

Friend, how fast or slow or how technical or nontechnical you can play means nothing. Whether you can read music or not doesn't matter. I don't care if you can only play three notes. All that matters is how you play those three notes and if it's real and if they come from deep inside your heart and soul.

It's all about your soul, your sound, your aura, your heart, your spirit, and your touch coming out through your music. It's not about the gear. It's not about the latest technology. It's not about being signed to a major record label. It's all about letting "you" come through in your music. When you do that, you will be in the company of the greats, and you're going to be someone I'm going to dig listening to.

Making a Hit Record

If I knew what makes a record a hit, I'd be writing this to you from my yacht taking a colonic, but the truth is no one knows for sure. Half the hit records I've played on—and there have been a lot—I'd think they sucked, but lo and behold they'd become hits. Who knew?

You don't have to be on a major label to have a big hit. I'd say, do it with your own independent label, because you're going to have complete control of your music, you'll own your creation, and you'll make a boatload more money.

And you need to realize that you don't even need a hit record to be a musical success. If you're doing what you love to do, perhaps able to make a little money at it, and you're loving your life, then in my book, you're already a great success.

By all means, use technology to help you create your own "real" music, but don't get hung up on technology and worrying about what kind of guitar, amp, or little blue wire Mr. Rockstar has in the back of his effects rack. All of that shit means absolutely nothing and almost everyone could care less.

It's all about the song. Some of the greatest songs the world has ever heard and are still timeless (like Motown or any of The Beatles's work) were done without all the high-tech computers and software you have today. It's not about the technology. It's all about the song. It's about the music. It's about your soul. It's about keeping it real.

Enjoying Your Gift of Music

The musical road you travel down always turns out to be way different from the one you originally thought you'd take. And in the end, it's all good, even though at the time, you could be going through some experiences that really suck.

Over the years, I've had many great successes and many great disappointments, yet through them all, I've always kept a few things about life in perspective: Live for today. Enjoy every moment. Deny yourself nothing. Have a great time. Try to be nice to people. Try to leave a little love behind. Small little gestures make you feel good inside. Respect others. My friend, all the fame and fortune don't matter. It's about caring for the people who care about you.

My parents thought I was insane in 1967 when I was 10 years old and announced I wanted to be a musician, as I held up Jimi's [Hendrix] album *Are You Experienced* in my hand. I've never wanted to be a rock star, but always wanted to be a lifer who played music from that magical day until the day I die.

I'll be the first to admit that I'm an overpaid guitar player who's a happy guy that's mystified by my own success and is grateful to any and everyone who has been and will be important in my musical road and this journey and experience called Life.

In the big picture of life, what I do is insignificant. It really is. I mean, c'mon. We don't know if we'll be here tomorrow, and a long time ago I stopped caring about the little stupid things that used to upset me. Really, what we've got to do is enjoy the moment.

I care nothing about material things. What matters to me is not how many Grammys or awards I get or what the critics say. What matters most is my family and my friends. Everything else is expendable. That's my philosophy: Everything in life is fleeting except the people I truly love and care about. I love my family. I love my friends and everything else is just bullshit.

I know I'm blessed and so lucky to do what I do. I mean for heaven's sakes, I'm a guitar player and able to earn a good living at what I love to do. What more do I need?

Websites: Toto99.com and Stevelukather.net

Lesson 5
Building Your A-Team: Who You Need
and Who You Don't

If you want to take your music out of the bars and into a bigger market, you need a good team behind you. A good attorney and CPA can save your money and maybe even your hide. Along with an attorney and CPA, you may think that you need a manager or an agent. But as you read through this lesson, you'll be surprised how many doors you can open by yourself—and save some money to boot.

So who do you really need and how do you find "the good ones" for your team? The road to success in the music business is littered with bad experiences, broken promises, and a lot of money gone up in smoke chasing the "You're really going to make it, kiddo" come-ons tossed out each day to the wanting-to-believe by the conniving.

Attorneys

We live in a litigious society. No longer are the courts viewed as a place where big corporations battle big corporations. If two people can't resolve a dispute to both parties' satisfaction, then civil court is often the next place they'll meet.

Thank goodness for attorneys! While there's plenty to not thank them for (e.g. huge damage awards that have helped drive insurance costs through the roof), when it comes to having the law on your side, it's tough to do without a good attorney. That's why you need the right attorney on your team, one who can make sure you're legally protected, both personally and professionally. He or she can help you structure and negotiate good deals and prevent you from getting into bad ones.

There are some first-class attorneys who do great work and truly care about helping their clients succeed. Of this I am absolutely sure, and in a moment I'll tell you how to find them. You also need to be aware that there are some attorneys you should absolutely stay away from, and you need to know how to differentiate between the two. You need to know how the legal game is played as well.

The first must-have member of your A-team is going to be an attorney, but not just any attorney. You want what is known as an entertainment attorney, one whose specialty is music, media, and entertainment. As you'll soon read, lots of lawyers call themselves entertainment attorneys, but only a handful are both true specialists in the field and also of the caliber you want on your team. But first, you should understand how attorneys operate and how they charge for their time. Attorneys either charge a flat fee (say, $500 to draw up a simple agreement), or a commission or percentage (if they think you've got serious star power potential), or on an as-needed/per-hour basis, or a combination of any or all of them. It's the as-needed/per-hour basis I want to tell you about first.

It's All About Billable Hours

If your attorney is charging you by billable hours, it means that every time you call him or her, the clock is ticking—just like a cab driver who turns on the meter as soon as you get in the cab. You're being charged for every minute of your attorney's time, and it goes something like this:

Attorney: Hi Matt (20 dollars). How have you been? (25 dollars).

Matt: I've been good, thanks. I just wanted to see if you heard from that record label about our demo we sent to them?

Attorney: Well, Matt (30 dollars), I put in a few calls to them and the A&R's assistant told me (35 dollars) they were out of town this week, but they'd be back in touch next week and let us know (40 dollars) what they think.

Before you've spent 60 cents on your call, you've just racked up 40 bucks worth of attorney charges you could've used for 2 months of Webcasting access or new gear.

You see, attorneys (especially the ones who work for the big firms with prestigious addresses, great-looking offices, and lots of attorney names printed on their letterhead) have a huge monthly nut. As much as they come across as wanting to be your buddy, they are paid to do one thing, and that's produce income for the firm. And unless they're in litigation, winning lawsuits and jury awards, or on retainer doing work for big companies, they're watching the clock and billing—big time—for every minute they're working for you. A lot of them have a quota they've got to meet of billing × number of hours for the firm, and if they don't meet it, they're out on the street looking for another job.

Music is a big money business, and the major players want to deal with those who already have deals, will soon be getting deals, or need help getting out of deals. Rarely will the handful of "My Calls Get Taken by Record Label Presidents Every Time" attorneys ever get back to you unless you can make the cash register ring (for them and the record company executives who'll take their calls) in a big way.

Many firms ask for an up-front advance fee for work they are promising to do. You have to be very wary about agreeing to such a fee, especially if it is preceded by promises of a big financial return for you. The following story illustrates what can happen if you are not careful.

One of my companies owned some rare video footage of a very famous person, and at some point we found out it had been pirated and copies were being sold all over the country by some of the biggest retailers out there. I called one of the largest music and entertainment law firms in Los Angeles and asked about handling our case. Their response was classic. Here's how it went:

RW: Hi, my name is Robert Wolff. My company owns Famous Person video and we have gathered evidence from a number of sources that such and such and so and so have been illegally manufacturing, distributing, and selling our intellectual property. I'd like to discuss the merits of our case with you.

Big Name Law Firm: We've got you on speakerphone Mr. Wolff, and we have (attorneys) Mr. X, Mr. Y, and Ms. Z here. We'd like to know how long this has been going on and how much money you estimate this has cost you.

RW: We just found out about it a few months ago, and based on the preliminary research we've been able to do, they've been illegally selling our property for over a year. Until we can find out the full extent of the piracy, it's going to be difficult to come up with a figure of damages.

BNLF: Well, based on what you've told us thus far, it sounds like you've got a strong case. You could be entitled to anywhere from $_ to $_ for damages for violation of this copyright statute, along with $_ to $_ for damages for that copyright infringement, plus other damages.

RW: Well, that's interesting. What do you suggest as the best way for us to proceed?

BNLF: We think the award for damages if a suit is filed and it goes to court—but it most likely won't and would be settled out of court—could be quite significant, and possibly much more than the figures we just quoted you. We'll do a search within the firm to make sure there is no conflict of interest and that we do not have the companies you named as our clients. If we don't, then we'd need you to send us $5,000 to get started.

RW: And what will that $5,000 cover?

BNLF: Probably a couple of calls and a couple of letters to "cease and desist" to the people who are infringing your copyrights and illegally selling your property.

RW: What if we find that there are more people involved in illegally selling our property than we know about now?

BNLF: That would obviously cost more. But you would also have excellent potential to collect even more money in the settlement.

RW: Tell you what. The more I think about this, sure, we can pay you $5,000 now, and perhaps another $5,000 a little later, but it's really unfair to you guys.

BNLF: What do you mean?

RW: Well, think about it. If you took our case on a contingency basis, you'd get a percentage—say one-third—of any damages and money we recovered, and with the numbers you just quoted, your firm stands to make far more money than if we just pay you $5,000 or $10,000. This is a real win-win for our company and your firm.

BNLF: [After a long silence] We'll have to talk about it and get back to you. What are your telephone and fax numbers?

The next day, I received a fax from Big Name Law Firm saying that they had to devote their resources to cases they were already busy with, so "regrettably" they could take our case only if we paid them a flat fee up front. So much for having a strong case with a big money payoff potential.

Finding and Hiring the Right Attorney

The point of the story I just told is that before you enter into any agreement with an attorney, you've got to weed out the fast talkers, quick promisers, and "I can do it for you's." The first step is to compile a list of likely candidates. Then you've got to put each one through your own Pass This Test before you trust them with your time, talent, and money.

There are a number of ways that people in the music business find others in the business:

- Friends, referrals, and contacts in the business. If they're in music, they either have an attorney or know someone who does and can get that attorney's name for you.

- Trade publication stories naming attorneys involved in deals made or cases won.

- Mainstream media news or else feature stories in which attorneys are involved.

- The Internet. Check out two sites in particular: Lawyers.com is a website devoted to helping you find attorneys anywhere in the United States. It lists those who specialize in various aspects of the law, including entertainment and music. The site has a search engine that lets you choose the type of attorney you need, and once you type in the city where you'd like to find one, it gives you a listing in that area and information about each. The second good Internet source is on abanet. org, the official website of the American Bar Association (the granddaddy organization to which all legit lawyers belong). It's easy to find lots of references for your area or for any area you wish. Go to the organization's home page, point and click on General Public Resources, click on Find Legal Help, and you'll be directed to their Help page, which will offer Hiring a Lawyer, Online Lawyer Referral, Handling Legal Matters Yourself, Legal Information Services, and more.

Once you've got a list of attorneys who advertise themselves as music/ entertainment attorneys, you need to narrow it down. Here's how you need to deal with anyone who's a potential candidate to be your attorney:

Make sure they are not a music/entertainment firm in name only. Ask how long the firm has specialized in music/entertainment law and ask to see their client list.

Check out their client list. Make sure it's current. I know some "music/ entertainment" attorneys who proudly list the names of clients on their websites who haven't been clients of theirs for many years. Believe me, there's a reason why these people aren't their clients anymore. Find out why. Be alert.

Ask them for references. Specifically, ask them for names of three people or companies who are current clients whom you can contact to get feedback about the work their firm did for those clients.

Ask them to tell you about three of the most recent deals they've made. Who were they with, and for what? A reputable attorney (while being ever mindful of attorney/client privilege and privacy) won't mind telling you about recent success stories that he or she is proud of. They don't need to divulge dollar amounts and deal details. Those should remain private. The good ones will have a file full of successes. The turkey attorneys? Well, they'll have a file full of "that deal almost happened."

Get It in Writing

Some attorneys do not like putting things in writing because written agreements can come back and bite them on the ass. You need to get attorneys to make a written, signed commitment to you that they can be held to. The good ones won't have a problem with this. The ones who do should be immediately crossed off your list.

The first thing you need to get in writing is the basis of your agreement. Ask them to put the following five things in writing:

- What specifically they will do for you.

- How long it will take and when they will begin. Put a completion deadline on it.

- How they will do it.

- What they will need from you in order to do the things they're promising they'll do.

- How much everything will cost. There should be no surprises, or "Oh, by the way's," or "I forgot to tell you's" coming back at you.

Let me tell you another quick story—another one involving piracy—from my company's personal files about how not getting things in writing can end up costing you big money.

We were referred to a "great attorney" by a friend (usually, but unfortunately not always, referrals by friends are good starting points in finding someone) who told us Mr. Attorney was a specialist in the entertainment field.

We called him at his swanky law firm in Los Angeles and told him that we had discovered that a group of infringers was ripping us off and we wanted him to go after them.

Oh, man, after we filled him in about our case, this guy came on like a tiger with big teeth, ready to go after those bad people and get us the lost income we deserved. We were stoked! He said he would look over our files as well and register whatever additional papers needed to be filed in order to bring us up to date and totally protected. He also said to send him a check for $3,000. So we did.

After weeks of Mr. Attorney's calls and letter writing to the infringing party, he bluntly told us that they were digging their feet in the sand and were not going to budge anymore on their offer of restitution. All this after telling us that, based on his years of experience with similar cases, he believed we could expect to receive an amount five times greater than the amount he said they were now being very firm on. Imagine our surprise. When we asked him how things were going regarding the papers he said he was filing for us, he assured us everything was on track.

So another month goes by and nothing's happening, and this guy is asking us to send more money so he can continue! We thought, continue what? His time and money-wasting with no results? So we fired him. Canned him that day. We told him to send all our files back, along with the confirmation of the papers he had filed for us, and to stop his "negotiations" with the infringing party.

The next day, I contacted the infringing party's attorney directly and informed her that we had fired our attorney and that all negotiations were to be done between her, myself, and my partner. Within a week, we had settled out of court for more than three times the money and "best deal" Mr. Attorney said he had been able to get. My dealing with the other attorney was smooth, and based on what she told me, far more enjoyable for her than dealing with the abrasive and seemingly incompetent goofball we had just fired.

This got us thinking: If one attorney is being so negative about another attorney (and usually attorneys don't talk crap about other attorneys unless there is something really wrong), just how competent had this guy been in carrying out our instructions to him to file the papers we asked him—and paid him (up front)—to file? As it turned out, not very.

After nearly three months of letters, calls, e-mails, and faxes demanding the return of our files, Mr. Attorney finally did send them back (after we had to provide our FedEx number so that he wouldn't have to pay for it). It wasn't until two years later that we discovered that he hadn't filed the papers correctly. In the end, his errors and incompetence ended up costing us tens of thousands of dollars in recoverable damages from future copyright infringers.

Needless to say, since that time we've hired a group of top-notch entertainment attorneys (not based in Los Angeles, thank you) who have us protected six ways to Sunday and they are worth every cent we pay them. The best ones always are. Never forget that.

Negotiating a Fee

You've located a good attorney, so now what? When you're first starting out— perhaps you haven't lost enough money yet or been stung enough times through other people's lies, or you've fallen for the pompous windbags who love to tell you what you want to hear—any kind of negotiation may seem overwhelming. But don't worry. It's a piece of cake, especially if you understand a big factor that motivates attorneys, and everyone else in business— making money.

If you can make an attorney some money, then you've got a listening ear and a new best friend who'll have you wondering where in the world they've been hiding all these years. You want your attorney to make money. This is only fair and right. They have dreams. They have a family. They have a business, and they should be paid for helping you. However, you don't want to give away the farm.

If you've traveled to a foreign country and shopped in the stores and outdoor markets, you know how the negotiation game is played. You see something you like, ask the owner how much, and they give you a price. You tell them the price is too high, and then they tell you they will lower it. This back-and-forth bargaining goes on for a while, until the owner says that his or her last price is the lowest they can go. If it's still not the price you want, you begin to walk out of the store. However, just as you almost reach the door, they yell at you to come back and—big surprise—they can go a little lower.

It's all about testing limits: theirs and yours. Their job is to sell you their services at the highest price, and your job is to buy it at the lowest price. The middle point is where they've come down low enough and you've raised your offer high enough so that both of you can walk away happy.

In the business of You, Inc., regardless of whether you're shopping for an attorney, a CPA, an agent, or anyone else you'll either be making money for or giving money to, always remember that you don't get what you want; you get what you negotiate. And the better your negotiation skills, the more value you'll receive, and the wiser businessperson you'll become.

Almost every negotiation involves some trade-off. If you're in negotiations to use an attorney's services, the attorney may say he or she is quoting a "firm" price, but nearly everyone will negotiate from that price. He or she may say, "We charge $200 an hour and we need you to pay us a starting retainer of $1,000 within 30 days," to which you might counter, "I can pay you $175 an hour and a $500 starting retainer today." That's today money, that's a done deal, and don't be at all surprised when they say, "Okay, when can you come in?"

It's all about give and take: You give a little, they give a little. Anytime anyone wants something from you, don't just give it to them. It's a fact of human nature that things quickly and easily gotten are likely to be less appreciated and more quickly taken for granted—like your music and your life. It's also a fact of human nature that the more we have to work for things, the more we appreciate and value them.

So make your attorney work for whatever he or she is getting from you. After all, you've had to work your butt off many long years and long hours to get to where you are right now. Chances are slim that anyone, anywhere, will ever call you or knock on your door one day and say, "Gee, you're so talented. We'd like to give you money and opportunities just for being you." Be sure to write me if that happens.

Setting Deal Parameters

Being the wise businessperson you're now becoming, you already know what kind of deal you want and don't want. You want the best terms, you want the most money for your services and product, and you want to give up the least amount necessary to make the deal happen. You also want to feed your attorney a script that he or she should follow. Understand that no one knows, wants, or understands your dreams better than you. And no one can sell you better than you. This is your life. Don't give the keys to your future to anyone for any reason.

Never give a blank check to an attorney—or to a CPA, manager, agent, or anyone else who's "going to be looking after you." Whenever an attorney is negotiating something for you, be absolutely certain that he or she knows what you want and don't want in your deal. Make sure that everyone who works for you understands that unless you're happy, they don't get paid.

For any deal you're thinking of getting into, tell your attorney your must-haves as well as your would-like-to-haves. The must-haves are points you will not and cannot budge on. If you don't get those must-haves—if the deal is asking too much from you, doesn't feel right anymore, or is no longer keeping you excited and happy—you won't make the deal.

The would-like-to-haves are negotiable points that would be great if you can get them but it won't be a deal killer if you don't. This is ammunition that your attorney needs for those give-and-take negotiations with the other party. Just like our street vendor in that foreign country, the seller is the party with whom your attorney will be negotiating, and you are the customer who walked in. Always remember that you can just as quickly walk out the door if the price and deal are not right.

Giving your attorney your dealmakers and breakers also saves you a wad of cash. No longer will you be paying for their "get me up to speed" educational lesson at $200 or more per hour. He or she will have a specific understanding of what must be negotiated, and the results that must be achieved, and won't be charging you for chit-chat/feel-good calls back and forth with the other party "to see what they are offering."

Good attorneys know that time is money, and the more time they take with you, the less time they have to spend with their other clients who are bigger, richer, and more famous (for now) and can bring in more money. Do yourself and your attorney a favor: Know exactly what you want, write it down, explain it in precise detail, reach a mutually acceptable fee and performance arrangement, and let him or her help get you that deal.

When You Need an Attorney— And When You Don't

Have you ever heard the story of an artist or band who decided that they didn't need an attorney when they signed their music and lives away, and for the next 20 or so years they were stuck with such a bummer of a deal that their attorney, manager, agent, and practically everyone else they dealt with made more money than they did? Better get out your calculator, because you don't have enough fingers and toes to count how many times this has happened in the music business.

Stories like this used to be more common than they are today, but they still happen. In the past, artists' contracts and deals were closed books that only the privileged few were privy to, so you just needed to trust that your attorney, agent, and manager were getting you the best deal possible.

Thank goodness that's not the case anymore. Now, if you want to see what a record contract, management deal, or other legal document looks like, you can go to the Internet and do a search on Google. In a matter of seconds, you'll have your pick from hundreds, if not thousands, of them to look over and learn from. This brings me to a subject many have asked me about: What should I use an attorney for and what can I do on my own?

Think of attorneys as people who protect you. They are the guard dogs who stand at the gate of your future, and anyone who wishes to enter has to first get past the guard dog. Guard dogs protect you and keep people from taking things from you, unless of course you knowingly or unknowingly neutralize your guard dog and give something away.

In addition to offering guard dog services, legit music and entertainment attorneys will have a Rolodex of names and contacts that can be worth far more than the hourly fee they charge. Music, like any business, is all about networking and contacts, and the more people you know who know people who know people, the better chance you have of getting what you want and making your dreams come true.

Here's a list of areas in which you may or may not need the services of an attorney, depending on the circumstances.

Copyrights. You can always register your own copyrights. Any music you create will be a copyright intellectual property that is yours, and there's a good chance that someone, somewhere down the road will rip you off. It happens every day, so get used to it. But you can protect yourself and your composition from the get-go by having it formally registered, in writing, with the copyright office. It's quick, it's cheap, it's easy, and in Lesson 12, I'll show you how to do it. In the meantime, keep this in mind:

After you receive your "filed" copyright papers back from the copyright office, you need to file those copyright papers away in a safe place.

Make at least two copies that you can keep in different locations. If you ever need them, you'll have them, and it'll be just the evidence and protection you'll need to protect your songs and your income and to recover damages from those who need a big bank-account-draining lesson should they or anyone else ever rip you off.

Down the road, if despite your meticulous registration procedures people are stealing your property, you will need an attorney to take charge of going after them.

Goods and services. When you're making minor purchases, like supplies and gear, obviously you don't need an attorney holding your hand and running "the meter." For those types of purchases, save your money and negotiate the best deals by yourself. Likewise, for simple equipment repairs, there's no need for an attorney to be standing next to you. However, if you're thinking of signing any kind of contract, including leasing a car, equipment, an office, or a home for your business, you want your CPA (more about them in a moment) and your attorney looking things over and making absolutely certain you're not locked into something that can come back to bite you in the ass down the road.

For services beyond straightforward repairs—such as a photographer shooting photos for your album cover or an engineer who's mastering your record—you can use a standard release and work-for-hire agreement. You can also have your attorney write one for you which you can use anytime in the future, saving yourself fees down the road. Another source for useful agreements is legal forms books, which you can find online or in your local bookstore. My advice is that if your budget allows, go the attorney route. You can probably get an attorney to provide you with a release and work-for-hire agreement specific to your needs for a couple of hundred dollars. If you prefer do-it-yourself, look at several of the online or in-print forms and check to see whether they cover all the bases. Bottom line: Always seek competent legal counsel before signing any legal forms.

Deal negotiation. This is the area where too many people spend too much money needlessly bringing in an attorney too quickly. The "let's get things started" call they're making on your behalf could just as easily be made by you, saving yourself a few hundred dollars. At $200 or more an hour, that gets to be expensive chit-chat.

The bottom line is, make the calls and talk to the people who are interested in doing business with you yourself. Keep those conversations going between you and them until you reach the point where you no longer feel comfortable doing it on your own, where the conversation and deal are now above your head and beyond your level of understanding. That is the ideal place to bring in an attorney. And for heaven's sake, do not orally promise or sign anything unless and until an attorney has looked everything over and given you the legal okay to proceed.

Great Advice and Free Stuff You Can Get in Seconds

The Internet makes it easy for you to do many things you used to need an attorney for, such as getting answers to legal questions. You can also get tons of information and downloadable agreements and contracts for free. Check out the following four sites before you go spending hundreds of dollars in attorney fees for answers you might get for nothing.

Nolo.com. This is an excellent site with loads of information on a variety of legal topics. It includes a reference library of articles, free legal forms, dictionaries and encyclopedias, and answers to over 400 of your legal questions.

Legaldocs.com. I'm all for saving you lots of money, so if you're looking for a terrific place to find legal documents that you can simply download, print out, and complete yourself, look no further than Legaldocs.com. You'll find plenty of free legal documents along with others that can be downloaded for a very small fee.

Law.com. If you're looking for a website that can give you a quick and very basic understanding of the law, your rights, self-representation, and a host of other topics, then check out this site. It has just about everything you could ask for (easy topic menus, links to lots of other law-related sites and information) to get you up to speed in a hurry.

Lawinfo.com. Let's say that after you've created your music, filed your copyright registration, and done all the right things that I just told you about, you find someone or some company ripping you off. They've sold your song all over the place without asking or telling you, and now you need an expert to tell you what that song is worth, and to put a figure on how much they've damaged you. Would you know where to look? Your attorney most likely will (the great ones always do), but how about you? Click on this site and you'll find all the legal expertise you'll need.

For more information, answers to questions, resources, documents and links about copyrights and U.S. Copyright Laws, check out the following five sites:

Law.cornell.edu. This site is maintained by the Legal Information Institute of Cornell Law School. You'll find lots of full-text documents, including the U.S. Code; U.S. Constitution; the Code of Federal Regulations; federal, state, and international laws; and directories of lawyers, organizations, and journals.

Loc.gov. This is the main site of the United States Library of Congress. There's plenty of information on this site, including an exhaustive database on U.S. copyright law.

Iu.edu/copyright/resources.shtml. This site, the Copyright Management Center from Indiana University, has lots of good copyright information, including a Copyright Quickguide with basic information on protection, registration, rights, ownership, and duration.

Benedict.com. This website covers some of the same ground as the Cornell and Indiana sites, but it also has interesting cases of copyright use and infringement involving celebrities.

Weblawresources.com. This website features information on protecting your copyrighted works on the Internet. It offers packages (some with more than 50 legal form documents for the Web, copyrights, etc.) that you can purchase for a fraction of what it would cost to have them each created by attorneys. However, the site advises that you secure competent legal counsel to review your documents prior to use.

Good CPAs: Worth Their Weight in Gold

The second must-have member of your A-team is a good (emphasis on good) accountant. For the sake of keeping things simple, I recommend that you find a CPA (certified public accountant), as CPA experience, training, and certification are the skills you want when it comes to keeping your taxes at a minimum and the records of your money coming in and going out up-to-date and precise.

A good CPA can offer advice and services that can help you become and remain wealthy. All CPAs deal with numbers, and in your world that means income and expenses. The more money you make and the less money you spend, the wealthier you become. It's that simple.

But knowing what to do with your expenses and how to treat your income can make all the difference in just how much money you keep and how quickly you'll reach financial independence. A good CPA knows this. A good CPA also knows the latest tax laws and deductions (which change all the time), and how those laws and changes will affect you and your business. If you would rather spend your time making music than studying tax code, the fees you pay to your CPA are a wise investment.

Over the years, I've met many people who fill out their own tax returns. They think they're saving money, but when they add up the cost of their time to learn the newest tax laws; the number of hours they spend going over all the previous years' records of income, expenses, and deductions; the frustration of not knowing whether they took the right deduction and filled out the forms correctly (and then sometimes having the IRS send back the return because it was filled out incorrectly)—when all is said and done, they're losing money big time. This is money and time that could've been saved (with the difference invested!) by letting a CPA do it. Not just any CPA. As you're about to read, the right CPA.

A Cautionary Tale

The music business of a friend of mine had enjoyed a blockbuster year. It took him years of struggle and small paydays before his name and his business finally paid off and his phone was beginning to ring off the hook. Although he knew he had the makings of a good year, it wasn't until its end, when he finally got a breather and had an opportunity to sit down and look at his bank account, that he nearly fell out of his chair—he had had a great year. He had made more money in that one year than in the previous 8 years combined.

My friend needed some help, though. Not in spending his money, mind you—he was already great at that—but taking advantage of all his expenses and deductions to minimize his taxes. Because he was now in a new city and devoting his business to music, he believed he needed someone who specialized in music business.

One day, during a phone call to a friend also involved in music, he mentioned that he needed to find a CPA who was a music specialist. Without hesitation, his friend gave him the name of someone he had heard was excellent. My friend called Mr. New CPA. Everything sounded great. The CPA specialized in the music business, had a large staff, and had lots of industry clients. New CPA told my friend that his firm would be perfect for what he was looking for, as it was "right down our alley" and "the very thing we do each day."

Within a few weeks, my friend had gathered all his papers, invoices, check stubs, bank statements, and records and sent them to New CPA, along with a detailed letter explaining his business and his purchases and expenses for the year. He called New CPA's office and told them that everything was on the way. "Perfect" he was told; they'd get back to him soon.

Weeks went by. No call. No letter. No e-mail. No fax. My friend started getting concerned, so he called them. He was told that New CPA was "out of town," but he'd be given the message. My friend sent e-mails, then more e-mails. Still, no reply. After two more weeks, he received a reply from New CPA apologizing for the delay in getting back to him as "things have been just crazy this time of year." Another two weeks went by and he received a call and message from New CPA with news that he had my friend's taxes ready and wanted to go over the numbers with him. He quickly called New CPA and the conversation went like this:

> **Friend:** Hi. This is Friend. I got your message that you wanted to go over my tax returns and some numbers with me.

> **NCPA:** Hey, How's it going? Sorry for not getting back to you sooner. Things have just been such a &!$#*! around here. We've been swamped.

> **Friend:** No problem. What did you come up with?

> **NCPA** [sound of fumbling through papers]: Just a second. I thought I had your returns right in front of me. Damn. Where in the heck are those. [long pause] Ah... there they are. Okay, here are the numbers. Your company made x dollars last year. You had x in expenses and you owe x(here gives a number in the tens of thousands] dollars to the IRS and x [thousands of dollars] to the state."

> **Friend:** You can't be serious!

> **NCPA:** Yeah, man, I'm sorry but that's the way the numbers came out.

> **Friend** [still in shock]: What about all the expenses I had? The equipment I bought?

NCPA: Sorry. I took everything you sent me and that's what came out. Hey, look at the bright side; you've just had your best year ever and with your income, it'll be easy for you to get a mortgage. I'll go ahead and put everything in the mail to you. Oh, and I'll also send you my invoice and would appreciate if you could pay it as soon as you can. Talk to you soon. By the way, start getting this year's tax receipts together and send those to me so we can get started on those.

Friend: Yeah, sure. Talk to you later.

After he hung up with New CPA, my friend felt really angry—both with the numbers he had just heard and with the whole experience of trusting his business and financial (and dare I say, emotional) life to a firm that had more clients than they had time for and treated their new client like the number he certainly felt he had become.

When the "taxes due" forms arrived a week later, instead of signing and mailing them, my friend decided to get a second opinion. He called a CPA he knew who had done his taxes in the past but wasn't a "music CPA" and told his tale of woe. "Old" CPA told my friend to send him everything and let him take a look at it.

About two weeks later he got a phone call, and it went like this:

OCPA: Hi. I've had a chance to go over everything. Are you sitting down?

Friend [thinking he's going to owe even more money]: Yes.

OCPA: First I'd like you to verify that you had major equipment purchases [names them], laid out major dollars for business-related travel [names a big number], and had x [another big number] business expenses last year.

Friend: Yes. All of that.

OCPA: Well, New CPA failed to record any of those in the categories they needed to go in.

Friend: How could that be?

OCPA: It looks to me like he just didn't spend the time to give you the attention your business and you deserve.

Friend: Geez, I knew there was something wrong.

OCPA: I hope you're still sitting down, because you owe $40,000 less than New CPA said you did.

Friend: Are you sure?

OCPA: Absolutely.

Friend: You are the best. Wow! Thank you a million times!

OCPA: Not a problem. But I do have one piece of advice. Keep your old CPA.

That's a happy ending to what could have been a very sad story. Unfortunately, for every great story like that, there are countless others that aren't so great. Too many of us spend too many of our waking hours thinking of all the ways to create money and too few thinking about ways to keep what we make. Having a great CPA, one who knows his or her business, and truly cares about your business and about you as a person, is one of the most effective ways for you to keep most of your money, pay in taxes no more than you honestly need to pay, and invest the rest.

One of the best CPAs I've met is a man named Larry Cohen. He's also the Old CPA in the story you just read who saved my friend over $40,000. He doesn't work for a firm that has hundreds of CPAs and accountants. He doesn't drive a flashy car. And he doesn't talk about all the big deals he's working on. He simply happens to be one of the best CPAs you'll find anywhere—not only for his knowledge of money, taxes, and accounting, but because he truly cares about his clients and about helping them become successful. Larry has this to say about why it's a good idea to have a CPA on your team:

> People ask me which is better when it comes to handling their business and personal taxes: a CPA or non-CPA accountant? Even before I became one, I've always felt CPAs were the best choice. First, they go through a more extensive educational process than non-CPAs. Second, they must be accredited and have passed numerous tests. Finally, there are only three people who can represent you in front of the IRS should you or your business ever get called before them for an audit. The first is an attorney. The second is an Enrolled Agent. The third is a CPA.

Tracking Expenses on Your Own

Many years ago, when I first started my own business, I came up with a simple way to keep track of my cash expenses. I do use a corporate charge card for most of my travel and business-related expenses, but I sometimes also pay cash. Charge card statements provide plenty of information on what, when, and where a business expense occurred. Here's an easy way to record cash business expenses.

Get a small spiral-bound notebook, and at the top of each page you use write the words "Cash Business Expenses for Year 2xxx."

Whenever you have a cash business expense, write down on each line what the expense is, when and where the expense occurred, the date of the expense, who (if anyone) you were with and the amount.

On the front of a letter-size envelope, write "Cash Business Expense Receipts for_(month), _(year)." You can use a new envelope for each month, or do what I do and make each envelope cover a 2-month period.

Each time you create a cash business expense, record the expense in your journal notebook and place the receipt in the envelope.

At the end of your tax year, simply remove the pages from that year's Cash Business Expense notebook and record the totals for each category of expense you had.

Send copies of those pages and your year-end summary of expenses in their categories, with total amounts for each category, to the accountant or CPA who is doing your taxes.

Agents: Do You Really Need One?

It's been said that agents (also known as managers) are more interested in your numbers than in your potential. Perhaps. Yet if they're smart, and if you've got potential, they'll definitely see how the two can become one. Many of the people I've spoken with have mixed feelings about needing an agent. This is especially true for an artist whose real-world ability to become a commercial success may not yet warrant having an agent.

Regardless of where you currently stand on the agent/no agent question, if you do decide you need one, you need to make your choice on the basis of the same kind of test you would give to a prospective attorney. Do not sign with an agent just because he or she is telling you all the things you want to hear. Time and time again I see and hear the stories of smart and talented people signing over their talent to people who don't have any talent of their own for making things happen. Here's just one among many that I could tell.

A singer I know who writes his own songs and has a unique voice was part of a band that had opened for some once-famous name acts, but, it seemed to the singer/songwriter, wasn't going much of anywhere. So he called a friend of mine who runs a very successful music business in a major music city and told him that while it would be great to get some big things happening with the band, he would like to see what could happen for him as a solo artist. My friend told the singer to send him a demo. He'd listen to it and let his other music friends (who are in the studios on a daily basis producing and playing on major label records) listen to it, and he'd get back to him with their honest opinions. No promises. Just a "let's see what happens" kind of thing.

The singer sent the demo out, and after a few weeks my friend called the singer back to give him the promised feedback. He began by saying that while there were many good points about his demo, the people who heard it agreed that it didn't stand out enough to make a major label want to offer a development, demo, or record deal. My friend also explained that what he was telling him was simply their opinions and that someone else could have a very different opinion.

A few weeks later, my friend found out that the singer who had sent him the demo, and his band, were seriously considering signing with an "enter-tainment attorney" who is also an "agent/manager" and who was "really interested" in "doing big things" for the singer and his band. Out of curiosity, my friend checked around and found out that this "entertainment attorney" was fresh out of college, had just passed the bar exam, and had no other clients. But he's really interested in doing big things for this guy and his band.

Sadly, the singer and his band bit. They signed an agreement with this attorney that had ridiculously low performance guarantees; exclusivity clauses that locked them up for multiple years; too broad a control of the use of their names, likeness, and image; and way too much in out-of-pocket expenses that they (the band), and not the attorney, would be responsible for. Feels good to have a deal, eh?

Don't get me wrong. There are good deals and good agents. But you need to know why you need one and when. Like attorneys, there are some terrific agents who really know this business. Yet there are only a small number who have the creative genius to know how to create the next stars. And not all of these people have years of experience or Rolodexes full of contacts.

Remember that all those great and high-priced people you hear or read about who are at the top right now all started at the same place—the bottom. It was through effective work, personality, and great ideas that these people quickly rose to the top. And it's the best ones who've stayed there.

Go after the ones at the top first. If they can't take you on right now (once your star rises, you'll be surprised at how many people who wouldn't give you the time of day suddenly have an opening for you), have them refer you to a few people they admire who can take you on. I've done this for many other aspects of the music and publishing business a number of times.

Case in point: I needed to have some photos shot for a book project we were working on, so I found out who was the best photographer in town for the cover shoot we were doing. The photographer also turned out to be one of the best album cover photographers in the world, who works with the major record labels photographing their artists.

I called him, and after we talked and he told me his fee began at $20,000, I asked if he could recommend someone who could do the project within our budget. He said he'd be happy to, and referred me to one of his assistants, who, by the way, was great to work with and did the entire project for a fraction of the price. Don't be shy. Ask… Ask… Ask!

When it comes to hiring an agent, you should really give some serious thought to how great you could be at being your own agent. As

I've said time and again, nobody, but nobody, can sell you to the world better than you.

Throughout my publishing career, I have pitched my book ideas to major publishers—this book included—by myself. When agents find out that I have sold all of my books without help, they ask, "How in the world do you do it?" "Well," I answer, "I identify an editor at a publishing house that does books like the one I am working on. I pick up the phone, call the editor, and give him or her a rundown of my ideas and ask if they would be interested in seeing more specifics. When the answer is 'yes' (and you'd be surprised at how often it is), I send an e-mail with details of the proposal. That's the beginning, but I do all follow-up calls and e-mails myself, and the publishers make their offers to me, not to some agent." It isn't such a complicated process, is it? So why would I want to give up 15 percent to someone who could've done the same thing?

When it comes to needing or getting an agent, my advice is simple: Unless this individual can bring big things to the table that will significantly help you and your career, keep control and do it yourself. If you meet someone you think can truly help your career rise and you don't mind giving a percentage of royalties and money to that person, then consider it. Until that time—until you are sure the person you are signing with can contribute something to whatever it is you are doing that you could not do on your own—don't give away the keys to your life or music to anyone, for any reason.

PART 2

Writing Your Songs, Getting Your Sound, and Mixing, Mastering, and Recording Your Music

Lesson 6
It's All about the Song: Advice and Inspiration from Diane Warren

Where were you when you heard DeBarge's "Rhythm of the Night"? Diane Warren could tell you where she was. Driving down Sunset Boulevard in Los Angeles with the radio blasting, the windows down, and the biggest smile you could imagine on anyone's face.

Who could blame her? She's the one who wrote it. That and over 1,000 other songs, including such hits as Aerosmith's "I Don't Want to Miss a Thing," Faith Hill's "There You'll Be," Celine Dion's "Because You Loved Me," Toni Braxton's "Unbreak My Heart," Starship's "Nothing's Gonna Stop Us Now," Belinda Carlisle's "I Get Weak," Heart's "Who Will You Run To?" Chicago's "I Don't Want to Live Without Your Love," Cher's "If I Could Turn Back Time," Bad English's "When I See You Smile," Taylor Dayne's "Love Will Lead You

Back," Michael Bolton's "How Can We Be Lovers?" and Trisha Yearwood and LeAnn Rimes' "How Do I Live," which became the longest-running song in the history of Billboard's Hot 100 and Country Singles charts. And that's only the beginning.

Diane's songs have been sung by Beyonce, Justin Bieber, Elton John, Tina Turner, Barbra Streisand, Aretha Franklin, Patti LaBelle, Roberta Flack, Roy Orbison, *NSYNC, Gloria Estefan, Britney Spears, Christina Aguilera, Reba McEntire, Whitney Houston, Enrique Iglesias, Ricky Martin, Mary J. Blige, and many, many others. Diane's music has been heard in over 100 movies from *Mannequin* to *Coyote Ugly, Armageddon* to *Moulin Rouge, Gone in Sixty Seconds* to *Pearl Harbor.* And her first television theme for *Enterprise* was also the first theme song for the Star Trek series.

Okay, let's forget the hits. What about the awards? Diane has done what no one else has ever done; she's had her songs on nine different Billboard music charts at the same time. She has won the coveted ASCAP Songwriter of the Year six times (and is the only writer to win in both pop and country) and Billboard's Songwriter of the Year four times. Diane has also won a Grammy Award, a Golden Globe Award, and a NARAS Governor's Award. She's been nominated for five Golden Globe Awards and six Academy Awards. In 2001 she got her own star on the Hollywood Walk of Fame and was inducted into the National Academy of Music/Songwriters Hall of Fame. Whew!

Diane is also the global A&R consultant for all of Universal Music Group's recorded music artists.

Diane's publishing company, Realsongs, is considered one of the most successful publishing companies in music and the most successful female-owned publishing company in the world. It has won walls full of awards, including being named Billboard's Number 1 Singles Publisher and Top 10 Publishing Corporation and American Songwriter's Number 1 Pop Publisher.

Quite a feat when you consider that her publishing company only has one songwriter: Diane Warren.

Realsongs is the name of her publishing company, and make no mistake about it: When it comes to songwriting, Diane Warren is the Real Deal. Word has it that record mogul and legend Clive Davis has a standing appointment with her each month when he visits Los Angeles. As famed Hollywood film director and producer Jerry Bruckheimer says, "I think she is on the top of her game. Where she goes, the public goes."

The life of Diane Warren is one of intense focus. It's an inspiring example of truly following your muse. She writes the hits that touch millions of people's hearts. With such a consuming passion and zeal for what she does, and so much time and attention devoted to her craft, she rarely has the opportunity to fully appreciate the impact of her gift on the millions who are touched by it. But you won't hear any complaints, for Diane Warren is one of those truly rare people who loves what she does and lives for each moment she's able to do it.

As you're about to read, Diane's life was changed forever when as a young girl she heard the magic of music speak to her from the speakers of the radio. Her destiny would be to hone and develop her gift and calling—despite incredible rejection from the music meisters who "knew" music and the audience they said "listened" to it—to become the premier contemporary songwriter of our time.

With the world's biggest music stars ringing her phone each day for just one more magical Diane Warren song, life is indeed very good for the songwriter whose words may inspire you to follow your passion and gift for a song, wherever it may lead you.

Diane on Starting Out

I started out just wanting to be a songwriter, even when I was little. One of my earliest memories of wanting to be a songwriter was when my two sisters—one being 11 years and the other 14 years older—had lots of 45s, and for some reason I always wanted to know who wrote the songs. I didn't really care who sang them. I just wanted to know who wrote them. Perhaps it was some sort of psychic thing that at that early age I just knew one day I would be a songwriter.

When I was growing up, probably around the age of 9, a bunch of us girls in the neighborhood wanted to start a band. One friend wanted to play the drums, another wanted to play the guitar, but I wanted to be the songwriter. I just wanted to write the songs. The band never happened, but the dream of becoming a songwriter did.

As I look back on it, I guess you could say I was one of those kids who loved listening to the radio and would spend hours upon hours each day doing it. I loved listening to songs and escaping into the music. I'd imagine if you'd talk to Steven Spielberg he'd probably say he lived in movies when he was a kid. It was the same thing for me. My world was the song and radio was my escape into it.

People ask me what kind of music has had the most influence on me, and I must say it was pop music and hit records. Back when I began listening to radio, the hits of the day were everything because radio was so different than it is today. It wasn't fragmented and formatted, and you were getting the best of everything. I grew up loving Top 40, and Top 40 back then was a lot of different kinds of music—great songs, and great artists.

I was influenced by lots of artists and different kinds of music, but The Beatles were up there at the top. The songs really hooked me, and to this day those songs are still great. It's always been about the songs for me, and that's never changed.

As I look back on things, I realize I was very lucky when I was growing up to have so much support from my family. When I was 14, my father got me a subscription to *Billboard* magazine and I would study each issue from first page to last. I knew who wrote everything, who produced everything, and who sang everything. Forget school textbooks. Music and *Billboard* magazine became the only subjects I was interested in.

My father recognized my love for music from the start and encouraged me so much. The first guitar I got was this real piece of junk 6-string from Tijuana, and I was just dying to have a 12-string. So my dad made a deal with me. If I could get all A's and B's for one semester, he would buy me a brand-new Martin 12-string. For the first time in my life, I didn't get D's and F's. I was a terrible student because I just didn't care about school. Music was all I was interested in. For that one little brief semester, I got a lot of A's and B's and dad paid $500—a lot of money at that time—for my new Martin 12-string. Next semester, my grades slid right back down, but hey, at least I got the guitar [laughs]!

My mother was supportive of my music dreams. She wanted me to be happy and follow my heart's desire, but she thought the music business was a very tough business to make it in. And she was right. Understandably, she was always a bit reserved in her support. She only wanted the best for me and I knew her concern came from love.

My dad was a dreamer and he saw the same thing in me. It was his encouragement I knew I could count on that helped me through those struggling early years of my songwriting career.

The Big Break

My big break came in 1985, shortly after I began working for Jack White, who produced Laura Branigan. Laura had cut a few of my songs with some success, but it wasn't until someone at Arista Publishing, who administered my early songs, gave my song "Rhythm of the Night" to DeBarge to do for the movie The Last Dragon that things started to happen.

DeBarge recorded the song and it became a huge hit. I was 28 years old at the time. That song was my first big hit, and the one I had written by myself. I did have a Top 10 record with the song "Solitaire," but that was a song I had only written lyrics to. "Rhythm of the Night" was the song that got things started for me as a songwriter of both music and lyrics.

I remember the first time I heard my song on the radio. I was driving down Sunset Boulevard in Los Angeles and heard "Rhythm of the Night" playing on two radio stations. I was just freaking out in excitement. People must've thought I was crazy when they heard me yelling "Oh my God, that's my song! That's my song!" Heaven knows how I didn't hit anybody [laughs]. To this day, I still get excited and love hearing my songs on the radio. I'm such a kid when it comes to that kind of stuff.

The Learning That'll Never End

I can honestly say that even though I've had wonderful success as a songwriter—which I'm so incredibly thankful for—I still don't know if I've learned how to be a songwriter. That may sound a bit strange, but with every new song I write, I learn something. It could be about me, about others, about music, about life, about writing, and the magical creative process that it is so hard to describe. Perhaps I've gotten better at what I do, yet, it's just so hard to explain to anyone how to become a songwriter. I just do it. I just write. I just create, and the end result happens to be a song.

It seems that for so many things in life, we want to have specific answers and the how-to's. Yet what I have discovered about songwriting is that it cannot be described like "Put six words here for the first bar, then four words on the second bar, then pause..." or anything like that. Songs have to come from inside, at their own time, in their own way, and they can't be forced. Coaxed, yes, and a great way to do that is by writing a little bit each day. But forcing a song to happen today or three hours from now, has never worked for me.

The Diane Warren Songwriting Process

I love to work and come up with concepts, ideas, melodies, and lyrics. I'll sit at the keyboard and play around with different ideas. I might turn on the drum machine and find a good groove and build some music around it. I might get out the guitar and play some chords and see if anything flows.

When writing a song, I gravitate towards ideas that interest me first. I'm inspired by everything, everywhere, and have notebook after notebook filled with ideas. An idea could come to me when I'm playing chords or driving my car. I just never know when or where it'll happen.

I always like to write about something. It needs to have a meaning for me. I like interesting key changes, and you'll hear them in a lot of my songs. Strange rhythmic things are interesting to me. Shifting keys and awkward bars and measures are fun. I like making my songs deceptively simple when you hear them, but when you sing them, you realize they aren't. I think that's cool. I laugh when I hear artists or producers who get my songs say "There are too many words here. How do I sing this?" All those words and weird rhythmic things I put in my songs sometimes throws them a curve ball, but I like that [laughs].

The way I write songs today is the way I've always written songs. Technology may make things like the demo and recording process easier, but it doesn't change the process of how I write a song. I still use my old piece of junk cassette player—that's broken—that sits next to me on my seat when I'm writing. I have nice keyboards with great sounds and have drum machines with lots of different beats, but that's about it. Don't know much about technology and don't really care. I just write songs.

People have asked if my environment plays a big part in influencing how I write a song. Honestly, I don't pay attention to the environment or scenery around me. I haven't cleaned my writing room in 18 years. The scenery won't change what I write. I write every day, but I don't write a song every day. I just feel compelled, perhaps pulled, to write a little something each day.

Writing is so magical for me that I don't like to talk about it, because it takes away the magic of how it happens. I love to write songs and I don't know how you learn, except by just doing it. It's a lot like being an athlete. You work out. You practice. You get good at it. You just do it, and you learn by doing it. As a songwriter, you leave your antennas up for inspiration, because each day, no matter where you live, or what you do, you're going to find it. Inspiration is everywhere you look, and it's just waiting for you to discover and make it your own.

When I write a song, every note has a reason. Every word, every "and" and "though," has a meaning. To me, a powerful song should contain great words and a great melody that work beautifully with each other and almost cannot work without each other. They're just meant to be together. A powerful song has to touch you and make you feel something. Whether it makes you cry or get up and dance, a powerful song needs to move you inside.

Some people are inspired to write from either a painful or pleasurable experience or event. I'm one of those people who believe you don't need to feel miserable to write a great song, and I've discovered that while I've written some of my songs at times when I wasn't feeling good, or at trying times in my life, most of my songs have been written when I feel good about myself and life. The better I feel, the better I write.

Protect Yourself and Your Music

Besides following inspiration wherever it leads you, and writing it down in a song, the one piece of advice I give to people who want to be songwriters is to protect your music. That means not signing away all your publishing to anyone or any company.

Granted, when you're first starting out, you don't have the stature to get The Deal you want, and you may need to take the best publishing deal you're offered. But you need to hold on to as much of your publishing as possible, and have whatever publishing rights you do give up revert back to you at some time in the near future.

My advice is that before you sign anything, to make sure you have a good music/entertainment attorney look things over to ensure that you're protected. If you need help finding one, just call ASCAP or BMI and have them give you a list of attorneys to choose from.

When I got my first publishing deal, I didn't own 100 percent of my songs. But as soon as I was able, I started my own publishing company, which began as a one-person business—me—in my home. From day one, that company, Realsongs, has and still publishes only one person, and it's me. Once it makes sense businesswise and financially, I think having your own publishing company is a good idea for any songwriter who wants to keep control of their music.

If you're an unknown songwriter, and you want to get your music recorded by artists and heard on the radio, the most important thing you can do to get your foot in the door—besides writing great songs—is to get hooked up with a music publisher. Bring them your best songs and try and get a publishing deal. Try to get anything you can at the beginning, because you don't yet have the clout to ask for a lot of money or any crazy kind of terms. I've seen more potentially great careers stopped right at the beginning because some artist or songwriter asked for too much too soon. Be smart. Be patient. If you're writing good stuff, you'll get your big break.

You just need to find the right person who'll believe in you and your music. When I started, I had meetings with, and got my music out to, as many publishers as I could, just to find the right one who believed in my ability and me. They're out there. You'll get rejected a lot—I certainly did—but you're going to find the right one if only you don't quit too soon and give up on your dream.

Think of joining a performance rights organization like ASCAP or BMI. You'll need them when your songs get recorded and played. They essentially do the same thing—collect money—so the choice of which organization feels best to you is a personal thing. I've been with ASCAP since day one and I always liked the fact that the great old-time songwriters, like Irving Berlin, were also ASCAP writers. You can't go wrong with either organization.

Radio and the Music Business Today

As I look back on what radio was when I was growing up, to what it has become today, it's changed so much. It's so corporate and rigidly formatted now. Years ago, a radio station program director in a city could pick up on a record and break it and the artist in that city. Things like that don't happen as much now.

The stations of today do so much research and focus group things, that if a song doesn't research well at one station, it might go through the corporation's whole system of stations and not get played in other cities as well. I think that's one of the reasons why so many records get dropped so quickly from airplay. I've always thought that was a bit unfair, since some records do take a while to break, and perhaps, just in that one city, it might not be working, but in another city, it could work great.

The music business has changed in a big way, too. I think there are two big reasons: downloading and corporate buyouts and mergers. The record companies are shrinking to the point where there might be as few as four major companies. To a songwriter, that can be frustrating, especially if it means that with so few companies, if they turn down that individual's music, does that also close the door to their music in the future?

Yet, I think there could be some great news in all of this. I think the way the music business is changing will mean it's going to be good for independent labels again. There's going to be a lot of great talent out there that some smart person is going to sign. I get a sense the music business is going full circle and is going back to the way it started: Lots of indy labels and great artists making great music. That's exciting for everyone, especially for songwriters. The new music business will be such that while the distribution, promotion, and delivery of music may change, people will never stop loving songs.

I really believe that one of the ways the record companies have hurt themselves is when they cut out the singles market. When I was a kid, I wanted to buy artists' singles and if that single interested me enough, I'd want to buy the whole album. Singles were like an appetizer, and more times than not, after having the appetizer, I wanted the whole meal—the album.

Yet record labels began changing things, and many times they wouldn't put out a single because they wanted people to buy the whole album. But I ask you, why would anyone go out and pay all that money for an album, only to get one or two great songs, and the rest of the album would be crap? That kind of thinking really turned people off to music and to the record labels in a big way. And wouldn't you know that not too long after that, the Internet thing and Napster happened, and it forever changed how music will be distributed.

I think the great record legend Clive Davis said it best when he was asked about technology and how it will change music. Clive told the interviewer that while he didn't know too much about technology, he simply wanted to create the kinds of artists and great music people will want to steal. For Clive, it's all about the artist, the music, and the song. Ah, once a music person, always a music person.

The record business has changed so much, to the point where there are now more suits and bean counters in positions of power than those like my dear friend Clive Davis, who is the last of the dying breed of record visionaries and music mavericks. Clive is the man who keeps reinventing himself with great new music and artists—even after more than 40 years in the business.

A Song Is a Part of Who You Are

I'll be the first to admit that I'm a bit of a control freak when it comes to my music. Songs are so personal. They're almost like little children you've created, and it can sometimes be difficult to let them go. But you've got to let them go. Once my song gets into the artist's hands, they take my creation, put their own unique spin on it, and that song becomes their own. Which is as it should be. But I'll admit that when it does leave my hands, I always hope the melody is sung right and that too many things aren't changed around. Over the years, I've been very lucky that the artists who record my songs have kept them close to the way I originally wrote them.

Sometimes I do enjoy being in the studio when an artist is recording my song, especially when I'm working with a great producer like David Foster. The process of watching and hearing the song come alive is exciting. For me, it's always been that as long as an artist respects my song, then I'm okay with what they do to it.

For me, being a songwriter is the only thing I know how to do. It's so powerful of a passion for me that I have no choice but to be a songwriter. To choose not to do this, for me, would be like deciding not to breathe. Each day, I just want to get better and better at it. I want to keep writing songs that people want to take into their hearts and into their lives. It's that much a part of who I am. I don't have time for any other kind of life and probably wouldn't know what to do with it if I did [laughs].

The power of words and music can be so intense. For some people, finding the words to express their feelings and emotions can be tough. But a song can express those things in ways unlike anything else. A song with the perfect words and melody can be as true to revealing the soul and essence of who we are as anything else we may say or do.

I've always thought of my songs as my little creations that I want to be everywhere bringing a smile to someone's face and a good feeling inside someone's heart. I want my music to make them happy. So many times in life we get so caught up in what we're doing that we don't stop often and long enough to see just how much who we are and what we do impacts others.

Heaven knows I'm guilty of being a workaholic, and being so focused and caught up in what I do, often, make that too often, I don't stop long enough to realize many things. Yet the way life can get our attention can be so amazingly wonderful. Sometimes, all it takes is a smile, perhaps a good word at the right time, or something as unexpected as reading the inside of a fortune cookie that says, "You'll never know just how much you touch other people's lives."

Websites: Realsongs.com and DianeWarren.com

Lesson 7
Developing Your Sound:
Advice from Bob Bradshaw

When it comes to music, the greatest thing you can give to someone is your sound. Sure, all of us start out learning and copying music from those we admire, be they composers, singers, or musicians, but for many of us, that's a phase we soon outgrow. As we all know, cover bands are everywhere, but very few, if any, are ever remembered except for sounding "like so-and-so (fill in the blank famous artist)."

There comes a time in your journey when you have to decide which road you want to take. Do you want to be a copy or do you want to be an original? You see, when it comes to music, you have choices: either play the music other people write or write the music other people play. The choice you make can change your life.

I'm betting you choose to follow your passion, your calling, and your desire to compose and perform the music that's inside of you. After all, no one but you has the distinct abilities, the combination of influences, and the experiences to compose, sing, and/or play in your own way. Friend, you were born an original so don't die a copy.

Now that it's been decided you're going to write and play your music, you're going to need your sound. Just as singers like Mariah Carey, Bono, Whitney Houston, Bruce Springsteen, Bob Dylan, and Celine Dion have their own signature vocal sound, you, too, as a singer or musician, need to possess your own voice.

How you sing and how you play are only one part of getting your sound. The other part is in the equipment you use or don't use. Some musicians, like U2's The Edge, use technology as an important element of their sound.

Just listen to all those layered delays in his guitar work and you'll hear what I'm talking about. Other musicians like the raw sound of an acoustic guitar or prefer one cable going straight from guitar to amp or microphone to mixing board and recorder.

Whichever equipment path you choose, you'll save lots of time and money if you know how to get the sound you want. To help you learn how to get the sounds that you hear on radio and on records, though, you'd need the guidance of a handful of people with the experience to teach you the tricks of the trade. Among this handful of people is Bob Bradshaw, the granddaddy and king of Custom Audio Electronics.

To the guitar world, Bob Bradshaw is the Einstein of sound. His work and sound architectures are legendary. They've been heard on countless hit records and in concerts all over the world. His clients include—and this is the short list—Trey Anastasio [Phish], Babyface, Walter Becker [Steely Dan], George Benson, Vivian Campbell [Def Leppard], Bill Champlin [Chicago], Kyle Cook & Adam Gaynor [matchbox 20], Tom Delonge [Blink 182], The Edge [U2], Peter Frampton, Sammy Hagar, Warren Haynes [Gov't Mule], Lenny Kravitz, Steve Lukather [Toto], Yngwie Malmsteen, John Mayer, Steve Miller, Dave Mustaine [Megadeth], Dean Parks [studio legend], Joe Perry and Brad Whitford [Aerosmith], Tom Petty, Prince, Nigel Pulsford and Cavin Rossdale [Bush], Lee Ritenour, Richie Sambora [Bon Jovi], Neil Schon [Journey and Bad English], Seal, Franz Stahl [Foo Fighters], Johnny Rzeznik [Goo Goo Dolls], Steve Vai, and Edward Van Halen.

Although much of his work has been for guitarists, Bob's advice is going to be a real godsend to you whether you're a keyboard player, drummer, percussionist, singer, etc. He's about to teach you the secrets to discovering and achieving your sound, and doing it cheaper and easier than you may have thought possible.

Bob Bradshaw on Starting Out

I started out loving music. It all began when I was just a kid. I'm going to have to blame my sister for this, because as soon as she started playing all the Beatles and Motown stuff in our house, I was hooked. It was a love of music that blossomed into a curiosity about how it was made.

I always loved sounds. I was the kid in school who had the biggest stereo and the first guy to have an 8-track recorder. I would record everything from records to bands, and loved pretending I was the recording and sound engineer for big concerts.

I was fascinated by sonics and sounds. What can I say: Turning all those knobs was really cool. Yet I never played an instrument. I had a guitar and fiddled with it a bit, and I can even play a few things, but I'd consider myself a guitar owner and not a player. However, knowing how to get great guitar sounds was the big thing for me.

The first audio project I built was a 2-12 speaker cabinet. I was 14 years old. I grew up in Florida, and since I didn't grow up with musicians or knew anyone who was, I knew I had to get whatever sound knowledge I wanted on my own. Let me tell you, I read and experimented with anything and everything I could to get what I was imagining in my head out into the real world. But there remained one problem: I didn't know enough about how electronic things worked.

One day in the mail, I received something about electronics from DeVry Institute [a technical school] and it caught my attention. I realized that school could be my chance to learn about electronics and I hoped, how sounds were made. The school was located in Atlanta. A friend and I enrolled and off to Atlanta we went. While there, and for the first time in my life, I applied myself to studying and quickly found how easy the electronics stuff came to me. Also for the first time in my life, something else happened: I graduated at the top of my class with a 4.0 grade average. I was hooked.

Yet there was still one problem: Here I was, a young kid with all this technical knowledge, but no practical hands-on knowledge of how to apply what I knew in the real world of music and audio. I knew I had to get out to Los Angeles and be where all the music was being made, but there was one big obstacle: I needed a way to get out there. As fortune would have it, Hughes Aircraft hired me as an electronics technician and they paid for my move. Bingo!

Not long after my arrival in Los Angeles, I went to work for Musicians Service Center. This was a place that repaired music equipment, and it wasn't long before I was meeting lots of musicians and studio players. There were guys in L.A., one in particular named Paul Rivera, building pedalboards for players. While his [Rivera's] designs were good and players liked them, I was thinking of going in an entirely different direction. Inspired by Craig Anderton's *Guitar Player* magazine column, I wanted to create a switching system—with the effects into loops—that could give someone immediate access to multiple pieces of gear with a remote control foot switcher.

I began building a prototype switching system. The first prototype consisted of a rack mount unit whereby all the pedals would be on a sliding tray connected to a floorboard controller which would offer a uniform way to select various effects. Keep in mind, this was years before MIDI.

I wanted an individual switch and a light for every effect in the rack which would tell me when an effect was off or on, and also keep everything in the rack to take the place of having all those pedals on the floor that people were having to dance around and stomp on to either turn them off or on. I wanted a system whereby I wasn't modifying any effects but, rather, could interchange effects whenever I wanted simply by unplugging the old effect and plugging a new one in its place. Would you believe the basic prototype model I developed in 1980 is the same one I use today? Hey, if it ain't broke, don't fix it.

Great Combinations = Great Sounds

An important lesson I've learned over the years is that to get the greatest combinations and types of sounds in any system, it's all about instant individual direct access to any piece of gear you have—that is, using that gear in any way you want simply by use of multiple footswitches, and then being able to create individual presets and/or combinations, with one, two, three, or all the pieces of gear in your system. Truly amazing sounds can be created in this way.

To me, it's always been about allowing musicians the ability to choose whatever kind of gear they want to use in order to make their system and sound unique, regardless of the kind of equipment or manufacturer. If you plug your instrument directly into your amplifier, great. But as soon as you put something between that instrument and your amplifier, then I can help you. Even your cable is an effect, because different kinds of cables can color your sound due to their capacitive quality. Yes, even something so simple as a cable can make a big difference in your sound.

The Bob Bradshaw Sound Philosophy

Much of my sound philosophy revolves around how things would be configured in a studio. Such as taking a dry [no effects] amplifier, mic it up, then process, blend, and mix it through the studio's effects to create lots of great sound combinations. That's why I make the line mixer an important part of many sound system setups I build.

Whether a player is well-known or not known, people looking for their own sounds come to me for the same thing. Typically, a player will call me and say they've got this kind of delay, that kind of reverb, this kind of overdrive pedal, that kind of amp, or any other pieces of gear and/or amps, and they'll want to put them in some kind of system that will allow them to use all the gear they've got, but in an easy way, and with the most options for sounds.

For me, it's always been about working with the players directly. I'm hands-on, and sound design is my forte. When people in Los Angeles started hearing about my work, some didn't know what to think. I was the guy wanting to change the way things were being done, and some people shied away from me. However, there were a few forward-thinking folks who wanted to see and hear what I was all about. That's when things started to happen. I was dealing with studio players and it was all word of mouth. It was, as they say, "the best advertising."

I began designing sound rigs for studio players like Buzzy Feiten, Michael Landau, Steve Lukather, Dean Parks, Paul Jackson, Jr., Crant Geisman, and many others. Word quickly got back to me that because of this new-found power of creating sounds like never before, arrangers were writing more complex parts just to take advantage of what the studio players who were using my rigs could now do. That was really cool.

Over the years, I've learned from the top players in the world—those whose career depends on their sound—that a great guitar, bass, or keyboard sound is one that has feeling behind it, is unique, and grabs you. It can be anything from thin and tinny sounding to big and in your face. Anything goes and it's all cool, as long as it works for you. A favorite kind of sound is such a subjective thing. There's no such thing as "the best" sound. One person will totally dig a sound while another will totally hate it. The bottom line is, if it's your sound, if it's what you like, then that's all that matters. It's all good, so don't limit yourself.

Years ago, it used to be that people took the time to really learn their instrument and craft. They took lessons, they studied, copied licks from great records, and all of these things helped develop their style. Today, and with technology the way it is, I see too many people using that technology and effects as a crutch to cover up bad playing, laziness, lack of ability, or musicianship.

In the past, the kind of effort you needed to put into your chosen instrument was enormous compared to what people can get away with now. Today, anybody can buy a drum/beat box, keyboards that have all of these sounds and instruments in them that are immediately accessed at the touch of a button or piano key, sequencers and samplers that make it so much easier to create music without having to be a good player in order to do it. But what kinds of great music are being created? Of course, music is all in the ears of the listener. However, when you see the decline of the record labels, radio stations, and the kind of stuff that gets made and played, it really makes you wonder where it's going.

People tell me they think the same is true of Pro Tools and other digital-do-everything-on-a-computer ways of recording and mixing music. If someone is singing or playing off key or not in time, it's not a problem; they just put it through the auto tune, timing device, other software program, and everything's fine. It's almost as if cut and paste has become the must-have solution to making records. All of that may make things quicker and easier, but it doesn't help one become a better singer or player. I think for too many people, it's become a crutch they can't or won't do without.

Whether it's old classic analog gear or the newest digital whiz-bang in a box, the sound is everything. Yet, when you go back and listen to older records, the records I and so many of the pros I work with grew up on, there's something to be said about those analog recordings. In my mind, there's nothing like having an analog signal path you're recording into for sonics, then, using the ease of editing in the digital realm. It's the best of both the analog and digital worlds and it's a combination that's tough to beat.

I read a letter in a magazine called *Tape Op* [for a free subscription go to Tapeop.com] that really caught my attention. It talked about how we've stopped listening to the music and have instead become computer screen watchers when making music. It's a fascinating account by a reader that proves the stimulus of the visual takes precedent over the audio in the processing by the brain. Here's what it said:

I made the switch about a year ago to hard disk computer record-ing. Since the switch and move of home and studio, I've had some major problems in monitoring—hearing properly. I have my com-puter monitor set up in front of me with the audio monitors off to each side about six feet apart. The speakers have been shielded so no interference can come from the computer monitor. I'm using Event 20/20's and EV 100A's. My console is at the side of me be-cause I can really mix mainly in the computer itself.

I thought the room was causing problems and needed tuning. I had it checked and done. No help. Then one fine day about a week ago, I was experiencing eye strain from looking at the com-puter monitor for so long. I said, "Screw it. I'll just shut it off and listen to give my eyes a break."

Well, lo and behold, I could hear again. I could sit back and gaze into each audio monitor and hear like I used to. I could almost see where the musician was standing in the audio field! The apparent volume seemed louder and the field was wider, just like it's sup-posed to be. Now, I know you may think it's because of some hum-ming or masking of sound from the monitor/video itself. Not so.

I tested the theory by leaving [the monitor] on and covering it with a towel. Same result. And this listening test was confirmed by every client who passed through the studio that week: about nine musicians and three engineers. Many a mouth flew open. The only down side is now I have to rewire and reconfigure the damn studio.

The reason for the more accurate listening with the computer monitor off seems to be the battle between audio and visual. Visual, being a stronger medium, seems to win out when the monitor is on. Attention is diverted away from the listening so can watch a stupid wave file and general scrolling go by. That also explains what happened to music because of MTV. Hope this helps some readers.

When searching for your sound, be patient. You'll try some things that sound good and others that don't. You'll buy the hottest piece of gear today and two months from now, you could be selling it because it no longer sounds good to you. It's all a growing, experimenting, and learning process that never ends.

Whether you choose to plug your instrument straight into your amp or recording console, or choose to use effects to color and embellish your sound, just remember they are choices and tools to help you get whatever sound you want. Each is valid and each is good and there's not one way better than another. It's all up to you because in the end, you and your sound are all that matter.

Getting a Great Sound

I have people ask me what the must-have elements are to getting a great sound. To them I answer, a well-tuned and well-maintained instrument. After that, anything goes. Your instrument is the first and most important thing you make music with, so you need to have one that feels good in your hands and fingers. Your instrument is the first step in your music, and your style, and your sound, and all else follows from there.

I tell people don't get caught up in thinking you need to have every new piece of gear that comes out. Technology and gear change so fast. Build your sound around two key pieces of equipment first—your instrument and amplifier—then add whatever kinds of effects sound good to you. Effects will change, but a good-sounding instrument and amp won't. And everything is good. Even a crappy-sounding piece of gear can be a great-sounding piece of gear, if it has the sound you like.

As much as we like new and modern sounding stuff, players will always go back to the old and vintage pieces of gear because they have a vibe and sound uniquely their own. My advice is if you have a good mix of pedals and rack gear, you won't go wrong.

I've never been the guy who tells people what kinds of sounds they should use. It's not my music and style. It's theirs, and they need to listen to the records and things they like that will help them put together elements that will create their sound.

Many times, people will tell me that they want to get Van Halen or some other rock star's sound and I'll ask them, "Do you play like them?" Also, what you hear on a CD and how the musician got that sound in the studio can be very different than a live rig. People need to be realistic, know their ability and needs, and think more about creating something unique to them instead of trying to copy someone else and simply becoming known as another copycat. There's so much great gear, options, and possibilities for creating your own unique sound that you don't need to sound like someone else.

Over the years people have also asked me for a Bob Bradshaw sound. I tell them there isn't one and there can't be. You see, I help people get their sounds by using whatever kinds of gear they want, and then putting all that gear together for them in ways that'll give them the widest possibilities for any kinds of sounds they wish to create.

Having said that, I do, however, have certain ideas about sound that I apply to how things are ordered in the signal path. For example, I like to put my delays after the reverbs, whereas a lot of people will put the reverb at the end of the line. To my ears, I like the delay after the reverb because of the distinctness of the decay.

When looking for your sound and access to lots of sounds, the first thing I want to know is what's the purpose of your rig? Do you need it for the studio? The road? You need to know why you need the sounds you're seeking. Next would be, what kind of effects do you need and why? Unless a piece of gear has its own unique sound or thing it can do that cannot be duplicated by anything else, I say keep the duplication of gear to a minimum. Ultimately, it all comes down to getting the equipment that you like and that sounds good to you.

You need to keep in mind that, for example, guitar gear is built for guitar, and there can be problems between one manufacturer and another as to how well different types and brands of gear interface with each other. You also need to keep in mind as you design a sound system that what you are putting in it today could be very different a year from now, when new gear comes out or when you're at a different place musically and looking for a different kind of sound. This happens all the time. Be flexible and open so that you can easily change things should you ever want to.

A big decision you'll need to make is whether your sound system will be a pedal-based rig that you'll put between your instrument and your amp or whether it will be a preamp/power amp type configuration, where there are effects between the preamp and power amp. Will it be a rack-mount gear-based system or a combination?

Some people's needs are pretty simple. Once they know what kinds of effects they want, they can go the off-the-store-shelf route and they're fine. Others need more versatility and options. They want to be able to create a set of sounds they can't get with off-the-store-shelf gear. For them, my switching system is unlike anything else they'll find anywhere, and it's perfect for their needs.

Amps and Speakers: The Keys to a Great Sound

I think it helps when people understand sound from the perspective of how the amp and speaker work with or against each other. For example, with an amplifier, you have an output transformer and with a speaker you have a coil. When the amp sends its signal to the speaker, that speaker is loaded in a cabinet and its resonance depends on the damping and its cabinet and, along with that, the resonance within the cabinet itself. And as that speaker pushes back at the amplifier, it creates a reactive load.

Of the amps we first experimented with, Marshall's were much more sensitive to having a reactive load and the sound difference was immediately apparent. In comparison, Mesa Boogies were more forgiving. So, even though an amp can be the same wattage or use the same kinds of tubes, there can be big differences in how they'll react to your gear, your system, or ways you'd like to use it to record.

Years ago, when we were interfacing effects to amps, there weren't effects loops, so all of the effects went right into the front [into the inputs] of amps. And we weren't using preamps either. We were using regular amplifiers. A good example of that setup was the early Michael Landau rigs.

We designed a rack of effects and pedals that went right into the front end [the inputs] of the amps. There would be two amps and two cabinets for the clean sound and another pair of amps and cabinets for the dirty [overdriven] sound. The effects were smacking the front ends of these two setups of four amps all at the same time, so he could get a clean and dirty sound both at once. And that was a cool thing at the time.

Then I had a revelation of sorts. I began thinking about using load resistors along with speakers within the signal chain. A load resistor is a fixed impedance and not a reactive impedance like a speaker, meaning that depending upon the frequency the amp is trying to reproduce, a speaker will give and take from the amplifier's damping and reactance from the coils. A load resistor won't, but using the two together could create some interesting results.

I wanted to know what would happen if we just took one amplifier and put a load resistor on it so it could be turned all the way up to give the whole sound of the amp and without needing a speaker. I also wanted to find out what would happen if we also used a speaker to give us the wet/dry [speaker/no speaker] sound, along with the amp's slave out, which would allow us to take a portion of the signal and then re-amp it any way we wanted. In essence, what would happen if we used the load resistor, padded the signal down to line level, then through the effects, and we took the signal out through power amps and into the speakers, or a direct out into a mixing board?

I tried it and a whole new set of sound possibilities opened up. Now the effects had that whole amp sound they were processing, whereas before, when an effect, like an echo, hit the front end of the amplifiers, the repeats and decay died off because of their lower output levels. Those effects weren't hitting the amp as hard, and the result was a thinner sound.

However, with this new way of routing things—having the amp first with the gain cranked up and then processing the echoes—the sound you'd get was this great overdriven/distortion sound with the echoes on it. And along with it, as the overdriven/distortion sounds died off, so did the echoes at the same time. A way thicker sound.

And that brings up a good point about using and recording speakers: A 16-ohm single speaker in a single-speaker cabinet will act as a different load than four 16-ohm speakers placed in a 4-12 cabinet. The same is true for single-speaker cabinets versus double-speaker cabinets. Keep that in mind when recording or playing live and you're wanting a tighter vs. more open sound.

Let me tell you a great story about Van Halen. For years, Ed always felt a 16-ohm load was the way to go, for example, a 4-12 16-ohm Marshall cabinet that had two sets of two 12-inch speakers wired in series with all the speakers connected together in parallel. When we built the first rig for Van Halen back in 1986 for his 5150 Tour, I built this elaborate load box that allowed him to switch amplifiers and a bank of load resistors simply by turning a knob on the front of the box.

When Ed came to check out the rig for the first time, I had this thing set up with a 4-ohm load and not 16 ohms like he always liked, and he freaked out. "Oh no, it won't sound good on 4 ohms and we've gotta set it back to 16" were the first words from his mouth. I told him that there wouldn't be any problems and all he had to do was set his amplifier for 4 ohms instead of 16 and everything would sound great. But no, he wanted it 16 ohms, so I went back into his system and rewired everything to 16.

Ed goes out and does the tour with his favorite hallowed Marshall Plexi amp head now being plugged into a static load box and not going directly from there into a speaker. Instead, we took that loaded signal through his effects, and then into his power amps, and then into just two speakers, and not all those speaker cabinets people would see on stage. He had the dry sound and the effects sound coming out in stereo. It was a big huge sound and Ed loved it.

Then one year later, in 1987, he's getting ready to do another tour, and in the meantime we come across the wonderful revelation that this static load resistor thing isn't happening anymore, especially on a Marshall. Sound from the amp needed to be heard on a reactive load. So one day I'm with him at a rehearsal and I'm coming to him with this amazing sound revelation. I was thinking to myself, Ed, you're going to be amazed at how unbelievable this is going to sound. This is it, pal. Now, it's really going to sound like the amp. I go in there and hook this up for him and I'm all excited and he hates it! Didn't like it at all. I was crushed. I was thinking, are you nuts and out of your friggin' mind? Just listen to how this sounds!

But I learned a powerful lesson that day and it was, he was used to the other sound and in his mind, that was the only sound there was. It wasn't until a year or two later that we finally convinced him to use our new setup. And when he did, and when we brought out that other speaker that had the effects coming out in stereo on either side of it, Ed realized he had the wet/dry approach and his new sound system was really happening. He was hooked.

Regardless of how much or little you spend, or how famous or not famous you are, getting a great sound is not having Ed Van Halen's or anyone else's setup. It all goes back to plugging your instrument into your amp. After that, the possibilities are unlimited, be they as simple as miking the speaker cabinet(s) and having that sound go into the studio mixing board and through the studio's effects units or anything else. It's how and where you use your effects, amps, preamps, and anything else that can give you lots of possibilities for recording your own cool sound.

Over 20 years ago, I started out interfacing pedals with high-end studio-quality rack-mount gear, like Steve Lukather using API EQs, which were right from the studio and very pricey. My clients back then—again, Ed Van Halen comes to mind—weren't into MIDI program changes. Ed simply wanted combinations of gear to come on and off and he used my foot controller with four presets to get his great sound. The sound that people today still want to get.

And you don't need a lot of amps to get a great sound. Ed used lots of amps for years before I started working with him, and the inconsistencies of sound and power from multiple amps and from stage to stage weren't worth it. With Ed's rig, I got him into using one amp that we would take a signal from, then run the signal into the effects, from which [it] would go into a power amp—in Ed's rig, they were HH V800 solid-state MOSFET power amps—and then line out into a cabinet. It's the wet/dry approach. Keep in mind that it takes a doubling of power [e.g., going from 100 watts to 200 watts] just to get 3 decibels more loudness, so you might want to save your money next time you think you need to have all these amps and power. Look at what Ed Van Halen did with just one amp. It's how you use your gear that makes all the difference.

Years ago, when I was touring with Steve Lukather and Toto, he was using a Mesa amp for a clean sound, a Marshall amp for a crunch sound, and a Soldano SLO-100 for the lead sound, and all of these amps were on load resistors. The freight costs of taking all those amps, cabinets, and effects racks overseas were outrageous.

There had to be a way to get a Fender clean sound—which was what we were using the Boogie for—a Marshall crunch sound, and the SLO sound, but in one unit. Make that a double rack space unit that had individual gain, EQs, and individual output levels for each channel that would offer three totally independent amplifiers. Working with Mike Soldano, we built the first prototype of that very thing into one of my switching system chassis.

One day, I brought the prototype into the studio for Steve to play and told him to check this out. There were all the amp sounds he was using, but in a double rack space! He loved it. We then began using this new prototype along with flat frequency-response Mesa M-180 tube power amps. Yet, it still wasn't there in terms of the sound I wanted. We still needed to beef it up and EQ it, because we weren't using guitar-voiced power stages.

Then came the proliferation of guitar preamps. Bogner made one. Soldano took my prototype and design and turned it into the X-88R. But as good as all these sounded, there was still work to do for the sounds I was looking to get. That led to my collaboration with famed guitar maker John Suhr to build the Custom Audio Electronics 3+SE preamp. It became the preamp that took things further and just sounded right to us. It had more tone, more output drive capability, a more balanced sound between all three channels, and a switchable tube stage EQ that gave players plenty of low and top end.

I've always believed that a good preamp is 80 percent of your tone with the other 20 percent coming from your power amp when the power amps are 100 watts or more. I prefer using lower-wattage power amps since you can really crank them up and allow their voicing to be more a part of your overall sound.

Getting a Professional Sound on a Modest Budget

Each week I get calls from all over the world from people who are planning to get one of our pro systems built for them, but, in the meantime, would like to know if they can get a good-sounding system without spending a lot of money. I tell them yes, if they know what to look for.

The more effects a piece of gear has inside of it and the more effects it can do simultaneously, the better chance the quality and/or options on how to use that effect will be limiting—unless that multieffects unit is a high-end product that'll cost you top dollar.

You need to know that when you put all your eggs in one basket for your sound—like having only one piece of gear that you want to do everything— you're also at the mercy of two things out of your control: the possibility of something going wrong with that piece of gear, and getting that gear manufacturer's idea of what they think a chorus or a delay should sound like. As many people have found, it may be very different from what your ears tell you sounds better.

If a company is selling a unit that'll do 10 effects at once and it's priced at 200 dollars, for the most part you're simply not going to get the best-quality and realistic-sounding effect. The company has to cut costs somewhere in the manufacturing to be able to give you all those goodies at such a low price. And many of them cut costs in the processing system—the very thing you don't want to be compromised.

If you're looking to go the cheaper route, I say stick to the basic sound groups—delay, reverb, compressor, chorus, vibrato, flanger, overdrive—and get a unit, from a good company, that does these things well. You might want to add a wah-wah pedal and another distortion/overdrive pedal. That should give you the basic tools to get you on the road to getting your sound. And remember: Nobody says you have to turn everything on at once. Pick and choose what sounds best to you and focus your sound around those effects [or no effects].

Going the Custom Route

If you go the custom route, that is, having us design your sound system, the kind of service you'll get will be the same, regardless of whether you spend a little money or a lot. The only differences are the size of the system, how elaborate it is, and what kind of tools it's going to take to realize the sounds you need to get. When we're building your system, you're talking directly to me and not to anyone else, and you and I will be the only ones who'll design your system.

For example, I'll build the hardware components, such as a rack-mount audio router/controller and the foot controller that controls it, and all of your effects and amps plug into this audio router—or several audio routers, depending upon the size of the system. This would be the basic building blocks from which we would create your rig.

Now you can take all of that hardware home with you and wire it up yourself, but no one does it better than us when it comes to designing, wiring, and interfacing all the various products you have, because this is all we do. That's why the pro players come to us and stay with us.

Back in the '80s, we were building giant rigs for pro players because there were certain kinds of gear that only did one thing and the player had to have that piece of gear. As you can imagine, putting all those unique pieces of gear into a system required a big system.

Things have changed. While we still build elaborate rigs for people who use them as their "A rig," we'll also build them a smaller version of that huge system for fly dates and road gigs. The cartage and freight of shipping these monsters around the world can be costly, and having a smaller, lighter, and more portable version is the ideal solution for a lot of people.

When it comes to sound, keep in mind that you're dealing with little input signals [i.e., –20 decibels or less from a guitar). You have to amplify it through screaming amps with tons of gain, and it's all an unbalanced circuit, which means there's all kinds of room for noise and other things you don't want to have going on.

Everything you get from us is hand-built and made to order.

Although we do have off-the-shelf products, such as the RS-10 MIDI foot controllers, most switching systems and products are built on a per-order basis. Each piece is built for each player and the player's needs. One of the things we do is take the music gear you have, go inside of it, and configure and program things to help you get your sound. When your rig leaves our shop, it will be a one-of-a-kind unique piece of gear that you will own, built entirely to your specifications, based on our circuit designs. We build tools; we don't build toys.

Twenty Ways to Get Great Sounds

I did sound system variations for Andy Summers [guitarist for The Police], whereby we designed a looping system when he toured by himself. Since it was only Andy, he needed to create real-time loops on stage by using his effects and then playing against them. And we didn't do it with loop devices, but by using infinite holds on delays. Today, there are lots of looping effect devices—Boomerang, Lexicon Jam Man, Oberheim Echoplex, Electrix Repeater, and others—that can do Andy's looping sounds.

For years, the pros had monitors on stage and that was their only way of hearing the sound and the band mix. Today, that's changed. With the advent of in-ear monitors, the pro players are very meticulous about being able to play on stage the sounds they used on every one of their records. And the guy who is taking creating record sounds live further than most is The Edge from U2. Every sound he has played, on every record he's ever done, needs to be recreated live on stage. Let me tell you how tough this can be.

We're talking about being able to create sounds, on records, with equipment he used 20 or more years ago [like a Korg SDD-3000] that spans U2's entire career. Lots of loops [more than 24 in a series chain], lots of programming, lots of effects, buffers in the signal path to keep the guitar signal sounding its best, a sound that must be quiet when switched off, and it's got to sound like he had plugged straight into his amp, with all of it going through a signal path that takes everything into the front end of a Vox AC-30 amp. We're talking 2-hour sound checks here.

Before in-ear monitors, there were lots of monitor/speaker sweet spots depending upon where you were standing or sitting when you played. Now you can't escape your sound and there are no sweet spots. What's coming out of your amp is what you hear in your ears and there's no running away from it like when they used to move away from a screaming Marshall stack. That's why it's important that you have the best-quality effects you can afford—effects that are quiet, switchable, programmable, and will give you the greatest possibilities for using combinations of those effects to create your sound.

Here's a list of 20 tips for getting your own great sound.

1. Use the highest-quality cable you can afford, because cable can make a big difference in your sound. Cabling is the pipeline from your instrument of music creation to recording or amplification.

2. Always use some type of buffering in the signal path if your cable coming from your instrument is more than 20 feet long.

It will help preserve the instrument's original tone before it gets to the amplifier.

3. Keep the signal path as short as possible, with the least amount of effects in between your instrument and the amp. The most critical link in the sound system is between your instrument and the input of the amp, whether it's a power amp, preamp, or an instrument into an amp with pedals. There's nothing more pure than to be able to put your effects into a looping system that allows you to get them out of the signal path whenever you desire The way we design our systems, not only do we bypass the effects, we also bypass the cabling connected to the effects, which allows us to take a lot more than just the effects out of the signal path. And everything you take out of the signal path helps to eliminate yet another connection that could create noise and/or problems.

4. When miking speaker cabinets, you can't go wrong with a Shure SM-57 up against the grill, although there are many other choices available. However, having a little "air" on things, giving the sound some room to "breathe," and keeping the mics not so close to the speakers also works great.

5. Multiple miking [i.e., close/off-axis/back of the cabinet], using different kinds of mics—that create phase shifting—can either be a good thing or a not-so-good thing, depending on what sounds good to your music.

6. Listen to the sound source and put your head and ears near the speaker [not when playing at loud volumes] where the sound is going to come out. When you find a "sweet spot" on that speaker that sounds good, put a mic there. Same thing when using a room mic. Get on a ladder and put your head where the microphone is going to go. Once you find a great-sounding place, put a mic there. Experiment with different mics, distances, angles, and positions. I've never heard any direct recording music that sounded convincing to me. There's nothing better than miked speakers to faithfully reproduce sounds, especially your sound.

7. If you're new to multiple effects and/or pedals, or combining things, remember that anything goes. When using a single effect, the order isn't an issue, but when you combine other pedals and multiple effects, where they are placed does become important. Give the following a try.

8. Put envelope filters and octave boxes first, because they work best when they receive a good, clean, pure signal. Then add overdrives and distortion boxes. Now add wah pedals, phasers, chorus, and tremelo. Finally, add in reverbs and delays.

9. If a volume pedal is used, I typically place it as far down the effects chain as possible, but just prior to the reverbs and delays. The reason? When you pull your volume back, the reverbs and delays will naturally decay.

10. This order holds true regardless of whether you're using pedals into an amplifier or rack-mount gear-type configuration with preamps and power amps and effects in between them.

11. When it's a preamp/power amp type configuration, and if there is compression and such involved as well, I like to keep the volume pedals as far down the path as possible, but just prior to the reverbs and delays, so that things that may be threshold-sensitive [like compressors, gates, and noise-reduction units], aren't affected by the volume fluctuation.

12. If you're using pedals, I like the wah and volume pedals to come after the distortions. Here's why. Let's say you've got an amplifier and you've got it set for a certain amount of crunch, but you like your volume pedal to clean that up a little bit, since by pulling your volume back, you're essentially using the volume pedal like an extension of the volume knob on your guitar.

13. If you put the volume pedal a little further down the effects chain, but after the distortions, now you've got another level in which you can help create your crunch. In other words, if your guitar signal comes out full volume and hits your distortion boxes, the distortion boxes then hit your volume pedal, the volume pedal then hits your amplifier, you've now got a wide range of adjustments in being able to control the amount of gain stages going to end the result—the input of your amplifier. The end result is you've got a healthy signal hitting your distortion boxes with your guitar wide open, your volume pedal will pull that amount of crunch back hitting the input of your amplifier, and if the distortions are not on, then the volume pedal can be used the same way to help clean up the sound of the amplifier.

14. Typically, people who wire their pedal boards do so in the most convenient fashion, such as plugging into a wah pedal first and then adding the rest of the effects from there. However, if you move the wah pedal and let your distortion boxes come first, and you combine the distortions with the wah, it gives the wah a thicker and more harmonically rich signal to filter. To me, the wahs sound better when they're hit by a distorted signal, rather than a clean one. Again, anything goes, and all these tips are just my personal preferences.

15. It's important to have some form of buffering/impedance matching on your pedal board, even if your pedal board has true-bypass switching. Regardless if all your pedals have true-bypass switching and you're playing a passive instrument [like a guitar], a cumulative capacitive buildup is going to occur. The flow of your signal from guitar to amp still passes through every cable, every effect and its switches, and the end result is it's going to suck your tone just like it would if you were using a 100-foot cable.

16. Find out what devices in your signal path are sensitive to any low-impedence buffer output. Often, discrete and germanium transistor-type fuzz boxes don't like to use a buffered signal. They work better with the high-output impedance of the instrument. One solution to try is to use any active pedal as a good buffer and put any active pedals—like any of the BOSS pedals including the BOSS TU-12 Tuner or Ibanez TS-9 Tube Screamer type pedals, since they are buffered and are active bypass—after these distortion boxes, and let your high-impedance instrument, like a guitar, feed the inputs.

17. To find out if any of your pedals has a hardwire bypass [not true 100 percent bypass], plug your guitar into the pedal and plug the pedal into an amp. Then pull out the pedal battery. If you have no sound, then you've got an active bypass pedal. If it does have sound when it's in the bypass mode, it's at least a hard-wire bypass.

18. If you have a rack-type system, be aware of the placement of certain types of gear. Keep the more sensitive high-gain-type devices—like preamps or low-level signal devices—away from other devices that have power transformers in them that could radiate hum fields and magnetic interference. I like to keep preamps away from power amps because a power amp often generates more hum than practically any other piece of equipment due to its large power transformers.

19. Take note of which side of the effects box the internal power transformer is on by looking at which side the power cable comes out. For example, you wouldn't want to put a preamp that has its input on the left side next to or close to any effects devices that have its power cable coming out the same side. The idea is to keep them physically apart, with the transformer of one and the input of the other on opposite sides.

20. Try using isolation transformers [available from companies like Furman or Custom Audio Electronics] to break ground loops rather than AC ground lifting devices. It's okay to use an AC ground lifting device in a multicomponent system as long as one device in the rack is grounded to ensure safety and proper shielding.

Website: Customaudioelectronics.com

Lesson 8
Finding the Best Recording and Creating Platform:
Using What the Pros Use

The world of computers, tablets, smartphones and software is changing so rapidly that it makes it nearly impossible to stay on top of all the day-to-day changes and choices you have.

So how do you decide what kind of gear you need to record your music?

First focus on the basics, the foundation of your studio, and then add the peripherals, apps, and software from there.

Just remember that you can be using the same exact things that your favorite singer, songwriter or producer uses, but get a totally different result.

It's *how* you use them that'll help you to create your signature sound (along with, of course, the tips you received from Bob Bradshaw) and perhaps open doors for you in the business.

So let's look at what you may want to consider as the good basics for your system.

Please keep in mind that it's important for you not to get locked into thinking there's only one or a few ways of using equipment. The ideal way to use any technology—old or new technology—is to pick and choose carefully from among them. Use analog hardware equipment in tandem with digital audio equipment to create something that says, "This is me. This is my sound."

And by all means, don't think that once you get any (or all) of these great tools you must become an island unto yourself, with no outside involvement, influence, or inspiration. Most of the producers and musicians I know use their home studios to work on new ideas, which includes having others send them hard disks, FTPs, or downloads of music projects so that they can lay down guitar, percussion, key and synth parts, produce remixes, add sound textures, and do anything else needed to help create the finished product. It makes collaborating with others lots of fun.

Along with that, many of these studio pros will take their work (many of them still like hard disks) with all their digital audio workstation (DAW) and plug-in data on them to a bigger studio that has compatible equipment and finish overdubbing and mixing before the final product is ready to be mastered.

Your Computer: The Hub of Your System

In the new music business, the brains, hub, and centerpiece of your recording studio is your computer. Creating, recording, editing, and mixing with a computer is the way a lot of music is made today. While big studios, big consoles, bulky tape machines, and racks of analog and digital outboard gear were once the key, today's key—and probably tomorrow's as well—is a personal computer. You can simply do more things musically with a computer than you can without one.

We're about to get into debatable territory here. That is, which computer should you use for recording? Both platforms (Mac and Windows-based PCs) have their die-hard devotees. And if you really want to know which platform more music pros use, I have the answer for you.

The operating system of choice of serious professionals who make their living and reputation creating music is the Mac (at least for music production).

The PC is still the most popular consumer computer; it outsells Mac by a wide margin. But you'll find Macs being used in very demanding environments. When I was the editor of a major international magazine, all of the layout designers and creatives used a Mac. For high-demand processing power applications, a Mac can do everything your PC does and better.

The Mac has always had plenty of loyal fans who love its innovations and user-friendly operating system. In the music world, third-party developers typically create innovative state-of-the-art software technologies for the Mac before creating them for any other type of computer platform. Why? Because when it comes to music, the majority of people who create the hits use Macs. Also, you can run Windows on a Mac, as well as share files between a Mac and a Windows-based PC.

In the years I've been in the music business and around those who produce music and artists for major labels, I've found that the Mac either is the main computer system that their studio is built around, or is part of their Pro Tools, Logic, and other computer recording workstation rack rigs, or is their laptop portable studio. These people get paid big money to make records. They also pay big money to the studios and musicians for sessions. And when there's so much money involved, the people and equipment (especially the often-joked-about "fickle computer") have got to be rock-solid and reliable. While no computer platform or manufacturer can claim 100 percent reliability, the Mac comes awfully close.

The digital revolution has changed the way the music business operates. Who would've thought that the computer would become such an important piece of equipment for musicians creating music? Lots of artists and musicians use a Mac onstage to run their rigs, trigger sounds, or create amazing music live and on the fly. Some call it their second instrument. But while guitarists are likely to have lots of back-up guitars in the event their strings break or something else goes wrong, you don't see many musicians with back-up Mac iPads, MacBook Pros or MacBook Airs. There's got to be a good reason for this.

Once you have your computer, we need to take you to the next step, and that's hooking you up with a computer-audio interface.

Your Computer/Audio Interface

Think of your computer-audio interface as the terminal where the outside world of audio meets the inside world of recording and processing. For example, audio interfaces allow you to take the analog signal from a guitar or from effects and then convert that analog signal to digital (A/D) and vice versa, from digital to analog (D/A), so it can be used by your computer's music software (DAWs, plug-ins, etc.) and hardware. There are lots of companies that make interfaces, ranging from those that cost a couple of hundred dollars to the higher-end gear.

Digital Audio Workstations (DAWs)

How should I record my music? Boy, has that question been asked untold number of times. It used to be that you needed the services of a recording studio to do it. Those $250,000 multitrack recorders and half-million-dollar recording consoles sure sounded good, but the hefty price tags put them way beyond many musicians' budgets.

Along came the personal computer. The first personal computers were expensive and lacked power and features. But, like all emerging technology, they soon became faster, better, and cheaper. And so did the software and hardware from the companies who created products for them. Music recording is a prime example.

Pro Tools and MOTU Performer were among the first major products embraced by the professional music community. Both offered sophisticated recording, mixing, and editing capabilities, as well as an alternative to outboard gear, large studio consoles, and analog and digital tape. As far as digital tape recording goes, Alesis's ADAT was a major innovation, but it was simply a cheaper way to record to digital tape, and it offered no extensive effects, composing, and editing capabilities.

Since then, much has changed—and for the better. The kinds of music you can create; the myriad ways you can create, mix, master, and edit it; the surround-sound capabilities; the seamless merging of audio to video; and the vast number and types of plug-in effects and instruments, all controlled through your home computer and accessed by the click of a mouse, are astonishing. Never in the history of music making have you been able to do so much for so little.

If you want to get serious about your music, you need to start using the DAW platforms that the pros use in almost every major studio in the world. They've been extensively tested, they're reliable, and they produce outstanding results.

That means Pro Tools, Logic, and Nuendo. Yes, there are others, but these are still the top go-to platforms that many of music's biggest names go to.

Plug-Ins

The world of digital technology changes incredibly fast. Almost as quickly as you learn the latest version of that hot new software, a new and improved version comes along, and this is certainly true for recording and music software and hardware.

In the world of computer-recorded music, one of the most-talked-about evolving technologies is that of plug-ins. Through a complex process involving mathematical algorithms, computer code, and amazing human ingenuity, today's plug-ins can virtually recreate (many times with breathtaking realism) instruments and effects.

There are software and hardware sound samplers that'll give you a studio full of symphony orchestra instruments and the baddest (read: great) sounding hip-hop beats and rhythms you can imagine, all at the touch of your computer mouse, keypad, or keyboard. There is software that'll allow you to create racks of studio equipment and instruments, patch them in any configurations you want, and adjust any of the knobs and controls. You can see all of this on your computer screen. You don't even have to have any real instruments in your home.

For many of us, the days of locating vintage gear or buying expensive outboard processing equipment—like a $30,000 Fairchild tube limiter—are over, as plug-ins come so very close to emulating the real thing. With many plug-ins priced in the neighborhood of $150 to $600, you can get software filled with instruments, effects, and recording capabilities unimaginable only a few years ago. Computer software plug-ins have become the way to create hit-quality music on a tight budget.

As plug-in technology is changing so rapidly, more and more companies are offering products with more features and for less money. Whether you're using a Mac or a Windows-based PC, plug-in music software essentially does one thing: It turns your computer into a recording studio filled with effects and instruments. All you need to add are talent and creativity. You do, however, need to make sure that what you're buying will work with your computer's operating system and your DAW software.

You may be asking, "Can a software program (effects, instruments, etc.) actually sound as good as the original hardware versions?" In many instances, the answer is "yes." And plug-ins can be even better than hardware when you consider all the additional capabilities, like improved audio specs, sound quality, and new options for use, to name a few, that they offer.

If you're making a list of which software to check out, you'd be wise to put Spectrasonics, Universal Audio, and Waves at the top of your list.

Outboard Gear, Sound Controllers, and Mixers

We've talked a lot about computers, DAWs, and software plug-ins that recreate real instruments and many great effects. However, lots of artists, engineers, and producers also use outboard effects gear. Some use them for signal processing prior to voice and music recording, others to process recorded tracks and give them effects. There isn't any "right" or "wrong" when it comes to choosing equipment. Great joy and inspiration can be found when you come up with your own combinations and create your sound in your own way. This section covers, albeit briefly, some of the outboard gear and sound modules you might want to check out.

Sound controllers. In addition to outboard gear, it's smart to have a sound controller (or two or three) that allows you to access sounds from a keyboard and not just from a computer keyboard or mouse. Some MIDI controllers are just that—a keyboard that is used to control, patch, or program sounds from your plug-ins and outboard sound module gear.

While other MIDI controllers have sounds (some of them, lots of sounds), you'll pay more for the added features. You can choose anything from a small, inexpensive Edirol or M-Audio MIDI controller, to a classic MIDI controller like the Roland A-70, A-80, or A-90, to a fully loaded Kurzweil. The best advice I can give you is go to a music store and have them demo MIDI controllers (even those with sound capabilities), then go with what works best for your needs and your budget.

Some of my musician/producer friends have racks of outboard gear and sound modules, and/or keyboards of classic gear like the Nord rack, Korg Triton Studio keyboard/rack, Roland XV series rack, E-MU sound modules, Access Virus, Waldorf, Kurzweil keys/rack, Parametric EQs, and others that they'll use along with plug-ins. Many of them also use the Electrix rack gear (cheaply priced, good quality and still easy to find on eBay or Harmony-Central. com) to shape music and vocals either before or after tracks are recorded, or during recording.

Ask others what they are using. Log in to a few of the gear chatrooms, and don't be shy about asking lots of questions. You'll find musicians like to help other musicians.

Mixers. If you've ever played live or been in a recording studio, you know what the recording console/mixer does. While the DAWs featured in this book allow you to use your computer screen, keyboard, and mouse as your mixer, you might want to give some thought to getting a dedicated mixer that's compatible with the DAW you have (or will soon be getting), as well as your outboard gear and keyboard/MIDI controller.

Many digital mixers (also known as DAW controllers or DAW control surfaces) are completely compatible with your DAW applications software and include lots of shortcuts for many DAW program tasks—a huge time-saver. Having a dedicated mixer also means that you don't have to be in the computer realm all the time. You can turn real knobs and move real faders—the kind of thing that makes it feel like you're recording and mixing music in a professional studio.

Storage Systems

As I said back at the beginning of this lesson, there are six components to your recording studio setup: your computer; your computer/audio interface; DAWs; plug-ins; outboard gear, controllers, and mixers; and storage systems. It's the last one that I want to talk to you about now. It makes no sense to spend money on the first five if you don't cover yourself by having a bullet-proof number six.

Storage. I know, it's boring, it just sits there, and it doesn't make any cool sounds. It's usually the last thing people think about while they're recording. But it's the first thing they think about if something goes wrong with it. Great sessions and ideas—great music—can be lost forever if you don't have a backup storage medium that safely and reliably records them.

Before going into the different backup storage options, let me emphasize an important point. Far too many people rely on a single internal hard drive as a storage medium. But as we all know, computers (and hard drives) can crash. If your computer crashes, and the only place you have stored your work is on that computer's hard drive, everything you've done can be gone in an instant.

Retrieving data (if it's even possible) from a crashed hard drive can be very expensive. That's why you need an external storage medium to archive your masterpieces.

I recommend at least two different types: cloud-based storage and external hard disk storage.

And some music pros add another layer: tape storage.

As Bob Clearmountain tells you in the next chapter, he uses a Sony 3348 digital tape machine for backup storage for several reasons: It's a good interface for his SSL console, the music can be played back without the need for a particular edition of a music editing program, and it allows him to mix right off the tape. I'd like to suggest that the 3348 is a good choice for you also. If the price of the 3348 puts it beyond your reach right now, you can still use a tape backup. There are plenty of great used 24- to 48-track tape machines out there. Check out the Internet for used analog and digital tape machines made by Ampex, MCI, Otari, Revox, Sony, and Studer. Read the reviews and note the prices, and as soon as your budget allows, pick one up. It'll be a smart move.

Lesson 9
Mixing Your Music: Advice from Bob Clearmountain

I'll admit it: At times, I can be a liner note reader. You know, someone who picks up a CD and goes right to the inside liner to find out who engineered and mixed the songs. And wouldn't you know, on many of my favorite songs and albums, the name that has popped up over and over again is Bob Clearmountain.

Although I heard the magic that Bob Clearmountain worked on records in the 1980s, I think the first time I really stopped to give a good listen to what this guy did was when I played Bryan Adams's 1993 greatest hits album *So Far So Good*. The production and mix of those hits would make even the lamest of stereo systems sound terrific. It's how a great rock album should sound. And perhaps the greatest compliment is that it still doesn't sound dated today.

Now add to that his work on Simple Minds' *Once Upon a Time* and Hall & Oates' *Big Bam Boom* and INXS's *Kick* and Bruce Springsteen's *Born in the USA*, as well as records by Aerosmith, Bon Jovi, David Bowie, Jackson Browne, The Clash, Shawn Colvin, The Corrs, Crowded House, The Cure, Dire Straits, Melissa Etheridge, Goo Goo Dolls, The Kinks, King Crimson, Kiss, Huey Lewis & the News, Elton John, Edwin McCain, Paul McCartney, Willie Nelson, The Pretenders, The Rolling Stones, Carly Simon, Sister Sledge, Ringo Starr, Tears For Fears, Toto, Tina Turner, The Who, and many others, and you'll get a good idea of what this guy is capable of.

But don't stop there. Bob's also done the music for movies like *9½ Weeks, Ace Ventura, Bridget Jones's Diary, Four Weddings and a Funeral, Philadelphia,* and *Stuart Little 2.* And add to the mix such special projects as Bruce Springsteen & the E-Street Band in *Live in New York* [HBO Special], *Live Aid* (live worldwide TV and radio), *Saturday Night Live: 25 Years* [NBC],

The Concert for Nelson Mandela [live worldwide TV and renamed *Freedom Fest* in the United States on Fox TV Network], *The Concert for New York City* [VH1], *Woodstock 94* [live pay-per-view cablecast], and *The Rolling Stones and The Who* [live pay-per-view and Fox TV], and you have an amazing body of work that has defined a man, a genre, and an approach to mixing music and records that people will be going back to years from now.

To meet Clearmountain, as he often signs his e-mails, is to get a quick lesson in humbleness and not letting a name, a reputation, or even vast amounts of success go to your head. There's nothing pretentious about Bob or his work. What you see is what you get, and what you hear is what so many people would like to get.

I had the opportunity to sit down with Bob at his home studio in Pacific Palisades, California, and for the next few hours he gave me tape after tape of inspiring advice. In this lesson Bob offers a gold mine of information that's bound to help anyone wanting to produce and mix music in today's new music business.

Bob on Starting Out

I grew up in Greenwich, Connecticut, and was an amateur musician, playing bass in a couple of different local bar bands there and in Westchester County in New York. The last band was doing a couple of demos in a studio in New York City called Media Sound with an engineer named Michael Delugg. In the middle of doing that, the band split up.

So, I started coming into New York and hanging around the studio, bugging them to hire me. In fact, the first time I had ever been in a studio was with my band when we were doing those demos. I was 19 years old.

The studio experience was fascinating to me. I was always the guy in the band who was recording the rehearsals and the gigs. I was kind of the producer, too, who was telling everybody what to play and doing the arranging. The first time I walked into the studio, I knew I could spend all my time there. It had everything I wanted.

The studio experience was a real turning point for me. For one thing, I really didn't feel I could depend on other musicians for my living, which is what you have to do when you're in a band. And bands had let me down so many other times that I thought, okay, maybe it's time for a real job.

I never went to recording school or had any specific training to do what I do. I was in high school bands and in choirs and took a few electronics classes, but no formal music or recording training to speak of. It was just something I loved doing and I was always wanting to learn as much as I could on my own.

I even skipped college. My parents were just retiring at the time I was finishing high school and they told me to either go to state college or be on my own and pay for college myself. And at the time, I really didn't know what I wanted to go to college for, because what I really wanted to do was be in a recording studio. And since there weren't any college courses at that time for recording, I just went right to work. What I did was an old time hands-on apprenticeship in the studio.

So I started learning more about recording and what the studio did until the folks at Media finally hired me after bugging them over and over again. I was an assistant for a few years, but pretty early on, I got to do some recording sessions myself.

In those days, studios would assign staff engineers to sessions. One day I was assisting on a Kool & the Gang session with an engineer who was mainly a jingle guy and he said to me, "Hey, why don't you go ahead and do this session?" As he just sat there and read the paper, I did overdubs and mixed a couple of songs. That happened only after three months of working there, so I was pretty lucky.

About six months later, Kool & the Gang were working on its next album and I was the assistant once again. However, the engineer was sick this time and

I recorded basic tracks for them for two nights. The two songs I engineered ended up being hits. One was called "Hollywood Swinging" and the other was called "Funky Stuff." I think "Hollywood Swinging" reached number six on the charts. It was the first song I actually ever recorded from scratch.

I ended up doing a lot of R&B records and I worked on a lot of things like jingles and movies. Media did most of the music for *Sesame Street* as well.

Then, in 1977, two guys from Media Sound opened a studio called Power Station in New York. I went over to work at Power Station for a few years and helped design that studio, which is now called Avatar. Once I started working at Power Station, I began producing. At first, it was some punk rock bands for Sire Records. Soon thereafter, I began producing Bryan Adams and lots of others. The mixing thing quickly followed.

The first client at Power Station was a band called Chic. It was a big disco act at the time. I got a reputation at Atlantic Records for the work I did with them because Chic was quite successful. The Rolling Stones were on Atlantic at the time and so was Roxy Music.

The Rolling Stones were looking to do a dance mix of a song called "Miss You," and someone from Atlantic Records recommended me. I mixed the 12-inch of that song and got to mix the single as well. That was sort of my introduction to big-time rock music. After that, I started doing some stuff for Bruce Springsteen, because the E-Street Band played on an Ian Hunter album called *You're Never Alone with a Schizophrenic* that I had engineered. I also did more things with the Stones and with Roxy Music, whose song "Dance Away" and album *Avalon* were big records for them.

Things just picked up from there. I was doing more mixing, I became independent, and began producing and mixing in other studios in New York, London, San Francisco, and Sydney. I eventually moved to Los Angeles, where I built my own home studio, which I work out of today.

Early on in my musical career, I was really influenced by The Beatles, The Rolling Stones, the Who, Traffic, and Led Zeppelin. Hendrix was a big thing for me in terms of influencing my producing and mixing.

When I was a kid listening to Hendrix records, I didn't know anything about recording, but I noticed he would do wacky things like crazy panning and flanging effects. The environment of the records always managed to match his incredible lyrics. I wondered what that was and how they were doing it. I knew somebody, besides the musicians, was in the picture, and I wanted to be that guy.

To this day, Beatles records still amaze me. It's almost depressing, because with such basic tools they got amazing sounds that we still can't get—even today. Geoff Emerick, George Martin, and The Beatles were one of those rare combinations of talent with the unbelievable creativity to come up with many of the best pop records ever made. Everyone should listen to those records carefully if they're wanting to be inspired and learn a powerful lesson: Modern technology can be great, but you don't need it to create brilliant records.

Being Successful in Music Is Doing the Best You Can

My philosophy about being successful in music is just simply to do what you do and do it the best you can. I was never much of a schmoozer, and I don't hang out with people and try and sell myself to them and explain to them why they should be working with me. I'm terrible at those kinds of things.

All I do is mix records the best way I can, and if people hear them and like what I do, hopefully they'll ask me to mix their record. I mean, I don't even have a manager going out getting me gigs, whereas a lot of other mixers and producers have managers that are always in the faces of record labels.

My manager, Dan Crewe, is off the beaten path and lives up in Maine. In fact, in the 1980s I had to talk him into managing me. He had managed his brother, Bob Crewe, who was a big record producer in the 1960s, and Dan had had it with the record business. But he was the only one I knew that knew anything about the business. He was a down-to-earth guy. He wasn't a hustler, which I liked. And it's worked great. He does the deals and makes sure I don't get ripped off.

I've always told people, whether you're a composer, musician, engineer, producer, or anything in-between, just enjoy what you're doing. I always have, and I was pretty amazed that I could make a nice comfortable living doing what I do. Years ago, it never occurred to me that I could make money doing what I do. I would've done it anyway, regardless of whether I made a little or a lot of money. The only thing I ever wanted to do was make records for the rest of my life. And if I could do that and earn a living, even live in a little studio apartment somewhere, then I'd be totally happy.

A Constantly Changing Approach to Recording and Mixing Music

You never know what song or record you're working on will become a hit or not become a hit, and which ones will still be touching people's lives 20 years from now. Chic had a record called "Good Times" and it was obvious it was going to be a hit. I knew for sure that Bruce Springsteen's Dancing in the Dark would be a hit. Yet for the most part, you just never know.

The album *Avalon* from Roxy Music that I mixed in the '80s is a good example of how a record has a big impact on a lot of people, and I wouldn't realize it until many years later. It wasn't until a few years ago that it went platinum, and surprisingly it's been the record that I get the most compliments about. I mean, people tell me that their child was conceived to that record [laughs]. You just never know.

I remember when we mixed Shawn Colvin's "Sunny Came Home." As soon as I heard it I thought, wow, that's a great song. In my opinion, it was the best song on the album. Then the record company released "Get Out of This House" as the first single and it did absolutely nothing. They finally came out with "Sunny Came Home" and it was a big hit. Go figure!

There have been plenty of other times I thought songs would be hits and nothing happened. And a lot of times it was because they weren't promoted and the label didn't do anything to get the record out there. Yet who's to say whether they weren't hits because nobody heard them or possibly because the songs weren't actually good enough?

My philosophy about mixing records has gone through many changes over the years. Even though a hit song is a hit song, I like to look at it as an evolving process, because music and styles are always changing. My criterion for a well-engineered, mixed, or recorded song is simple: Does the song come through? If everything in the mix and the music enhances the feeling and the thought behind the lyric, melody, and music, then I'm doing my job.

It isn't the best drum sound or guitar sound that makes a great recording. It's all about how everything fits into the mix. If you're doing a rock record, you're looking for a certain kind of excitement. If you're doing a dance or hip-hop record, you're looking for something that's going to make you dance, get up, and move around.

If it's a Springsteen song, you want something that's going to make you think and not take away from the power of the song's lyrics. You want it to make you think about what is the state of the character in the lyric. You don't want your mix to get in the way of that, and you want everything in your mix to enhance those qualities.

When I was producing, it was all about being transparent and enhancing each of the song's most important qualities, bringing them to the surface for everyone to hear, so the message was easy to get at by the listener.

I go back and listen to stuff I mixed in the '80s and it all sounds like there's way too much reverb and delay. Nowadays, I mix a lot drier. I'm always learning so much from working with many different producers, artists, and kinds of music.

People like Bryan Adams and Bruce Springsteen taught me about how important the song is. It doesn't matter if you're playing, mixing, or recording. The song is the most important thing, and nothing should ever get in the way of that. It's an important lesson I've learned, and I hope it's been reflected in everything I've done since then.

Whenever I listen to a new song on the radio, my ears go to the melody first and the way the melody relates to the chords. After that, I'll listen to how the words work with the melody and what it's about. The production and the mix are the last things I listen to. On a lot of pop records, what the words are saying really doesn't matter that much. But it is really nice when you hear a hit record and the words actually mean something.

I think that's what's so powerful about someone like Eminem. Even though a lot of what he's saying is irritating to a lot of people, whether you like it or not, you immediately get exactly what he's talking about—the songs are actually about something. For a lot of records, you don't know or don't care what they're saying, but with Eminem, there are two listeners: those who are pissed off at what he's saying and those who agree with him. He's making a statement and it's very powerful. That's the kind of thing that makes a hit record.

Some people have asked me if I think less is more when it comes to mixing and recording music, and I say sometimes, but not always. A philosophy I've always had is that there aren't any real rules about recording and mixing music.

I noticed that whenever I've done lectures or seminars and tell people, okay, in that kind of situation you want to do this and in this kind of situation you want to do that, there's always the exception where you do just the opposite. Never get locked into thinking you must always do something a certain way, because you'll find a situation where that's completely wrong and you need to go the other direction.

There are some things that I find myself preferring when I mix a record in regards to vocal and instrument placing. However, pop music styles have changed and the emphasis on even those things shifts over the years. I'll give you a couple of examples.

In the 1970s and '80s, emphasis on the drums and bass was the big thing. Then, when we got into the '90s, the drums weren't that important. In fact, it sounded stupid to have big overpowering drums. Rhythm has always been important, but the rhythm now comes from other things and not necessarily just the drums.

Along with that, my tastes change as well, and I think that has to be if I'm wanting to stay current and a little ahead of the curve. I'll hear stuff on the radio that I like and I might take some of that inspiration and use it on a project where it could be just what the record needed. I think it's a good thing that one's taste changes over time. You can't keep making the same kind of records you made in 1979 or else nobody's going to hire you, not to mention boring yourself to death. As John Lennon once said, "So who says I have to be consistent?"

I've had people ask me over the years if I have a signature sound and I tell them, I hope not. I don't think I do and I try not to, because to me, the signature should be the artist and whatever the project is I'm mixing. I try not to impose any signature of mine on what they do. The only thing I want to give them is a great record that's fun and enjoyable for the listener. Hopefully, that's my signature. There are records that I hear and I can tell who mixed them. For me, I just hope people can't tell I'm the one mixing the records. I really do not want to have that sort of identity. I just want the records to be great.

Always remember that there really is no right or wrong way to record music. It's all a matter of perspective and taste. The way I record and mix records could be very different than someone else. That's what makes records interesting and hopefully enjoyable. We all have different styles, as we all like different types of music. If I turned on the radio to find every record sounded like one of mine, I'd just switch to the news station!

I think a mixer or producer should approach each record as if it's the only one he'll ever do. Give it all you've got, and you'll always be able to say you gave it your best. Where it goes from there, only time will tell and the listeners, or the label, will decide.

The Bob Clearmountain Mixing Process

One of my biggest pet peeves is a rhythm track that's mixed really dry—where the drums and the guitar are right up front and in your face—and then the vocals are swimming in reverb way off in the back. I just don't understand that. The mental picture gets very confused, or is simply nonexistent. The band sounds like it's in this little anechoic chamber, but the singer is in the Grand Canyon or Carnegie Hall—it doesn't make sense. It's usually much easier to picture the vocalist up close to the listener and fairly dry, with the band behind him or her.

It's as if the engineer soloed the drums and said "Oh, this sounds good" and soloed the guitars and said "This sounds good" and then soloed the voice with a lot of reverb and said "That sounds nice," then put it all together and didn't bother to really pay attention to hear if it all worked together.

It's really obvious to me that you would want everybody to sound like they're coming from basically the same place. Of course quite often you'll use a unique massive 'verb on an element of the mix simply for contrast. See, I told you there are no hard and fast rules about mixing. When it's done purposefully to be interesting, that can work. It's when it doesn't make any sense, and when it's all thrown together without much thought, that I have a problem with it.

I think you need to be careful about using too much compression. Yet for some records and styles of music, it can work, especially modern rock records where maximum excitement is the goal. So many of these songs are mixed for hit radio where they're trying to make things as loud as they possibly can to grab your attention and using lots of compression can help do that. Unfortunately, using too much compression tends to homogenize everything and when you lose the dynamics—particularly on records with more dynamically open arrangements—you can suck the life out of what could have been a great-sounding mix. For some records, lots of compression does work really well. However for others, you want to hear less compression, you want to hear the dynamics, and you want to let the record breathe. You want to hear the space between the instruments instead of having every moment constantly filled.

Nowadays, almost every project we get comes in on hard drives or CD-ROM instead of tape. And there's a lot of bad editing from people who don't know how to use the music software, were very rushed to finish the project, or are just lazy. On a lot of projects, we'll spend several hours just fixing pops and clicks, redoing crossfades, and things like that. The other problem we see is tracks not labeled correctly, so working out what's what can take a lot of time.

Once the tracks in the DAW session are reorganized and all the edits are cleaned, we'll digitally transfer everything over to my Sony 3348 HR, which is a 24-bit 48-track digital tape recorder. They don't get used much anymore since most people mix directly off of their digital workstation. I like using the 3348 because it interfaces well with my SSL console and it also gives me another degree of safety. I now have another backup to what's on the hard disk. Not to mention, the record labels like that there's a safety master and it's on a format that's easy for them to deal with in the future, without needing the right version of some music editing software in order to play it back.

Another bonus in having the tape backup is that it allows me to mix off the tape, while my assistant can work on doing some additional editing, such as moving vocals around or adding a bass drum sample if needed.

As I start mixing, typically the artist, the producer, or both will come into the studio in the morning and give me a rundown on what's on the tape and what I should be watching out for. They'll also tell me what the thought was behind the recording. I'll take some notes and ask questions about the song and what's important to them about the track.

What the artist and producer say is the important thing to me. I try to think like they're thinking. Once I get a good idea of where they're coming from, I'll then spend a few hours and give them my interpretation. If theirs is different, they'll tell me "No, this is the kind of thing we were thinking about," and I'll change it to give them the record they're wanting.

To me, what I think about the record is just a suggestion. Take it or leave it. If they see it differently, that's what's most important. I'll never get married to an idea unless it's the right one for the artist and producer.

After our meeting, they'll usually leave for a while, or just go outside and hang by the pool, and I'll begin the mix. At first I'll spend a couple of hours just getting to learn what's on the tracks. I'll do a quick rough mix and try to get what the song is all about while really listening closely to the vocal. I'll then spend a good amount of time soloing or featuring individual tracks, learning what each instrument or vocal contributes to the overall picture. If it's a song with only 20 tracks, then it goes pretty quickly, but some songs will have 80 tracks, which might take a bit longer.

Next, I begin working on sounds and perspectives, such as panning, EQ, compression, effects, and figure out what sort of environment the song should be in, what sort of reverbs, if any, I should be using, or maybe adding some effects, such as a delay on a voice.

As far as sounds go, sounds are sounds, and rarely are things good or bad. It's bad if it's totally the opposite sound of what the producer had in mind. Yet a "bad" sound can be a good sound if it works in the record and it's what the producer and artist want.

The other day, a project came into the studio that was based on a bunch of loops that were all distorted and filtered. Fifteen years ago I would've thought "What the hell is that?" Nowadays, that's a really hip sound, so the sound of records is always changing.

Once I get a mix that I'm generally happy with, I'll fire up the automation and do rides to get the elements in perspective for each section of the tune. I'll then play it down a number of times with the automation in "trim" or "relative" mode, usually carefully riding the vocal to keep it properly focused and featuring melodic moments from various instruments.

Later, the producer and/or artist will come back and I'll play them what I've done. They'll either say, "Wow, that's great. Just put it down" or "No, that completely sucks. Start over!" [laughs]. What usually happens is that they'll like the mix, but perhaps would like a few things emphasized or de-emphasized.

It Doesn't Take a Lot of Money to Mix Great-Sounding Records

You can make records on just about anything these days, so don't think you need to spend a lot of money to make a good-sounding record. And while the SSL G Series mixing table is what I would call "my axe," I've made good records on equipment that was far less expensive. Remember, it's all about the song and the way you record that brings out the best of that song, and you can pretty much use any kind of equipment to do that.

If I was starting out today and wanting to record my own music, chances are I'd be going the DAW route, like Nuendo, Logic Audio, or maybe even Pro Tools, since they're the formats so many people are using right now. You see

Pro Tools rigs in nearly every major studio these days. But that format could change. The way technology changes today, it's tough for anyone to say this or that's going to be the recording format for the next 10, 15, or even 2 years. Formats come and go, and chances are in a few years it'll be something else.

As far as the recording medium goes, it's probably going to stay in the digital domain from this point forward. As good as analog can sound, there's just certain advantages that you can't deny about digital. Even a lot of the old analog die-hards aren't using analog anymore; they're doing most of their work digitally. With the converters always getting better with higher bit and sample rates, this stuff keeps sounding better all the time.

I think things will always be digital but not necessarily Pro Tools, because there are other systems around that are getting to be better now. Like Nuendo or Logic Audio. Here at Mix This! we have them all and can use everything that's brought to us, whether it's Nuendo, Logic, Cubase, Soundscape, Pro Tools, or even ADAT and DTRS.

Most sessions come in on Pro Tools, which I transfer to the Sony 3348HR and then I mix them down to Nuendo at 88.2 kHz. I like Nuendo a lot, because it's got great editing facilities. It records broadcast WAV files, which is perfect since that's becoming the standard delivery format. Nuendo also interfaces directly to my Apogee converters, which I feel are the best on the market.

I'm also mixing to surround along with stereo, even when people don't ask me for it. I'm doing the surround mix simultaneously so, via the Apogee AD-16, I can record eight tracks at a time, ending up with multiple groups of eight. For example, if I have to do an edit for a single, there's always the choice—a vocal up-mix, a vocal down-mix, a TV backing track with just backing vocals and an instrumental—all mixed in both stereo and surround. I'll always have a minimum of five mixes—five groups of eight tracks. And because they're all locked to time code from the multitrack, if need be I can do an edit on all of them at once in Nuendo, which is quite convenient and saves time.

Not too long ago, I was mixing a pop record in stereo and it sounded good. Then I did the surround mix, where I broke things out a bit and put strings and horns in the back, and so on. When I heard the surround mix, it gave me goose bumps. It sounded that good! I mean, it was like a whole different record that really sounded amazing. For years I kinda thought it was a novelty, but it's not anymore. The surround sound thing, if it's set up properly, can be an amazing experience. Although having said that, until the home surround systems get easier to set up and use, it'll probably remain a novelty.

Whether or not I chose Pro Tools, Nuendo, Logic, Cubase, Performer, or any other kind of computer recording platform, I'd still go with some kind of tape-based recorder/playback system in addition to the computer stuff I'm recording into. I like the idea of having a backup and the option to use either one. I really don't trust any hard disk system by itself, and people who do are really taking a risk, especially if they're paying musicians when they're recording.

I heard about some sessions that went down in London where they had a whole orchestra and it was all going to Pro Tools and the thing crashed. The engineer just about lost his mind. When I heard that, I thought why was he even bothering with Pro Tools only, because at AIR Studios [in London], they have 3348's that never crash. I don't think any computer—MAC or PC—can say that.

My computer of choice would be a Mac, because it's been my experience that Macs are way more stable than Windows-based machines. When we first got Nuendo, [Steinberg] recommended we use PCs. But for us, every few minutes the PC just crashed. We had three PCs. We had one we had bought and one Steinberg had recommended and had set up for us—which crashed big time. We also had a PC whiz at Apogee bring over his hand-built PC that he used for Cubase. While his PC was better than the others, it still crashed. We needed the PC to lock up to the SMPTE. None of them would do it reliably.

Once we got on the Mac, it never crashed and it locked up perfectly to SMPTE. The only thing we wish would be a little better is the software. That can be a little sluggish when you're zooming in and out on the waveform, but other than that, Macs are really reliable.

If I was going portable and wanted a music computer I could take anywhere, I'd go with a Mac. Along with the Mac, I'd have a bunch of Apogee AD-16s [analog-to-digital converters], depending on how many channels I needed. Just for recording, I probably wouldn't need a D/A converter, so I wouldn't worry about getting one of those.

In my portable rig, I'd want to have some great sounding mic preamps like the Apogee Trak-2, which is an amazing pair of stereo mic pre's, or the Apogee Mini-Me, that I really love the sound of, or perhaps some Avalons, that are really good mic preamps. I'd probably want some good compressors, like a couple of Avalons or a couple of the Urei LA-3A's, and perhaps a Pultec EQ.

For people who want to get into Webcasting, one option I'd recommend would be the Apogee stuff. We did some experiments not too long ago by trying to make Web streaming digital audio sound better. We found that using Apogee UV-22 in the mastering stage to get from 24 to 16 bits first makes the after-effects of digitally compressed sounds much less irritating. It sounds clearer, more realistic, and a lot less of that swishy top-end stuff that you typically get from Webcasting audio. That's a big advantage.

Another option would be checking out some other compressors and processors on the market that are specifically built for Webcasting audio. Check out the Aphex 2020 Mk. II. Pieces of gear like this really do enhance Webcasting because they do a certain type of processing—like taking a digital signal and processing it in analog and then converting it back again to digital before it's Webcast—that makes the Webcast sound better. It's amazing what damage Webcasting can do—depending on the bit rate, of course—and how it can mangle your sound unless you're mixing your music specifically for it.

As far as plug-ins go, I'm not really excited about a lot of them. I do use the Mac DSP EQ and Compression, which sounds amazing and the realest to me of any of the other ones I've heard. And it looks kind of normal. Some of these plug-ins make me wonder why they spent so much time graphically duplicating the look of the front panel of a piece of gear the plug-in is trying to duplicate, instead of making it sound better.

My preference is more on the analog side of things, whereas, even though I use digital for storage, I like the hands-on feel of creating and mixing music from a mixing console and not a computer keyboard and mouse.

Sonically, I can't tell the difference between something recorded into Pro Tools or on digital tape, because all my gear has the same kinds of converters and that's the thing that makes the difference. As long as the clocking is really good, since it's all transferred digitally, I don't think most people will be able to tell any difference.

And don't get hung up on all the things people say about technology and recording. For example, a lot of people today say the recording standard is 24 bit—96 kHz and to me, I don't really understand where that's all coming from.

CDs are still recorded at 44.1 kHz and that's still what sells, right? Well, 96k isn't compatible in any way with a CD. We'll either record the multitrack at 44.1k or 48k and then we mix to 88.2, which is compatible with CDs because it's a multiple of 44.1 and a simple division by two gets you there. As a result, there's a lot less signal degradation. Whereas going from 96k to 44.1 is a very complex process and you can lose sound quality by doing it. If you're mastering analog, it doesn't really matter because you're converting it back to analog and then reconverting it to digital anyway.

And the big question if you're sending your music out to be mastered is, will the equipment they'll use be compatible with how your music was recorded and mixed? Bob Ludwig at Gateway Mastering usually does my stuff digitally, so I do everything at 88.2 and it works out great.

I challenge anybody on this planet to be able to tell the difference between something recorded at 88.2 and something recorded at 96k. The difference is so minute that it's just not audible.

If you're mixing for film work and DVD, then 24 bit/48k is the standard, because the video format for digital audio is 48k. On a video DVD, there's usually no room for audio sampled higher than 48k. Occasionally, they'll just want 16 bits on some of these DVDs, simply because if there's so much video content, the audio gets squeezed, and there's not enough room to put 24 bits on them. In these situations, I'll sometimes get asked for a 16-bit DAT [digital audio tape] recorded at 48k for DVD.

A lot of people see the latest gear that's getting all written up and talked about everywhere and think they've got to get rid of their "old" equipment and get the latest stuff that comes out. For example, getting rid of their older Pro Tools rigs and getting the Pro Tools HD system with the 192k sample rate or something like that. My question to them is, why?

First of all, do you realize how much disk space you'll need for a 192k system? It's incredible. Just shuffling that amount of data around and backing it all up can be a nightmare. Not only that, you better get ready to spend a lot of money for more tracks, because Pro Tools HD does 128 channels at 48k, 64 channels at 96k, and 32 channels at 192k. So now what do you do if you need more tracks? Link up multiple Pro Tools HD systems?

Think about it: You're going to spend more time just getting all of that to work and synched and you're going to have to have extra people just to deal with all that. Talk about a big distraction and taking away from the recording process. I mean, what are we doing here: recording for technology tweak heads or making records for humans? It's meaningless and it doesn't add to the music, not to mention it's a whole lot of grief, distraction, and expense.

Anything that people use that distracts from the actual musical recording process is what I don't get. Some of my friends do it and I've heard nightmares about their sessions. My advice is to keep things simple.

In today's digital world, there are some key pieces of gear I think people should have if they're wanting to make really good sounding records. Besides the digital converters—that I've probably mentioned too many times—there comes the regular toolbox of effects that people like to use such as reverbs, compressors, and delays. I've heard some good sounding units that weren't that expensive. I've also heard some bad sounding units that were, so instead of me recommending a certain brand and model, my suggestion is to go to a music store or studio, hear lots of different ones for yourself, and see which ones sound best to your ears.

When I make and mix records, I don't use anything that fancy. I don't need a ton of tube gear. There's a lot of people who think that just because something's got a tube in it, it's going to make it better. But there's a lot of really crappy sounding tube gear too. In fact, I think I have some of it [laughs].

Bob Clearmountain's Mix This!
Studio Equipment List

Dynamic processing:

UREI 1178 Stereo Compressor—Fantastic, but old and cranky; difficult to recall.

Focusrite Red 3 Stereo Compressor—Sounds and looks good but noisy and hard to recall; could use control markings.

UREI LA-3A Compressor—Classic and transparent on vocals; modified for low noise.

Empirical Labs Distressor—Excellent on acoustic guitars and
many other things; great knobs!

SSL FXG384 Outboard Stereo Compressor—Same as in the
G-Series Console; great for piano or submixed drums.

Avalon AD2044 Stereo Compressor—Great on bass and guitars;
difficult to recall.

BSS DPR-901 Dynamic Equalizer—For vocals, it's like cheating!

DBX 902 De-Esser—Quite handy, but not for lead vocals.

Drawmer DS-201 Dual Gate—Great problem-solvers.

Equalizers:

Pultec EQP-1A3—The best then, now, and always will be.

Avalon AD2055, Stereo—Excellent alternative EQ; extremely
posh sound.

Digital signal processors—reverbs, delays, and so on:

Yamaha SPX-990 Multieffects Processor—Not well-known, but versatile and sounds great.

Yamaha Pro-R3 Reverb—Very smooth and rich for long reverbs.

Yamaha SPX-90 Multieffects Processor—Not used much anymore.

Eventide H-3000 Multieffects/Harmonizer—The old standby; lots
of cool stuff in there—when it's working; great sampling.

Eventide H-3500 Multieffects/Harmonizer—Pretty much same as above.

Eventide DSP-4000 Multieffects/Harmonizer—Excellent for tuning vocals, "tape" flanging, and many other things.

Yamaha D5000 Digital Delay—The best DDL ever made.

Roland SDE-3000 Digital Delay—The second-best DDL ever made.

AMS DMX 15-80S Digital Delay—Vintage 80s DDL; I still use it every day.

AMS RMX 16 Reverb—Classic digital verb, a bit grainy and dark; used occasionally.

Lexicon PCM-70 Multi-Effects Processor—"Concert Hall" with some mods is the bomb on piano.

Lexicon 480L Multi-Effects Processor—Not my favorite, but very expensive.

Antares AMM-1 Mic Modeler—Makes most any mic sound better, or worse, which sometimes is better... or not.

Ursa Major SST-282 Space Station—Disgusting, grungy early digital reverb, for a raggedy garage band sound.

MXR Phaser/Flanger Rack (two of each in four-unit rack)—Classic analog effects from the 70s; quite rare these days.

Analog signal processors:

Sans Amp guitar amp simulator—The old, non-memory type; great!

Roland Space Echo 201—Great classic analog tape delay effects — until the tape jams.

Live Echo Chambers—You don't come across these much anymore; kinda like Motown verb.

UREI Filter Set—Great for removing hums or feedback. Mix this! would be a lame studio without this device.

Funk Logic Valvecaster 1960—This box makes everything better; very transparent, subtle effect; looks great!

Funk Logic Digilog Dynamicator—Of all the pieces of gear in the room, this is definitely one of 'em!

Tape Recorders:

Studer A-800 Mk.1, modified to chase code—Classic analog!

Sony PCM-3348HR 48 Trk. Digital w/remote meter—The best multitrack recorder ever made; even better with Apogee converters!

Sony 7030 DAT—The best DAT machine; chases timecode; not easy to operate.

Sony 7010 DAT—Looks like the 7030, but is very different; records code but won't chase.

TASCAM DA-88 Digital 8-Track w/timecode—Used with the PSX-100 for "bit-split" 88.2-kHz stereo mix safeties.

TASCAM DA-38 Digital 8-Track—Used for L-C-R stems for movies, but not much anymore.

ADAT XT Digital 8-Track w/BRC—I'm glad this spends most of its time in the closet nowadays!

TASCAM DA-302 Dual DAT Recorder—Great for double-speed DAT copies.

TASCAM 122 Mk. III Cassette—The best cassette machine, but hardly used anymore.

Digital converters:

Apogee AD-8000SE 8-Channel A/D, D/A Converter—Don't even mention anything else; perfect for the front end of Pro Tools.

Apogee Trak 2 Stereo Mic Pre & A/D Converter—The best mic pre going, with the best 2-channel A/D, 8-channel D/A and AMBus.

Apogee PSX-100 Stereo AD-D/A Converter—Great for mixing double-wide 88.2/96-kHz stereo to Pro Tools or a DA-88.

Apogee AD-16, 16-channel A/D Converter—On the front end of the Nuendo system.

Apogee DA-16, 16-channel D/A Converter—On the back end of the Nuendo system.

Apogee AD-1000 Stereo A/D Converter—That classic Apogee digital sound.

Apogee AD-500 Stereo A/D Converter—Even more classic Apogee digital sound, with "Soft Saturate."

Apogee DA-1000 Stereo D/A Converter—The old standby D to A.

Apogee DA-2000 Stereo D/A Converter—Cello used to sell this great box for about six grand.

Apogee FC-8 ADAT/TDIF Format Converter—They won a TEC award for a format converter!

Microphone preamps and DIs:

Apogee Trak 2 Stereo Mic Pre and A/D Converter—An amazing mic preamp that happens to have an Apogee A/D attached.

Avalon M5 Mic Preamplifier—Great classic-sounding mic pre.

Avalon U5 Active/Passive Direct Box—Perfect for bass and electric guitars.

Microphones:

Neumann M-49 Multipattern Condenser—Great vintage tube vocal mics.

AKG C24 Stereo Multipattern Condenser—Excellent on the Boesendorfer.

Royer R-21 Ribbon—Very warm and smooth.

Royer SF-12 Stereo Ribbon—The best for the top of the Leslie; works well with the Trak 2.

Mojave Multipattern Condenser, David Royer Custom—Handmade by D.R.; the power supply is in an ammo case.

AKG C460 B Condenser—Two of these live in the live chambers.

AKG 414 Condenser—Not thrilling, but OK on the piano.

Octavia MC 012 Condenser—Good, strong Russian sound.

Shure SM-98 Condenser—Great mic for toms.

Shure SM 58 Dynamic—The most versatile mic ever created.

Sennheiser MD-421 Dynamic—The classic tom or bass drum mic.

Speakers:

Dynaudio BM-15s Self-powered monitors—The bomb for 5-channel monitoring.

KRK S-12 Self-powered Subwoofer—Great for the ".1"

Audix N5—Really nice!

Yamaha NS-10M Studio—The old standard.

Monitor Audio—In the Lounge; the best, inexpensive hi-fi speakers I've ever heard.

Mackie HR-824 Self-powered—These make the live chambers sing.

Amplifiers:

Hafler Trans-Nova 9500—Excellent with the Audix N5s.

Yamaha P-2700—Standing by for whatever.

Yamaha P-3200—Perfect for the NS-10Ms.

Sony ES-444 Surround Receiver—Fantastic surround receiver; would be much better without all the DSP.

Computers, DAWs, and software:

Macintosh G4 733 MHz—For Pro Tools and Logic.

Macintosh G4 933 MHz—For Nuendo [see next entry].

Steinberg's Nuendo Digital Audio Workstation—I'm mixing
to stereo and 5.1 to this on the G4 with the Apogee 16s;
sounds excellent!

Macintosh 9600 w/Newer G4 400 MHz upgrade—Retired to the
machine room for playing Quicktime movies, doing sound-
file backups and making CDs.

Apple Macintosh G3 Powerbook—The original; runs
SessionTools—among many other things—in the
control room.

Apple Orange iMac—Prints SessionTools J-cards, labels, and CDs
in the Lounge; client's Web access.

Apple Macintosh Beige G3—Server for SessionTools, e-mail
router; now-up-to-date and remote file transfers.

Digidesign ProTools Mix Plus—On the 733 G4 and uses an
AD-8000SE and the two Trak 2s for interfaces.

Logic Audio—Uses the DAE and Apogees, if someone needs it.

Mackie HDR-24 24-track Hard Disk Recorder—Very stable,
reliable recorder; however, the editing software isn't quite
there yet.

Digidesign Universal Slave Driver—Great synchronizer, but only Pro Tools can use it.

Opcode Studio 3 SMPTE/MIDI Interface—Not used much anymore, but did serve us well.

Microboards DSR 8800 CD Duplicator, plus five slaves—Everyone in the band gets a CD in a few minutes; runs off the Mac 9600.

Yamaha CDR 1000 CD/CD-RW Recorder—Great for one-offs from the desk or DAT safeties.

Glyph Hard Disk/DDSs Tape Drive Combo—For backing up without that beeping noise; rather unreliable.

Kensington Data Express Hotswap Drive Bay—For when we need more disk space… NOW!

VXA Tape Backup Drive—Faster backups, and less expensive than AIT.

Aurora Fuse Video PCI Card—For getting Quicktime out of the Mac 9600 to the Video Projector.

Other studio gear goodies:

Dolby "Dolbyfax" ISDN AC-2 encoder/decoder—Incredibly handy when the client can't be here for the mix.

TimeLine Lynx Synchronizer Module—Still the standard.

Brainstorm Timecode Destripalyzer—Lets you know what you've got—but not what to do with it.

Brainstorm Dual Timecode Distribution Amplifier—Makes sure
there's enough code to go around.

Grass Valley Video Sync Generator—NTSC house synch.

Sigma Electronics Blackburst Video Sync Generator—PAL
house synch.

Little Labs Sample Switcher—Jonathan Little did this one up for
me special.

Russian Dragon—Tells you if you're rushing or dragging.

DTS CAD-4 Decoder—For checking surround CD refs; it'd be
nice if it had alternate output configs.

Studio Technologies StudioCom 5.1 Monitor Control—Crank up
all those six speakers at once; needed a mod for a prefade
line out to connect to the Lounge 5-1 hi-fi system for alternate listening. "We've actually done that mod with some help
from Lucas Van Der Mee at Apogee—works great!"

Mitsubishi X500-UProfessional Video Projector—We show
synched Quicktime movies with this when mixing to picture.

On How Long It Should Take to Make a Record

I've had people ask me how long should it take to make a record. I tell them as
long as you need to make the record sound the best it can. I've done records
that only took a couple of weeks and I've done some that have taken a couple
of years.

When we did David Bowie's *Let's Dance* record that my old friend Nile
Rogers produced, it took us 3 weeks from start to finish to record and mix, and

it was a huge hit album. Whereas, John Fogerty's *Blue Moon Swamp* took 5 years. I mean, it only took us 2½ weeks to mix it, but he took a really long time to record it. He probably went through every drummer he could get a hold of to try new arrangements for every song. I think Def Leppard's *Pyromania* record took a couple of years.

I would say the normal amount of time to record and mix a record would be 2 to 3 months. As far as cost goes, if you're not engineering or mixing the record yourself, I tell people to plan on spending anywhere from $50 to $75 an hour for the engineer. For mixing, figure on anywhere from $1,000 to $5,000 a song, with the higher-end mixers also getting points [a percentage royalty] of record sales. Typically, their fee becomes an advance against their royalty.

Having said that, I do believe fees are coming down, as the market and budgets are getting tighter and people have to adjust to stay competitive and working. So it doesn't hurt to negotiate a fair rate for you and them.

And if you don't have a lot of money, don't be shy about asking a producer, engineer, or mixer to defer their fees in exchange for a small percentage or royalty on your record. If you've got the right song, sound, and potential to make something happen, I know many people who'll do just that.

How Making Music and Records Has Changed

When I started recording it was really exciting, because it was always with live musicians and that's what I enjoyed the most. Early on, I thought mixing records was boring because you're just sitting there in this room with one other guy pushing faders.

I always liked having a whole band out in the studio where you're running around plugging in mics and getting the headphones to work. Then, when everything is all hooked up and working, and they start playing and you start recording, you'd get a great take and everyone would say, "Wow, what was that!" That was exciting.

Nowadays, that so rarely happens. Today, most records are made by someone sitting in front of a computer with a mouse. That's not exciting at all. In fact, it's kinda dull and I'm amazed people put up with it. How does making records like that actually interest anyone at all? I couldn't do it.

We have a guy here at the studio who runs our DAW system and luckily, he likes it, whereas, even though I know how to work the thing, I can't do it because I don't have the patience. At least when I'm mixing, I'm turning knobs and pressing buttons and stuff and I get to slide back and forth in front of a big mixing console!

New Thinking for a New Music Business

People often ask me what I would do today if I were just starting out. To tell you the truth, I don't know what I'd do nowadays, because the record business is in such a mess. It's dying because of downloads and people copying. It's literally getting sucked down the Internet! If I were starting out today, I'd probably get more into mixing music for films, television, and things like that. Perhaps I'd go into mixing live sound.

It just doesn't seem as much fun to make records as it did not too long ago. The fact that the record business seems to be disappearing now has really affected a lot of people who are serious about making records.

There's all these people who download and copy music who think music should be free. Yet, I just wonder what they're going to be thinking a few years from now, when there'll be a lack of new music because the record companies have shut down from people not paying for the records. Of course, it doesn't help that record prices are kept so high because of the astronomical costs of radio and other types of promotion. The creeps running Clear Channel will probably wonder why their thousand or so radio stations have no new music to play after they helped put the nails in the record business's coffin by demanding huge payments for record spins!

Whether or not that actually happens is one of the scenarios for the future of the record business. I mean, who's to say, but you've got to be thinking where is it all going to go if people keep doing what they're doing? To me, it's all leading in that direction.

Hopefully, there's still going to be enough people who don't steal and actually understand that downloading free music is stealing not only from the record company, but more importantly, from the artists who create the music they are downloading, and whom they're supposedly fans of. Make no mistake: the record business has been overinflated for years. And like the stock market, maybe the record business will take a correction and come back down to normal again. We'll all just have to drive cheaper cars. I'm in—it's worth it!

Website: Mixthis.com

Lesson 10
Mastering Your Music: Advice from Bob Ludwig

In the world of mastering engineers, none is as sought after as Bob Ludwig. Bob is to mastering what Enzo Ferrari is to cars. Mastering is that oft-heard term that few people really understand. Perhaps its obfuscation is deliberate. It is the mastering engineers who bring out the best in recorded audio, but few are willing to reveal their methods and trade secrets to those seeking but a taste of technique to help them create better recordings.

Consider yourself one of the fortunate few, because Bob is about to impart advice that's bound to help you think differently when it comes to that final—and many say crucial—component of your music.

I went to Portland, Maine, to interview Bob, and what I discovered was eye-opening, to say the least. Despite having mastered the recordings of music's greatest stars and legends, he still has the twinkle in his eye of a young boy who's met the love of his life—music—for the first time. Bob loves his artists and his music, and everything he does is done with a zeal and zest that any of us would do well to emulate.

Ludwig's Gateway Mastering studio is a sight to behold. From the album-lined walls and award-filled shelves to rooms packed with equipment and people who know how to work its magic, Bob's paradise is contained in the two stories he calls home.

Walk into his traffic control room—the room with a wall-sized bulletin board filled with client names in time slots of days and hours—and on any day of the week, you'll find names like Beck, Mariah Carey, Celine Dion, Faith Hill, John Mellencamp, Natalie Merchant, Bruce Springsteen, and the hottest new group and artist climbing the Billboard charts, booked to have their record mastered by Bob Ludwig.

Over the years, Bob has mastered thousands upon thousands of records for such artists as Bryan Adams, Rush, Dire Straits, The Bee Gees, Eric Clapton, The Band, Elvis Costello, Gloria Estefan, Bryan Ferry, Foo Fighters, Jimi Hendrix, Journey, Nirvana, Radiohead, Pearl Jam, Rage Against the Machine, The Police, REM, Lou Reed, The Rolling Stones (almost every album!), Paul Simon, Carly Simon, Peter Wolf, ZZ Top, Led Zeppelin, and… well, you get the picture. (For a more complete listing go to Allmusic.com or Gatewaymastering.com.)

A classically trained and inspired trumpet virtuoso who found his love in many kinds of music, Bob's enthusiasm for the song and the artist has never wavered. And his advice has never been more timely for anyone ready to make their mark in the new music business.

Bob on Starting Out

My music recording career started in the late 1960s. I received my Master of Music degree from the Eastman School of Music in Rochester, New York. Many wonderful things happened when I was at Eastman. I played trumpet for the Utica Symphony Orchestra, which was an amazing experience, and I received lots of great hands-on recording experience while working in Eastman's recording department.

About the time I was finishing up my master's degree, Phil Ramone came to teach the first recording workshop at the school. At the end of his workshop program, he asked me if I wanted to come work for him at A&R Recording in New York. How could I refuse?

When Phil arrived on campus to teach his workshop, I was working in the recording department, and while he was there I became his de facto assistant, which led to his job offer. Little did I know what I was about to get into. Even though I had already recorded thousands of student and faculty recitals and concerts prior to Phil's arrival at Eastman, once I was introduced to the pop music recording world it was surprising in ways I never imagined.

When I began my musical career, I never wanted to do anything other than be a professional symphonic player. And once it happened, it was tremendously fulfilling. The thrill of playing solo trumpet and performing many of the great works was immensely enjoyable. However, it wasn't too long before I had experienced enough of the symphony to realize it wasn't quite what I was looking for. And much to my parents' chagrin (they wanted me to be a music teacher), I decided to go to New York and work with Phil.

From the first time I had a tape recorder when I was 8 years old, I had always loved recording. All those concerts, orchestral, recital, and symphonic recordings I had done at Eastman were priceless experiences. However, working with Phil would be a learning experience like no other. And I would be in good company.

Although I originally wanted to be a mix and remix engineer while at A&R, I learned the art of mastering, which I found I had an affinity for. Every recording engineer at A&R was an apprentice; some have gone on to become legends in the business, like Eliot Scheiner [who worked with Aerosmith, Eagles, Steely Dan] and Shelly Yakus [who worked with B.B. King, Tom Petty, U2].

Working with Phil at A&R was a great training ground. I learned disk cutting, which for some genetic reason [laughs] came easy. It really was an art; either you got it or you didn't. There's also the patience that a disk cutter needs. There were many times when I'd be 23 minutes into cutting a 24-minute side and something would go wrong with the disk cutting lathe vacuum, and I'd have to start all over again. Sometimes it would happen four or five times in a row.

In addition to disk cutting, A&R kept me busy assisting on many recording and mixing sessions. And because I read music scores, I did a lot of work for many classical clients, including Nonesuch Records, who is still my oldest client to this day.

After working at A&R for a couple of years, Neumann had developed a highly advanced disk cutting system that was a major leap from anything we had seen or heard. Though management at A&R didn't want to buy the new gear at the time, I knew it would be impossible to compete against this gear, because it was just that good.

Right about the same time as the Neumann equipment was coming out, a new recording and mastering company called Sterling Sound was starting in New York. The buzz surrounding Sterling was exciting, and most exciting for me was the fact that they already had Neumann, Studer, and Telefunken gear. After much thought, I left A&R and went to work for Sterling.

It didn't take long for things to start happening. I cut *Led Zeppelin II* after just joining Sterling and things just snowballed from there. Some of the first hits I cut were Neil Diamond's "Kentucky Woman" along with albums from artists like Jimi Hendrix and The Doors.

Early on in my career, I was fortunate to have worked on some master-piece records with some musical legends. The Led Zeppelin records were unique in their time, and have held up all these years as timeless recordings. When I started out there were no oldies radio stations. The songs those stations would play years later were the ones we were creating.

It was a time when I was mastering records for Janis Joplin, Jim Morrison, and Jimi Hendrix—all at the same time! And talk about a scary moment. I was working on each one's record when they died. I thought, my gosh, I'm jinxed [laughs].

The Music Business, Yesterday and Today

When rock and roll was being created, practically all artists were on independent record labels, with the exception of a few artists like The Beatles who were on the huge record label EMI. Back then, the majority of the labels were independent. None of the conglomerates and corporate takeover of the labels and radio had happened yet. Elektra was independent. So were Atlantic, Warner Bros., and Columbia. The music business was filled with great independents, from large to small.

Since that time music has changed, and not always for the better. We've gone from an era when there were only independent record labels and radio stations to today, where we have five major labels and three corporations that own most of the radio stations in America—radio stations that are programmed by a handful of people, and it's horrible. Number one records are bought now and not created.

Years ago, before the conglomerates took over the record labels and business, I used to easily be able to pick out a number one hit record. It's different now. The first time I listened to Hall and Oates's "Private Eyes" or "Your Kiss Is on My List" it was immediately clear to me that what I was hearing would become a hit. Same thing happened for ZZ Tops's "Legs." I couldn't believe what was coming off the tape. It was just magic.

Working on those records and with those artists was a thrill from the first day I did it, and still continues to be to this day. Even after all these years, it's just as fresh for me to work on music today as it was when I first started. Each day is exciting. I never know whose record will come in for me to master or what great song I might hear. What better job can I have than working on a daily basis with such artists as Faith Hill, Beck, and Bruce Springsteen?

While the ownership and business of today's record labels have changed, when it comes to a record's success, two things have not: a great hook and a great performance. That's it. All you need is one microphone in a studio, and if it's a great song with a great performance, it will probably sell—even today.

Years ago, some record label did a survey to find out how much quality influenced the sales of a record. The number they found was something like five percent. The other ninety-five percent was the artist, the song, the publicity, the price, and other factors.

The Importance of Mixing in the Recording Process

When I look at the three parts of the recording process—recording, mixing, and mastering—without a doubt I think the mix is the most important part. The top mixers, if they're good enough, will actually get a royalty percentage of the record. That's how important they and the mix are to a record. The mix can make or break a record—no matter how well it's recorded.

There's nothing sadder to see than an engineer who's recorded great-sounding tracks coming into our studio and listening for the first time to someone's poor mix on them. Watching the devastation on the face of an engineer who's hearing how his work was trashed is tough. On the other hand, if the mixing is done by someone great, it can be an entirely different story. I've seen Bob Clearmountain rescue terrible recordings and make these amazing mixes out of them—mixes so good, you just can't believe anyone could be capable of pulling that off.

Some recordings have the same people record and mix their music, while others have a separate engineer and mixer. There are pros and cons to both. From a mastering point of view it doesn't impact me at all, since I work with the final product that I'm given, regardless of how many people worked on the recording.

The point can be made that the person who engineered the project is the best person to mix the project. He or she knows all the tapes, all the overdubs, and everything that happened on the session. The counterpoint to that would be the case of a record that's taken a long time to finish. Some records I've mastered took a year or more to record. In those situations, the engineer can be so close to the project that the perspective has been lost on what's good and bad, what the record needs or doesn't. When that happens, taking the record to a separate mixer can be a good idea.

The mixer is hearing the record for the first time, and he or she will have a vision of the many ways they can make it sound like what they're hearing in their heads. Many times, the mixer will come up with a whole different musical context of great ideas that the artist and producer never dreamed of.

I think the ideal recording/engineering/mixing situation is really quite simple. Bruce Springsteen comes to mind here. For his Grammy-winning album *The Rising*, the whole record was recorded in just a matter of weeks, which was the shortest time he ever took to cut an album. To put recording a complete album that quickly in some context, years ago I mastered a record for James Brown. When I received the tapes, James called me and said, "We really care about this record Bob, and I want you to know that we spent a week on it." That was recording and mixing it [laughs]!

For *The Rising*, Bruce was working with Brendan O'Brien, who is one of the most successful musical producers today, as well as being a great engineer. As Bruce was recording, Brendan was also mixing the record. So every time Bruce was working on the record, he was also hearing a mix that was becoming more finely honed. Then, when it came time to do the final mix, all it needed was basically just a few slight adjustments to what he had been hearing over those last few weeks. To me, that's an ideal recording, engineering, and mixing situation.

Taking a long time to record a record, hearing the same thing over and over, and then hearing how that record can sound with a fresh new mix can be a bit traumatic to some. Whereas, doing everything in a shorter period of time, like Bruce did for *The Rising*, can be a very gratifying and enjoyable way to make a record.

The Importance of Mastering
in the Recording Process

With so many people doing home and project studio recordings, mastering is more important now than it's ever been. Mastering is the last creative step, where the final sound of the record will be determined. In many instances, when costs may have been cut during some part of the recording process, people are amazed at how poorly recorded music can be made to at least sound normal through excellent mastering. Many times, it can sound better than ever imagined. Mastering can make that big a difference.

Sometimes our job as mastering engineers is to take a really bad-sounding tape and make it sound normal. On the other hand, when we get a tape to master from one of these really great mixers—like Tom Lord-Alge, Jack Joseph Puig, Andy Wallace, Eliot Scheiner, Bob Clearmountain, and others like them—the mixes are so good that simply adding a small amount of mastering in a certain place will make it sound like you've made huge sonic changes. The extraordinary mixing work these great mixers do before their music comes to me is so carefully balanced that, many times, the slightest adjustment will make a radical change to it.

Recording has changed so much and so fast in just a brief period of time. Years ago, we used to be able to pick out all digital recordings very easily. They were brittle sounding and a bit one-dimensional. As time has gone on, and as the quality of analog-to-digital converters has gotten so much better, some of the best-sounding music now is completely digital. Again, regardless if you're using analog or digital, it all depends on how it's mixed.

The first commandment in the mastering bible is to do no harm to the sound. I think any gifted mastering engineer has the ability to hear a raw tape and imagine in their head how it could sound, and then know what kinds of gear to use and what buttons to move to make it sound like it does in their head.

The first time I hear new music from a client, my goal is to listen to the tape to hear what's really in there. After that, my job is to bring out and maximize the most musicality that's inherent in their music and on that tape. Having the ability to hear the raw tape and imagining in my head how it can sound, and then knowing what equipment to use and knobs to move to make it sound that way, is the essence of what I do.

My speakers are able to reveal things that people have never heard—even after they've been working on an album for months. There have been times when we've found ticks and defects on an album, and the studio where it came from can't hear them—even after they've been told where they are. Great speakers can reveal those kinds of things and are critically important to your music.

As a mastering engineer perhaps I'm like a painter, and the things that I use in order for me to get the sounds I do are the different colors in the palette. Those different colors could be the many different kinds of analog and digital equalizers, because they each have different colors, or capabilities to shape or paint the sound-scape. Some of them are extremely clinical and pristine, and others have a very musical color that can add a lot of life to the music.

The other colors I use may be the many different compressors we have, each having different sounds and arrangements in the signal path. Colors can also include the choices for the playback medium—whether it's going to be digital or analog—that influences the final sound.

We have five different kinds of analog tape playback here at the studio. We have Studer and Ampex stock machines. We have Ampex machines with discrete class A electronics. We have two different kinds of tube playback systems for the machines. And every one of those machines sounds distinctly different from every other one. Just to be able to choose the most appropriate playback for whatever kind of music comes through our doors makes a huge impact on the mastering and music.

And people can hear the difference. Sometimes a tape will come through the door, from a group I've never heard before, and I need to get acclimated to where they are coming from with their music. My goal as a mastering engineer is to make the musicality that they put into their project come through to the listener as much as possible. I want to get in tune with where they are, so I can forward their vision. One way we do that is by playing the artist's music on solid state versus tube playback electronics to see which they prefer. Some will say they like tube because it's so warm. Then when they hear solid state they understand what the trade-off might be, and they might not want their music to sound so warm.

When new music comes in, the first thing we do if it's analog is to align it to calibration tones that have been made for that particular project. We obviously won't know if the song has any sonic problems such as ticks and defects, etc., until we listen to it. The time it takes to master an album can vary, but for the most part, I'll typically begin mastering an album at 10:00 a.m. and will have it finished, edited, and deticked if needed by 7 p.m.

The first song usually takes the longest, I'd say roughly ninety minutes, since, before I work on the first song, I'll listen to certain parts of the entire album to get an idea where the band or artist is coming from. After the first song, the other songs may take a half hour or so, per song, to master.

These days, when working with a new artist or group, some A&R people will stack the majority of strong songs up front on the recording. Unless you spot-check the entire album first, you might think the first few songs are what the band and album are all about, only to find something different a few more cuts down the line.

After giving the entire recording a good spot check, I then set the bearings for the album. This is where I'll decide how much compression it does or doesn't need, along with making lots of decisions about the first song that will apply to the rest of the album. Mastering is the last chance to give your recording any of the elements it needs before the public hears it. And if you do it right, the results can be astounding.

I tell people if you want to record multitrack digital, then try mixing down into analog. It'll make a huge difference on how your record sounds. If you can mix down to ½-inch analog tape running at 30 ips [inches per second], it can really help gel a poor mix into a much better-sounding mix.

With digital-only, the highest-quality and best-sounding product you'll be able to achieve and say, is that it sounds exactly like it came off the console. With analog tape, many times, especially if you're not the world's greatest mixer, it sounds better than what came off the console. Why? Because analog tends to very musically glue the elements together in a way that's very satisfying to our ears. Even if you can't buy a ½-inch analog machine, I recommend renting one when it comes time to mix down your music.

People at the top of the mastering heap like Doug Sax, Stephen Marcussen, George Marino, and Greg Calbi will often get tapes from people who trust them completely to do whatever they want to their music. A good mastering engineer will have a vision and can give the client a finished product that will truly blow their mind.

I must say that even if you're a well-known mastering engineer, getting projects coming in from great mixers can be very daunting. At times, we'll get projects in from the best mixers on the planet, from people who will have worked on a record as long as they needed to—many times with little or no budget limits—in order to get the record as perfect as possible, and we are expected to make the record sound even better.

There's no question that a great mix locks in how great the final record will be. Good mastering is simply the icing on the cake. It makes a good record sound better. When it comes to mastering your music, paying someone else to do it for you is well worth the time and money spent.

The Biggest Mistakes People Make in Recording

Probably the biggest mistake I hear people making is using too much compression. Listen, you don't even want to get me going on the state of compression these days. It's one of the things that's hurting the music business. Artists and A&R people insist on having their music squashed way beyond anything they should. It only hurts the music and ruins its longevity.

If the digital compressors people use today had been invented and used at the time of The Beatles, their music would not have near the longevity to it. It absolutely makes that big a difference. Too much compression on music fatigues listeners' ears. You simply don't feel like hearing the music again.

Yet today it's a catch-22, because the music business is so highly competitive, with records competing against each other for chart position and sales. A program director, an A&R person, or even an artist will listen to one version of their record and then listen to the same record that's slightly louder—not better, just louder—from added compression, and the overly compressed record seems to have that much more impact. The extra loudness seems more attractive, so when you listen to the louder one for eight bars it does seem to sound better. Yet if you listen to the record from beginning to end, that same record now assaults and tires the ears, and you won't want to listen to it or put it on again until some time has passed.

Compare this to the original Beatles records. The only compression they used back then was during recording and mixing. Those Beatles records still have superb dynamic range, and that's critically important. When it comes to using compression, always remember that less is more. And keep in mind that when you're recording into the digital domain, using processing once is much better than using processing twice. And with cheaper digital gear, it doesn't like to be processed too much.

Tips on Setting Up a Recording Studio Workstation and Recording Platform

Pro Tools is a ubiquitous workstation for a good reason; it's fabulous. When compared to the older Pro Tools systems, the newer HD systems are, in my opinion, better for recording and mixing. And while there are many plug-ins to choose from, one of my favorites is the Waves plug-ins. The good news about plug-ins and digital recording is that things keep sounding better and getting cheaper.

Today you can literally replace a $250,000, 48-track digital open-reel tape machine with an Apple laptop and a FireWire I/O box for a fraction of the price. I have clients who will come into the studio with Pro Tools loaded into a Mac and they can play 48 tracks simultaneously off their Mac's internal hard drive. With a great song and performance, making great music has never been easier or cheaper, regardless of where you do it. It does help if you know what you are doing with it all!

When it comes to deciding whether you should spend extra money for software and equipment that can handle the higher sampling rates, such as 192 kHz, it's all dependent on how important sound accuracy is to you. The higher sampling rates for a given converter will yield a better sound.

Which format to choose and what kind of gear to buy are always complicated questions. There's no single answer, because what you choose must take into account your budget compared to your needs. For example, great older equipment can sometimes blow the doors off many new pieces of gear with the latest technology. There's no question that a Pacific Microsonics Model One digital-to-analog converter running at 44.1 kHz at 16 bits will blow away a $5, 192-kHz, 24-bit computer chip.

My advice to people who may not have the money for a high-end workstation system right now is to buy the best digital audio workstation you can afford, and spend the extra money on A/D and D/A converters. Get the very best you can, because excellent converters are crucial to making high-quality recordings.

Keep in mind that when you digitize your music, any distortions or jitter that is put into the analog-to-digital part of it cannot be removed in any fashion by anything further down the recording, mixing, editing, and mastering line. If your analog-to-digital conversion is no good, then the rest of the recording processing chain can't possibly help it.

Some Advice on Internet and Remote Broadcasting

With regard to Internet broadcasting, we use a dedicated FTP [file transfer protocol] system that allows our clients to send their music via the Internet to transfer non-data-compressed files. If we're doing a music project with a 100-megabyte song recorded at 88.2 kHz and 24 bits, it's completely lossless—no data changed or lost in the transfer process—when the other person receives it.

Broadcasting music works in a different way than FTP, since the method that it's broadcast by is streaming; it's received only bits at a time and not as a complete file all at once. As such, streaming requires mega data reduction on the order of something like 40 kbits per second, which is similar to what is used for satellite radio broadcasts. They use severely data-compressed signals, and some people under certain conditions, like using headphones while listening to classical music, will find that sound unacceptable.

On rare occasions we're asked to make an MP3 for use on the Internet. Sometimes we'll try different techniques to see if we can make it sound better for that kind of broadcast, but on the whole you're still pretty much beholden to the companies that make the software and hardware for Internet broadcast conversion. While MP3s can sound good, especially given the process they must go through before the listener hears them, many of the subtleties of the music are still lost.

With most codecs—code-decode, which is the process of coding your files for sending and decoding the files when received—we've found that if we do an **FFT** [fast Fourier transform] of the music with and without the codec in the circuit, store each in the analyzer, and subtract them from each other, the resulting frequency response ends up being about the same.

There is no EQ one can use to "correct" the codec. You might make a copy, hear it, and think it sounds brittle, but once it goes through these codecs—necessary for delivery of Internet broadcast files—and you try to change things and pre-EQ for it, you usually end up hurting some other part of the sound.

The high-quality codecs handle music with a lot of dynamics in it very well. However, most codecs do strange things to music files. It's tough to have some sort of global setting or fix that will work for all of them. My advice is to record your music at the highest sampling rate you can.

The Future of Recording

What I do is a lot like being a doctor. For one, you need to have a lot of dedication and love for what you do. There are always manuals to read, things to study, new technology and gear to learn. Over the years I've found that keeping up with changing technology is really important.

One of the things that has helped our business is that when a new technology is emerging, people usually knock on our door and tell us about it. Many times they get us involved before the technology or equipment is established. We're able to work with designers and manufacturers of these new technologies and understand and use them sometimes months before they hit the market.

For example, Sony came to us when they were developing the Super Audio CD. A team of Sony engineers from Tokyo came to visit Gateway Mastering twice during the development process for our evaluation. We were able to start working with SACD in the very early stages of its development, which helped both us and Sony a lot.

I think the future of recorded music is moving in the direction of SACD, DVD Audio, and surround. In automobiles, surround sound has the potential to be a big thing. A car is a very compelling place to listen to surround audio. Often I'll have record-label A&R people ask me how they can hear the surround mix in their cars. Whether it's in a car, studio, or home, when people hear 5.1 surround sound done correctly, most people don't want to go back to stereo. You can't go wrong by moving more of your music and recording work in the direction of these formats. In the case of surround, it's simply that good.

Website: Gatewaymastering.com

PART 3

Your Business in the New Music Business

Lesson 11
Launching the Business of You, Inc.:
Five Steps to Incorporation

It's time you become a "real" businessperson. It's time you get smart about protecting your assets, deducting all the business expenses you're entitled to, taking advantage of the immense saving and investment opportunities awaiting you and, finally, using the power of owning your own business to give you the clout that will change the way other businesses and people will see you from this point on. It's time for you to learn how to incorporate.

The Benefits of Incorporation

Why incorporate? In Lesson 5, "Building Your A-Team," I introduced you to Larry Cohen, one of the best CPAs in the business, who helped a friend of mine save $40,000 on his tax return. Larry strongly believes that the benefits of incorporation far outweigh any slight disadvantages. Here is some of what he has to say on the subject.

Let me ask you a question: Would you spend $500 to save $50,000? I'm imagining your answer will be yes. One of the best things anyone can do is to start a business. And over the life of your corporate entity, you will easily save thousands (perhaps tens of thousands) or more in tax deductions and saving benefits. This is a country built on small businesses, and so important are they that the government created all kinds of wonderful benefits designed to help small businesses get started and grow.

Many musicians simply start their business as a sole proprietorship. This is a simple and easy way to begin taking advantage of the tax deductions available for businesses, since the IRS acknowledges sole proprietorships as long as there is an intent by the business to make a profit within a specified period (i.e., the "ruling period").

However, many musicians find it more desirable to form a corporate entity. Some form limited liability companies (LLCs), and LLCs have their plusses and minuses. Here are a few things to keep in mind regarding an LLC:

- An LLC can be taxed as a partnership for federal income tax purposes. However, most of the time the profit or loss is reported on the "members'" individual income tax returns.

- The LLC is state-registered. California, for example, taxes the LLC on gross receipts, plus a minimum tax of $800.

- "Members" are not personally liable for the LLC's debts and liabilities.

- "Members" may participate in management without risking personal liability. No limitations are placed on the number of owners.

- LLCs have the ability to make disproportionate allocations and distributions.

For most of his clients, Larry recommends forming an S corporation. To read about the advantages of forming an S corporation, go to Incorporate.com and use promo code 4385, where it asks how did you hear about us.

Tax Advantages

One of the major tax advantages to having a corporation is the ability to invest up to 25 percent of your earnings or $30,000, whichever is less, into a SEP-IRA. Compare that to the smaller yearly limit for a with regular or Roth IRAs. It's a no-brainer as to which is the better deal for you.

Then there are the deductions. The IRS makes it simple for you as the owner of your business—be it a sole proprietorship, LLC, or S corporation—to deduct necessary and ordinary business expenses. Necessary expenses—those that are crucial to your business—include office supplies, professional membership fees (e.g. musician's union dues), magazine and book purchases, and the like. Ordinary expenses are any kind of equipment and gear you need to make music, like keyboards, drums, mics, speakers, effects, amps, guitars, and so on.

- *Business formation.* You can deduct the costs of creating your corporate entity.

- *Business use of car.* If you need a car to help you get to and from your business, to your practices, to the music store or studio, or in any other way for your business, the cost of purchase or leasing can be deducted.

- *Gas, insurance, and car repairs.* The business portion of anything your car needs to keep it running and insured is deductible.

- *Music equipment.* If you're a musician and you're making money by playing, writing, creating, or the like in the music business, you can deduct that amp, those strings, that new CD, your guitar, microphones, and any other music supplies or equipment from your taxes.

- *Leasing.* Your vehicle, an office, or any other equipment leased for your business can be a big tax deduction.

- *Insurances.* Health insurance, car insurance, equipment insurance, home insurance, and the like are all legit business deductions.

- *Services.* Repairs on your equipment including regular maintenance for your instruments and hiring others to perform work for your business can also be a deduction.

- *Business loan interest.* Unlike personal credit card interest, business loan interest charges can be a tax deduction as well.

- *Internet and its services.* If you use the Internet to inform yourself about and find the latest gear, to keep up with music news that can help your business, or to stay in touch via e-mail with other musicians, then you can deduct your monthly access fee and other costs.

- *Website.* If you've got a website or are going to put one up for your business, those costs are tax-deductible.

- *Computer and office equipment.* If you are using your computer and office equipment in your business, then those expenses can be deducted.

- *Computer software and supplies.* The latest plug-ins, as well as peripherals, disks, cables, and extra storage drives, can be a big deduction.

- *Clothes and shoes.* If you're a performer and your clothes are required exclusively for your gig, then you've got a deduction.

- *Books, magazines, other publications, and CDs.* If you need print media or music on disc to help you in your business, then they're deductible.

- *Moving.* If you relocate to a new town for a new job, a better job, or a different job, and it's related to your business, the entire cost of your move is deductible, including the costs of hiring a mover, as well as your gas, meals, lodging, flights, car rentals, etc.

- *Printing, advertising, and marketing.* If you had flyers printed to promote your band or music, bought advertising (print, television, radio, Internet, etc.), and paid for any other kinds of marketing to help you and your music business, then you've got deductions coming.

- *Continuing education.* If you want to take that latest Pro Tools class or go to recording school, or perhaps take a few classes at your local college to learn more about international business, go ahead and take them and keep your receipts. Continuing education is a tax deduction.

- *Food.* If you have lunch or dinner with a potential business client, or talk business with other people who could get you work or other business opportunities, then a portion of those expenses are deductible.

- *Travel.* If you travel anywhere on business, the cost of your trip is deductible, including flights, rental car, hotel, food, entertainment (that new show with great music and lighting that may help you create something good for your business), and other out-of-pocket expenses. Save all receipts.

- *Home.* If you use your home or apartment to conduct business, a portion of that residence is deductible. This means that a portion of what you pay in either rent or mortgage payments can be deducted, over and above your mortgage interest. A double benefit. The deduction is based on how much space and how many rooms you are using for your business, with a percentage formula applied to arrive at your total deduction.

- *Home utilities and insurance.* That same percentage formula can be applied to your home's utilities and insurance required for the areas you use for your home business.

- *Phone.* Your home and cell phone charges can be deductible if they are used for your business.

- *Parking.* Business-related parking is deductible.

- *Postage and shipping.* Any time you use any mail service—U.S. Post Office or private services—to send letters or packages for your business, those expenses are tax-deductible.

- *Office supplies.* Envelopes, printer paper, staples, pens, paper, etc., are tax deductions if you need them for your business.

- **Research.** If you write movie scripts and you go to the movie theater to see the newest film, your ticket is deductible since it's research that can give you new ideas for plots, characters, story, setting, and the like. And don't forget to keep your receipt for the Diet Coke and popcorn, too. Likewise, if you're a musician and you're looking for some great new ideas for songs and you want to check out the latest solo artist or group at a club or concert venue in town, go ahead and enjoy yourself. Just keep your receipts.

- **CPA and attorney fees.** The costs of professional services that your company uses are tax-deductible as well. Get the double benefit of using these services to help you, and then deduct the cost to help you reduce your tax liability.

And there are many more.

Other Advantages

As Larry told you, having a corporate legal business entity can also protect your personal assets as well as your business. If your business is a sole proprietorship, partnership, or, even worse, has no formal business structure at all, you (or you and your partners) are personally liable if someone sues you, as well as for any debts your business incurs.

However, if your business is set up as a corporation or LLC, it is the legal entity (and not you) that is responsible for the debts it incurs. While there are cases of illegalities of corporate malfeasance where both the corporation and principals can be liable, sued, and fined, these are the exception and not the rule. Having a legal corporate entity provides you (and your assets) maximum protections under the law.

Yes, incorporating does cost money, though not much as you may think, and it does take a little extra time (probably less than one hour a year) to fill out the yearly updates and corporation compliance forms that'll be sent to you, but I'm absolutely convinced that the benefits far exceed any cost and time.

When I first began my business, I did so as a sole proprietor. I didn't have any kind of corporate legal structure. I had a name for my business and kept good records of my expenses and income. When my taxes were filed, my CPA simply noted my sole proprietorship's income and expenses on them and that was that.

However, as I began to do more business with incorporated businesses, they would often ask me if I was incorporated. Often, when I answered that I wasn't, it was like bingo, the light went on for them that my business was a one-person, small-potatoes operation, and the way they treated me from that point on changed. You wouldn't think it would—after all, I was still the same person offering the same kind of service they enjoyed receiving—but in the real world of business, perception is reality. If you're perceived as operating out of your garage or bedroom, then more often than you may think, you're not given the same respect and treatment as someone who represents a larger company.

Once I figured out how that aspect of the business game is played, I decided to change my sole proprietorship to a corporation, and when I moved to California, I did just that. And sure enough, when people I was doing business with read the "Inc." after my company's name, they had no idea if I was working out of a home office or had a penthouse office suite and a huge staff. In a way, it leveled the playing field, giving me greater opportunities for good business deals.

That's why, even though you can do the sole proprietor thing, to save time, protect your assets, minimize taxes, and maximize wealth, opportunities, and deals, I want you to seriously think of incorporation. I'm about to show you how to save lots of money when you do it yourself and how quick and easy it is to accomplish.

Some years ago while traveling, I kept seeing a little ad in the pages of in-flight airline magazines for an outfit called The Company Corporation. The company promised that anyone could incorporate a business "over the phone," "in any state," "in as little as 10 minutes," and for under $500.

This caught my attention for a couple of reasons. One reason was the cost. At the time I was living in Los Angeles, and a partner and I had just set up a media/publishing company. To incorporate we used an attorney. The cost: $2,000.

There was another reason: aside from the promised ease, speed, and convenience, I definitely wanted to investigate the options of incorporating in states that could be more favorable (business and taxwise) than California.

I did more research on The Company Corporation and the legality of what they offered, and everything checked out. After speaking with my CPA about the best type of corporate entity for me (S corporation, C corporation, or LLC), I made the call; and the cost, the time it took, the services they offered, and the business entity I was able to set up were exactly as the ad promised. Since then, it's been the only company I've used to set up other businesses, and it's the one I recommend you use, too. They've been around since 1899, over 100 years, so there's a good chance they're not going anywhere. Incorporating businesses is all they do. You can check them out at Incorporate.com and use promo code 4385, where it asks how did you hear about us.

To show you just how easy it was to set up my own business, I'm going to walk you step by step through everything I did. Keep in mind that this was the first time I had ever done it on my own. Believe me, if I can do it, so can you.

Step One: Determine the Type of Business You Want

I knew I wanted to create another business that would be used for all my publishing, music, and entertainment business ventures. I wanted to be the sole owner and I wanted the business structure to offer maximum protection and great tax benefits for my personal income, too.

After discussing my needs with my CPA, he suggested forming an S corporation and basing it in a state with very favorable tax laws for business. Two states came to mind: Delaware and Nevada. I liked Delaware for these reasons:

- Anyone may form a corporation in Delaware without ever having to visit the state.

- Delaware has kept its fees low and is one of the friendliest states to corporations. Over 50 percent of all companies listed on the New York Stock Exchange are Delaware Corporations.

- The names and addresses of initial directors need not be listed in public records.

- The cost of forming a Delaware corporation is among the lowest in the nation.

- The annual Franchise Tax compares favorably with that of most other states.

- Delaware maintains a separate court system for business, called the Court of Chancery, so if legal matters involving a trial arise in Delaware, there is an established record of pertinent business decisions.

- No minimum capital is required to organize the corporation, and there is no need to have a bank account in Delaware. Just one person can hold all the offices of the corporation: President, Vice President, Secretary, and Treasurer.

- There is no state corporate income tax on Delaware corporations that do not operate within the state.

- Shares of stock owned by persons outside of Delaware are not subject to Delaware personal income tax.

- There is no Delaware inheritance tax levied on stock held by nonresidents.

A Delaware corporation can be formed quickly and easily by phone in under 5 minutes. Nevada has similar favorable business tax and corporate laws, but since my former magazine publisher had his publications business as a Delaware corporation, and knowing the owner to be a very shrewd and very wealthy businessman, I felt I couldn't go wrong doing the same. So a Delaware corporation it would be. Then came the next step.

Step Two: Choose a Business Name

Choosing a name for my new business took a little time. I came up with lots of names, but most didn't have a good ring to them. Many people believe that using your own name as the brand name for your company is a good idea. For many, it is. Others prefer using something a bit catchier, like Google.

I came up with three names I liked and ranked them in order of my first, second, and third choices. I figured there was always the possibility that one of the names would have already been taken, so it was better to have some options if I couldn't use my first choice. I was ready for the next step.

Step Three: Get Good Advice

I then called The Company Corporation's toll-free number (their website is Incorporate.com) and in less than 15 minutes, an associate and I had gone through the following process.

First, I told him I wanted to form a Delaware S corporation and asked him to explain the benefits (my CPA had already told me, but it never hurts to double check). He told me the following:

A Subchapter S corporation is a general corporation that has elected a special tax status with the IRS after formation. Subchapter S corporations are most appropriate for small business owners and entrepreneurs who prefer to be taxed as if they were still sole proprietors or partners.

When a general corporation makes a profit, it pays a federal corporate income tax on the profit. If the company also declares a dividend, the stockholders must report the dividend as personal income and pay more taxes. S corporations avoid this "double taxation" (once at the corporate level and again at the personal level), because all income or loss is reported only once on the personal tax returns of the stockholders. For many small businesses, the S corporation offers the best of both worlds, combining the tax advantages of a sole proprietorship or partnership with the limited liability and enduring life of a corporate structure.

If you choose an S corporation, your corporation must meet specific guidelines. They are:

- All stockholders must be U.S. citizens or permanent residents.

- The maximum number of stockholders for an S corporation is 75.

- If an S corporation is held by an "electing small business trust," then all beneficiaries of the trust must be individuals, estates, or charitable organizations. Interests in the trust cannot be purchased.

- S corporations may only issue one class of stock.

- No more than 25 percent of the gross corporate income may be derived from passive income (money received from business and real estate investment deals in which the person receiving the money is not actively involved).

Not all domestic general business corporations are eligible for S corporation status. The exclusions are a financial institution that is a bank, an insurance company taxed under Subchapter L, a Domestic International Sales Corporation (DISC), and certain affiliated groups of corporations.

I then asked him to explain what kinds of corporation-forming packages they offered and the costs. The prices ranged from about $200 to $500, depending on services and features. The more services The Company Corporation performed for you, the higher the cost.

The associate asked where the business would be based and its address. I told him that I lived in Idaho, but wanted a Delaware corporation. He said that would be no problem, and if I wanted to do business in my home state of Idaho, all I would need to do is simply obtain a Letter of Good Standing from the Delaware Secretary of State and then file it (along with payment of the Idaho state fee) with the Idaho Secretary of State office as a Foreign Corporation (i.e., a business registered in one state that wants to do business in another state.) More on this in a moment.

He asked me for the name and address of the person who would be in charge of the corporation and I told him it would be me. He asked how many shares of stock I wanted issued (in the event I ever wanted shareholders) and I said 20 would be fine.

He asked me what name I wanted for my corporation and I told him. He put me on hold for about a minute while he checked the Delaware Corporation name database. He came back online, told me that my first name choice was available, and asked whether I would like to register it. I told him I would and it was done.

The associate asked whom I wanted to use as my Registered Agent. For any corporation that is filed in a state outside the one you live in, you need to have a person or company with a physical address in that state who can receive official mail and notifications, should there ever be any sent. Since I didn't live in Delaware or know anyone who did, I chose to use The Company Corporation. The fee they charged for this service (which includes sending you advance notices of the annual Delaware Franchise Tax due date) was nominal and tax-deductible.

I picked a corporate package and he asked how I would like to pay for it. I put it on my corporate credit card. It, too, was tax-deductible.

That was it. I had given him all the information he needed. He said my new corporation package would arrive within 14 days and provided a toll-free number and Web address, should I have any questions.

Within 10 days, the package arrived and inside of it were:

- *Articles of incorporation.* Official documents from Delaware that say I own my own corporation.

- *Bylaws.* The rules and procedures I need to follow for my corporation.

- *Minutes.* The written record of actions taken or authorized by me.

- *Stock certificates.* The evidence of ownership of shares in my corporation.

- *Transfer ledger.* The record of people to whom I've issued shares of my corporation's stock.

- *Year in review.* The detailed summary of my corporation's state of compliance for the fiscal year.

- *Tax returns.* The file where I can keep copies of my federal, state, and local tax returns.

- *Miscellaneous.* The file where I keep forms and permits, leases, business licenses, and financial statements.

- *An official metal stamp.* A stamp like the kind a notary public uses, with my corporation's name on it. Cool.

Step Four: File with the IRS

Also included in the package were two forms I needed to file with the Internal Revenue Service, Form SS-4 and Form 2553.

- *Form SS-4.* Form SS-4 is the Application for Employer Identification Number. Think of an employee identification number as a social security number for your business. In business it's known as your Tax ID Number. It's easy to get. The form took less than 5 minutes to fill out and submit to the IRS.

- *Form 2553.* Form 2553 is the Election by a Small Business Corporation form. The IRS required me to fill out this form to officially register my business as an S corporation. After filling out the form in under 5 minutes, I submitted it to the same IRS Regional Headquarters I had used for the SS-4. So simple, and I just saved myself a bunch of money doing it myself. And don't worry; if you've accidentally made a mistake, the IRS won't knock on your door to hassle you. They'll simply return your form with instructions on what they need corrected. All you need to do is make the corrections and send it back. Done deal.

So, in less than 30 minutes, I had successfully completed—for the very first time!—all the paperwork the IRS requires for having a 100 percent legally official and protected business.

Step Five: File a Business in My State

After I had filed all the necessary paperwork with the IRS and received my official federal Tax ID Number, I needed to do one more thing: Get a Letter of Good Standing (that says my new company has paid its registration dues and is officially recognized by the state of Delaware as a Delaware Corporation) from the Delaware Secretary of State. This was easy, too. I simply phoned their office (you can now go online and do it) and requested the letter so that I could register my business in my home state of Idaho.

The Delaware Secretary of State's Division of Corporations office told me to send them a formal request by mail and to include the name of my company, the Delaware corporate number listed at the top right-hand corner of my Certificate of Incorporation, and a check for the small fee (I believe it was something like $20 at that time). I did, and 2 weeks later I received the Letter of Good Standing.

The day I received the letter, I went to the Idaho State Capital in down-town Boise (I lived only 15 minutes away) and found the Secretary of State's office. If you live in a city outside your state's capital, you can send your application and check via mail, FedEx, UPS, or any other overnight delivery service. I told them I had a Delaware corporation and that I wanted to file as a Foreign (a state other than the one you're in) Corporation so I could also do business in Idaho.

They asked for a copy of my Delaware Certificate of Incorporation and a copy of my IRS Form SS-4 with my IRS Tax ID Number. They had me fill out a simple Application for Certificate of Authority (for Profit), which took all of 3 minutes. I paid them $120 and my application was filed and stamped. I was now an official Idaho business!

After Incorporating

With documents in hand, I left the State Capitol building and headed for the bank to open my new business checking account. The process took less than 20 minutes, and 7 days later, I had a box delivered to me with my company's checks and deposit slips inside. I was ready for business!

I'll be the first to admit that math wasn't my favorite subject in school, and I did not want to spend endless hours doing balances and ledgers and all that accounting stuff. So after talking things over with my CPA, we decided that I'd keep track of my payables and receivables through the company checkbook ledger.

I'd simply send him my check ledgers, bank statements, and cancelled checks every quarter (though sometimes he doesn't get them until the end of the year... oops), along with a synopsis of what kinds of activities the business had for that period (deals made, money received, gear bought and sold, etc.). Everything has worked beautifully. And I made things even easier with a business accounting software package, QuickBooks.

Having my own business has given me freedom, independence, and many financial and personal rewards. I can't say enough good things about the considerable benefits of having incorporated. Over the years, many of my friends and associates have said, "I need to ask you about how to do that corporation thing." You don't even have to ask. Follow the steps in this chapter, and you'll be on your way in a hurry. I believe you'll find it to be one of the best business decisions you'll ever make. Here's a final suggestion: Go on over to Incorporate.com. There you'll find answers to any other questions you might have about incorporation as well as lots of helpful information that'll guide you as to what kind of corporation might be best for you.

Lesson 12
Real-World New Music Business Boot Camp: What You Need to Know about Copyrights, Music Publishing, and Licensing

A ll right, listen up. It's time for you to get in shape. I'm talking music business shape. It's time you entered boot camp. While this boot camp won't demand any tough physical challenges or make you physically fit, it will make you more business savvy and fiscally fit. Our boot camp is only going to talk about three things—copyrights, music publishing, and licensing—but those three things can help you to create a protected and enduring music empire.

The foundation of your music empire is copyrights. Copyrights are like a bank full of money. If you control the copyrights, you own the bank. Far too many people give away potentially valuable copyrights for the promise of great things to come. Rarely are they pleased with the results. You've got to run the bank.

Many of us were taught by well-intentioned family members, business associates, and friends, that if only you worked hard and long enough, success in life would be yours. But how many people do you know who've gotten rich working at their jobs? The real secret to wealth (if there is one) is to make one effort pay multiple times. And when you have copyrights that can be licensed, then you have something that can pay you time and time again. In this lesson, I'll give you the basics of copyright law—how it works, what your rights are, and easy steps to follow to register your work.

The second part of our boot camp is the music publishing business. In the music world, you need to have copyrights in order for a music publishing company (yours or someone else's) to license them. As music publishing is quite a different animal from other kinds of publishing, I'll give you the basics of how the music publishing business works, as well as tips and advice that you can use as you decide to work with a publisher or form your own company. If having your own music publishing company sounds good to you, I'll show you the simple steps to do it and also give you the music publishing vocabulary and lingo guide so you'll sound like you've been doing it for years.

Finally, we'll focus on licensing your work. You need to have a solid understanding of key points you want included in all your agreements. Far too many people don't read or include the fine points in their contracts, only to find out too late that they've given up too much or will receive too little. I'll also give you tips that'll help you get the best licensing deal possible. And I promise to make it all as simple as possible.

Boot camp has officially begun!

The "Get Smart" Quick Guide to Copyrights

Copyrights. I know you've heard about them, but do you know what they are and where they came from? American copyright law goes all the way back to late fifteenth-century England and the printing press. Back then, as the number of printing presses increased, authorities wanted to control the publication of books. So they gave printers what we would consider today to be a monopoly on publishing.

The Licensing Act of 1662 established that a register of licensed books was to be administered by the Stationers' Company, which was a group of printers with the authority to censor publications. A few years later, the Act did relax government censorship, but it wasn't until 1710 that English Parliament enacted the Statute of Anne that has essentially become the basic principles of our copyright law today.

The statute provided for an author's ownership of copyright and a fixed term of protection of copyrighted works (14 years with a provision to renew another 14 years if the author was still living). At that time, while this may have sounded like a big win for the creators of a copyright, it really wasn't. If authors wanted to be paid for their work, they had to assign it to a publisher or bookseller. In addition, the statute broke up the monopoly by printing press owners and established a public domain for literary works by limiting copyright terms. It also made clear that if a work was sold, then the previous owner of that work could not control how it was used.

Since then, much has changed (and for the better) for those who create copyrights. Instead of 14 years of protection, you now get the life of the copyright creator plus 70 years. Instead of formally needing to register a copyright work, it's no longer mandatory (although it's still a wise idea so that you're afforded the maximum protections under the law).

Today's copyright law gives the creator of a work the exclusive right to control who can make copies, or make works derived from the original work, along with full rights to license and sell the copyright. For a work to be copyrightable, it needs to be in tangible form. This means it needs to be recorded (words and/or music), written, painted, sculpted, or photographed, giving your copyrighted work some tangible form. It just can't be some brilliant idea floating around in your head. Under the Berne Copyright Convention of 1989 (a treaty to which nearly all major nations are signatories), every creative work is copyrighted the moment it is fixed in tangible form. No notice or registration is necessary, although registration can be greatly beneficial in the event of litigation, awarding of damages, settlement, etc. But keep in mind that ideas and facts can't be copyrighted. Your creative expression—in whatever tangible form you choose to express it—can.

When it comes to music, the first thing for you to know is that as soon as you've written your lyrics or your song, it's copyrighted. You are considered the "author" of the lyrics and/or music; and as the creator of that work, or intellectual property, you are entitled to the ownership of its copyright and all copyright protections under the law.

Now, let's talk about those protections. As I just told you, the work you create is legally protected for the life of the creator (that's you) plus 70 years! That's right. Whether you're 25 or 45, when you create your masterpiece, your creation is exclusively yours for as long as you live plus 70 more years! There is no automatic renewal once that term expires, but if you've got a younger brother, sister, cousin, or friend, or you have children (even a baby), you can extend your copyright term by naming one or more of them as a coauthor on your copyright. Once you include a younger coauthor, the entire protection is extended to the life of the youngest author on the copyright, plus 70 years. You've got automatic pass-through protection with nothing more that you need to do. Be sure, however, that when assigning a copyright or any portion thereof you put everything in writing: the percentage of copyright ownership, percentage of income derived from exploiting the copyright, effective date of assignment (e.g. your son/daughter will be assigned 100 percent ownership upon your death).

But let's not stop there. We want to protect your assets, and this involves officially registering what you've created with the Copyright Office. I'll show you how in just a minute. You'll find it to be something so quick and easy to do that you'll want to do it every time another masterpiece falls from your lips or fingers.

Your Copyright Is All Yours

How would it feel to create anything you want and then have the full power of the U.S. government (as well as the governments of many other countries) to protect you from anyone else's stealing, copying, or using your creation without your permission? Once you create your song and music, you will have that power.

Your work is your exclusive creation, and this means you can sell, lease, distribute, or rent your creation to anyone you want. It means you make derivative works of your creation or take bits and pieces of it to do with as you please. It means you can make copies and reproduce your creation as often and as much as you like. It means you own it and you can do anything with it that you please. Pretty cool, eh?

But what if someone else decides they want to use your creation and not tell you about it or pay you for it? Uh-oh, it's bad news for the other person. Remember what I told you earlier in the book about dealing with pirates and copyright infringers who take advantage of others by not getting permission or paying for using things that don't belong to them? Having your creation "officially" registered gives you added protection, and if you decide to take them to court, you have the potential to make a lot of money.

I'm talking statutory damages that can be anywhere from $500 to $20,000 for each infringement, and up to $100,000 if the infringement was willful. And, if the actual damages and profits you've lost because of the infringement would be greater than statutory damages, you have the option to go after those instead. In addition, the guilty party (the infringer) may be required to pay your attorney's fees. All of this is courtesy of, and enforced on your behalf by, Uncle Sam.

With Webcasting and Internet radio, which I'll be telling you about in Lesson 13, you should also know about a copyright law called the Digital Millennium Copyright Act (DMCA). The what-you-need-to-know lesson here is that if anyone steals, borrows, or uses your music from your website or any other website that you've given permission to use, or licensed your creation to, the person using it without your permission is in violation of this statute and, most likely, other copyright laws. The same goes for you. Note to self: Never record or use something that you don't have permission to use—free music downloads included. Check out Loc.copyright/legislation/dmca/ for more in-depth information about the DMCA.

How to Copyright Your Work in Two Easy Steps

The U.S. Copyright Office makes it easy to copyright your sound recordings in two easy steps. Here they are:

Step one: Make sure your work is a sound recording. Sound recordings are "works that result from the fixation of a series of musical, spoken, or other sounds, but not including the sounds accompanying a motion picture or other audiovisual work." A copyright registration for a sound recording alone is neither the same as, nor can it substitute for, registration for the musical, dramatic, or literary work recorded. The underlying work may be registered in its own right apart from any recording of the performance; or, in certain cases, the underlying work may be registered together with the sound recording.

Step two: Go to Copyright.gov/eco/ and register your copyright in only minutes with the Copyright Office *eCO Online System*. Before using the service, we recommend you first read eCO Acceptable File Types, eCO Tips, eCO FAQs, or eCO Tutorial (PowerPoint) or eCO Tutorial (PDF). For recently added features, see eCO Updates.

Advantages include:

- Lower filing fee of $35 for a basic claim (for online filings only)

- Fastest processing time

- Online status tracking

- Secure payment by credit or debit card, electronic check, or Copyright Office deposit account

- The ability to upload certain categories of deposits directly into eCO as electronic files

- Availability 24 hours a day, except for routine maintenance every Sunday from 12:00 midnight to 6:00 AM Eastern Time

The time the Copyright Office requires to process an application varies, depending on the number of applications the Office is receiving and clearing at the time of submission and the extent of questions associated with the application.

Copyright Issues Regarding Employment

On the journey down your musical road, there's a good chance that you will need and want to use the services and talents of other people, or that others will want to hire you. But as the creator of your own work, you always want to keep your copyrights. However, there may be times when you want to sell your music for other people to use (e.g. creating jingle music for ad agencies), and other times when you want to hire people to create music. So, here's what you need to know.

Independent contractor. If you are the person being asked/paid to create music, you want to perform your work as an independent contractor, which allows you to retain all copyrights. The person who hires you only gets the rights to use your creation for a specific purpose and in a specific way (that you'll make sure is specifically stated in an agreement you have your attorney agree to before you sign).

Works for hire. If you are the person who is paying someone else to create music for you, you want the other person to perform their work as a work for hire, which allows you to retain all copyrights and use their services however and whenever you wish. The person you hire gets paid only once for the work he or she creates for you.

The 1976 Copyright Act says that a work for hire is a work prepared by an employee within the scope of his/her employment, or a work specially ordered or commissioned for use by another person in accordance with a written document as a contribution to a collective work, motion picture, audio/visual, and other certain types of works, the nature of which is specifically defined in Section 101 of the Copyright Act. For more on this subject, read Courtney Love's advice in Lesson 3.

Remember: If you hire someone to perform any work for you, under the Copyright Act you, as the employer, are considered the author, and as such, own all the rights in and to the work.

The Basic Ins and Outs of Music Publishing

Over the years, I've heard many of the wisest and richest people in the music business say that the only people who make big money in music are the record companies, songwriters, and music publishers. What about the superstar artists and all their tens of millions of dollars the media loves telling us about? The artist only gets a small piece of the bigger split between the music publisher, songwriter, and record label.

My hat goes off to people like Shania Twain and her former producer Mutt Lange. Even though they don't operate their own label (yet), they wisely work the music business. Shania is the artist, Mutt is the producer, and it's only the two of them who write every song on her records. As such, they receive royalties from many different sources, but they created the work (song/album) only once. This is true whether they had their own label or signed to a major. Very smart.

Music publishers are important in the music business. In the early days, before the various ways to carry sounds were invented, the business centered on publishing sheet music. While that's still an important part of what music publishers do today, it's just one piece of a much larger and more lucrative business.

In today's music world, music publishers bring songwriters and recording artists together. They exploit songs for the songwriter and publisher's benefit. They also administer, manage, and protect music copyrights.

From the 1920s to the 1950s, artists sang and played songs written by professional songwriters. In fact, this is where the term A&R (artists and repertoire) originated. Record labels would find the right songs from a songwriter's repertoire and match them with the right artist.

Today, that's changed. Although there are still label A&R departments, artists are increasingly writing or co-writing their material. For those who do, owning a share of the publishing pie can mean huge financial rewards if they have a good understanding of just how the music publishing business works.

When people think of songs, many believe that the music and lyrics constitute the song. But that's not always true. A song often has three components: the lyrics, the music, and the arrangement. Songs are also different from a sound recording. A song can be recorded by 50 or more other artists and each of them can arrange it and record it differently, thereby creating 50 different recordings of that one song. As the creator and copyright owner, songwriters are the ones who grant permission for use of their songs. And the terms of the permission can be as limited or unlimited as the copyright owner wishes. While songs can be copyrighted separately from sound recordings, until a song is made into some kind of tangible form (remember our copyright lesson?), it is not a physical entity like a record. This separation of song from recording gives songwriters a potentially very lucrative source of income: publishing agreements with publishers who will, hopefully, have their songs placed with artists who will record them.

So how is this done? One of the many avenues that music publishers use is their relationship with record labels. They must get the songs they represent (e.g. their catalog) into the hands of any of a label's upper-level staff, such as A&R. This may be accomplished directly, through the publisher's relationships with the artist, the artist's management, or his or her attorney. In other instances an artist or record label may call the music publisher looking for a certain kind of song.

The biggest publishers—like EMI Music, Universal Music, Warner Chappell Music, Sony/ATV Music, and BMG Music—are typically the first call and go-to source for the best songs (since they have the biggest stable of writers and track record of hits). These publishers have lots of contacts in the music business and know who to go to and how to get songs placed.

How Music Publishers Generate Revenue

The ultimate goal in music publishing is to generate revenue for both the author of the work and the music publisher. There are a number of ways that this can be accomplished.

Sheet music. The sale of sheet music, songbooks, and reproduction rights for a song's lyrics in books, magazines, and CD jackets was the foundation of music publishing and it continues to be a big part of the business.

Broadcast and performance. Each time an artist's song is broadcast, that artist (and the publisher) must be paid. Publishers, along with performing rights organizations like ASCAP (American Society of Composers, Authors and Publishers), BMI (Broadcast Music Incorporated), SESAC (Society of European Stage Authors and Composers), make sure of it. A common way to cover performance of music is by issuing a blanket license. The venue—restaurant, broadcast or cable television company, programmed music company, etc.—pays a fee to the performing rights organization that represents the songwriter and publisher in return for which they have unlimited use of the music for a specified time. The blanket license income that the performance rights organizations collect is distributed to songwriters and publishers based on specific formulas, which are different depending on which organization represents the copyright owner. The performing rights organizations use various means of determining how often a song has been played and charge stations a set per-minute rate. After deducting their administration commission, the organizations pay out the money collected to songwriters and publishers. (Visit the ASCAP, BMI, and SESAC websites for more information about rates and services.)

Mechanical license fees. Under copyright law, once a phonorecord of a nondramatic composition has been distributed to the public with authorization of the copyright owner ("voluntarily and permanently parted with"), any other person may record and distribute phonorecords of the work after paying a mechanical license fee to the copyright owner. For example, an artist does not have to obtain permission to make a cover record of a song once it has been distributed, but will have to pay the requisite mechanical license fees to the copyright owner(s). The amount of the fee depends on the current minimum rate. (You can see the current rate here: Copyright.gov/carp/m200a.pdf) Payment of this fee is required for anyone who includes a copyrighted song on any physical product (including those designer cell phone ring tones). Most of the work of collecting and distributing mechanical license fees in the United States is handled by the Harry Fox Agency, Inc.

Controlled compositions. Record agreements include a provision that allows record companies to license your songs—the songs you write, own, or control in whole or in part—at three-fourths the statutory rate. In addition, the agreements usually say that the company will only pay 10 times the minimum rate for a CD even if the CD contains more than 10 songs. Using the current minimum statutory rate, that means that for a 12-song album (with each song under 5 minutes in length) that sells 500,000 copies, you, the artist (or you the artist and your publisher), have lost $127,000, which the record label keeps. Perhaps you should think of owning your own label, too!

Other license income. Other sources of revenue from licensing include:

- *Commercial use* (e.g., use of music in an advertisement)

- *Grand rights* (use of music in dramatic performance of a ballet, operetta, opera, musical comedy, etc.)

- *Nondramatic performance* (use of music in a public performance of a song on radio, TV, cabaret, hotel, concert, etc.)

- *Synchronization* (use of music on the soundtrack of an audio-visual work, e.g. background music on a television show, film soundtrack, multimedia work such as a video game, or a website)

- *Sampling.* Whenever anyone records and uses sound samples from another artist's recording, regardless of length, the person using the sample must have written permission from the copyright owner, and permission is usually not granted for free.

Writer-Publisher Relationships

If you're a new writer and don't have a name, following, or catalog (a collection of songs) yet, you need to find an outlet for your work to be placed with artists who will record it. Most songwriters use a music publisher.

You need to establish the nature of the agreement. If you're fortunate enough to capture the interest of a publisher who likes your songs and music, that publisher may want to enter into a publishing deal with you. This is where negotiations begin on how much of your song's copyright the publisher wants you to assign to them, and how much money you want them to pay you in exchange for it.

From the publisher's perspective, they would like you to assign them the largest percentage of your song's copyright, for the longest term, in exchange for paying you the least amount of money. From your perspective, you want to assign the smallest percentage possible, for the briefest term, and have them pay you the most money up front. The final deal usually ends up being some-place in the middle.

It is a big advantage for you, the songwriter (as opposed to a recording artist), to include in your written publishing agreement a provision that states that when the term of the deal expires, the copyright ownership reverts back to you, at which time you would be free to sign a different publishing deal with a different publishing company.

Once you've got a publishing deal, chances are that the publisher is go-ing to have to spend time and money to promote you and your material to people who'll want to "cut" one of your songs. You could get lucky and get a cut quickly. More often than not, this process takes time. Publishers realize this, and they realize that you need to eat, pay the bills, and keep the creative juices flowing. The solution? A publishing advance.

Much like a book advance, a publishing advance can be a few thousand dollars to tens of thousands of dollars. Typically, it's nonrefundable. This means that if a publisher pays you an advance and then decides to do nothing with your song, you don't have to give the money back.

If, on the other hand, you sign exclusively with one music publisher (e.g., to be a staff writer), you will most likely be paid on a bi-weekly or monthly basis. A staff writer typically agrees to write a certain number of songs per month, year, or whatever the length of his or her contract is. The publisher has the exclusive rights to all the writer's songs written during the contract period, and in return for paying the writer an advance, the publisher gets a percentage of any royalty income received.

If you are not a staff writer and you have a nonexclusive publishing agreement (for example, a single-song one-off deal, a multiple-song agreement, or an administrative deal where the publisher gets a certain percentage of your songs' income for taking care of the administrative, royalty collection, monitoring, and registration work), you may get an advance based on a specified number of songs you've agreed to write. This advance will, of course, be recouped by your publisher from any royalties generated from your music.

Because the publishing business is so lucrative, there are lots of… shall I say, less than reputable publishers who not only promise aspiring songwriters the moon and then some, but will charge them for the experience. I'm referring to the song-sharks who charge fees to hear and shop your music. The biggest and most reputable publishers don't do this. If you find a publisher who does, head the other direction.

In return for paying you up-front money and/or being assigned a percentage ownership of your song's/songs' copyrights, the publisher will exploit your material and get it out to as many people and places as possible in order to recoup their investment. Once you sign your rights over to the publisher, where and how your songs will be used will be at the discretion of the publisher, and not you.

How Your Publisher Works for You

There are a number of ways in which publishers say they will work for you.

Song plugging. In addition to the recorded demos of the songs a publisher will have in its catalog, some publishers will also have the songwriter perform the song in front of the interested party. Some songwriters I've talked to don't mind this, because it gets their names and faces in front of people who may be able to help them in a big way down the road. Others tell a different story; they felt paraded around town in front of many people who were simply "tire kickers" and not serious buyers and placers. It's always a good idea to know up front what will be expected of you.

Writing sessions. Sometimes publishers will pair two or more writers together to see what kind of magic it creates. This can be a good idea if one is a strong lyric writer and the other's strength is writing music. Some of these collaborations can be amazing, as in the case of Elton John and Bernie Taupin, so keep an open mind.

Divided publishing. Suppose you have a great song that would be perfect for a country artist but your publisher specializes in R&B (your usual genre). To get the song placed with a top country artist, the publisher may enter into a copublishing deal with a publisher who does specialize in country music. Large publishing companies are often able to make copublishing deals with multiple publishers. In addition, music publishers, like book publishers, have agreements with foreign publishers to exploit their songs in overseas markets. For a fee or percentage, these foreign publishers collect royalties and handle all licensing matters in their territory or country. However, be careful. With both your domestic copublishers and foreign subpublishers taking a share of your revenue, the amounts can add up quickly. To maximize your income and minimize double or more commissions, make sure all of your publisher's subpublishing deals include a provision that states you are to be paid your full royalty percentage rate "at source" from each publisher and subpublisher, territory, and deal, which means that you will receive the same percentage regardless of where the money was earned. For example, if you have a 50/50 publishing deal, you will get 50 percent of every dollar your song earns "at the source" of wherever it is earned.

Demo sessions. In some cities, publishers have their own recording studios and have a staff that specializes in cutting demos for its writers. Most publishers encourage their writers to demo their songs at their home studios, however, and if the material is strong enough, they'll record a master quality demo in one of the big studios in the city of the publisher. This more elaborate demo will often be the one the publisher will shop around, pitch, and plug to try to get a cut or placement. It's also the one that many times can make it on an artist's record—even in demo form.

If you're on the A-list. Publishers know that the big money is made when major artists cut their clients' songs. Even though they seldom admit that they have A-list or B-list songs, they do, and they set aside the real jewels in their publishing catalog and vault for the A-list artists and their producers, or their "people," who come in looking for material for their new album. Get a few moneymaking cuts under your belt and watch how quickly you graduate to A-cut status.

The hold. In the music world, making decisions is often a long, drawn-out process. With so much money involved and so many people reluctant to part with it, getting commitments can be like pulling teeth. However, publishers will sometimes allow A-list artists, producers, or labels to put a "hold" on a song. The way this works is that if an artist, producer, or label likes a publisher's song, they'll ask the publisher to put a hold on it so that they'll have exclusive right to use it. This does not obligate them to use the song, but as long as the hold is on, the song is effectively tied up so that no one else can use it.

Of course, publishers know that many of the songs that have holds placed on them are never used, and while they are just sitting there, the publisher is missing out on potential song placement opportunities. Therefore, some publishers have policies that put a time limit on those holds, but they may find themselves walking a fine line between wanting to move on with a song and keeping the hold on it in the hopes that the A-list artist will use it, generating major revenue.

For this reason, publishers will let other interested parties hear the song as well and place a second, third, or fourth hold on it. In the event that the party who placed the first hold doesn't use it, the song will be offered to the next artist on the hold list.

As you might imagine, this can be both exciting and frustrating for a songwriter. If a writer gets word that a major artist has put a hold on one of his or her songs, visions of mega success and big royalty bank deposits can be very heady stuff. Yet when the reality sets in as 1, 2, or 3 months pass and still no word has been received, excitement turns to disappointment. Have this happen to you a couple times and you'll better understand the adage "I'll get excited once the check clears the bank."

Administrative Agreements

Administrative agreements are different from agreements in which you agree to share ownership of your copyrights with a publisher. In administrative agreements, the administrative publisher—usually a publisher with offices and agents around the world—takes care of collecting royalties and other payments and handling legal documents and paperwork for you in return for a percentage of all income collected. The percentage varies depending on the nature of the services performed and on the bargaining clout of the songwriter. If the administrative publisher only does registration of songs with performance and mechanical rights organizations, the percentage is generally low, in the neighborhood of 10 to 15 percent. If, however, the administrative publisher provides a full range of services, including promotional efforts, recording demos and tapes, drafting agreements, etc., they may get up to 50 percent of all income collected.

Note that many administrative agreements stipulate that if the administrative publisher obtains a new recording of a song or a lucrative audiovisual use (a major motion picture or TV program), the percentage paid to the publisher will be increased. Increases may also be contingent on a cover version reaching a certain level on the charts.

Negotiating the Best Agreement

If you're ready to jump in headfirst and start your own company, you can skip this section and go straight to "Forming Your Own Music Publishing Company." If you're not, one option that may cross your mind is to sign a music publishing deal, learn the publishing business a bit better, and then go off on your own. If signing with a music publisher is the direction you're leaning toward, you'll find the following information helpful.

First and foremost, everything possible needs to be spelled out in the agreement. Always remember that one's assumptions are usually the cause of one's screw-ups. Make sure that your attorney has looked over the agreement carefully and, where necessary, made changes and inserted important clauses in your agreement that give you the best possible terms in the areas of advances, royalties, copyright assignment, territories, accounting and statements, governing laws, warranties, and subpublishing deals.

If you're entering into a copublishing deal rather than an administrative deal, don't sign away all your rights. Go for a 75/25 deal, whereby you control 75 percent of your publishing and the publisher gets 25 percent. If the publisher refuses, propose a 50/50 split. Under no circumstances should you take any deal that asks you to give up more.

If you are signing away a portion of your publishing rights to your publisher, be sure they will revert back to you in a short period of time. Some publishing deals are based on a two-tier arrangement, whereby one tier is the initial songwriting time period (e.g., 3, 5, or 7 years), and the second tier is a longer retention period, whereby the publisher controls your songs for more than 10 years. Negotiate to keep both periods as short as possible.

Have your attorney include a performance clause in your publishing agreement stating that you'll agree to write x number of songs in a specified period and that the publisher agrees to shop/place/promote that number of songs in that same period. If the publisher fails to abide by the terms of this clause, you can cancel the agreement ("without penalty," which means that no interest or additional funds are to be repaid to you beyond what was originally received) and all your rights immediately revert back to you.

Your agreement should state that there will be an automatic reversion of your copyrights if the publisher goes into bankruptcy or is liquidated. Plus you should have the option of canceling the agreement if the publisher sells the business or new management takes over.

In fairness to both parties, the agreement should state that if you breach the terms of the agreement, any advance monies paid to you shall be paid back by you to the publisher without penalty. If the publisher breaches the agreement, any advance monies paid to you by the publisher shall be kept by you without repayment or penalty.

Make sure the agreement gives you the right to audit the publisher's books. One audit per year should be enough, but if you can get two times per any 12-month period, all the better. One caveat: My advice is to not use this clause unless your songs are earning decent royalties ("decent" would be any amount over and above what it would cost to hire an independent CPA or auditor) and you have good reason to believe you are being cheated. In most cases, quarterly or semiannual accountings are sufficient.

Forming Your Own Music Publishing Company

As Diane Warren told you, when you're first starting out as a songwriter, it can be a good idea to hook up with a major publisher in order to get your songs recorded, placed, and administered. That's what she did, but only until she began experiencing success as a songwriter and making a name in the business. Once that happened, she quickly formed her own company, Realsongs. Her meteoric success is a powerful lesson that you can do it too.

Of course, many people dream of having their own music publishing company. But for this to make sense, you've got to be the right kind of person. By that, I mean a person who is disciplined and organized, enjoys taking care of business and details, and doesn't mind going after people, companies, and deals.

If you don't want to give up a percentage of your copyrights to a company to have them chase down royalties and the people who owe them to you, read on. Keep in mind as you read, however, that even if you're a songwriter who has no music publishing deal and you don't have any ambition to have your own music publishing company, you can still join organizations like ASCAP, BMI, or SESAC and the Harry Fox Agency and take advantage of their services.

If the idea of having your own music publishing company sounds good to you, there are some things you need to consider:

All successful music publishers have a catalog of songs they can exploit for commercial gain. If you don't have enough of your own songs (many people say you should have at least 20) and/or access to songs from other songwriters, you might not be ready to form your own music publishing company.

Let's say you've decided that you want to have your own publishing company. How do you form it? A company is a company, right? It's just the name and nature of the business that differentiates one company from another. And since what you'll be creating is a company, follow the advice in Lesson 11, "Launching the Business of You, Inc," and you will have completed the first step. You will have all the legal protections afforded to a corporation.

Music publishing is all about the exploitation of copyrights, and your corporation will need to have access to a team of legal advisers who thoroughly understand copyright law, can negotiate contracts, and can take care of litigation should the need ever arise.

You'll also need to have a top-notch accounting system and people in place who understand music royalties and publishing. Registering copyrights, contracts, licenses, royalties, compliance issues, and the like can be very time-consuming and costly if you're not properly prepared to deal with them.

Finally, you'll need to have the financial resources necessary for the successful promotion of your music—recording demos, creating promo packages, printing and distributing sheet music, etc.—all the things that will get you, your company, and your songs promoted and in the hands of those who can record and use them.

Down the road, you'll probably want to be able to sign new songwriters, which can be costly, so plan ahead.

Joining the Right Organizations

Let's say you've formed your company and are ready for business. One of the first things you need to do is establish the right professional connections.

As a songwriter you of course need to be affiliated with one of the top three performing rights organizations: ASCAP, BMI, or SESAC. Each offers a slightly different package, but all of them essentially do one thing: collect royalties for the performances of your songs. These organizations also offer publishers a similar service, so it might make sense for you to have an affiliation with one organization to handle both your songwriting and publishing collections.

Many songwriters who have their own publishing companies choose ASCAP, BMI, or SESAC for their songwriting and the Harry Fox Agency for their publishing. The Harry Fox Agency represents publishers and licensees and, like the other performance rights organizations, it also collects royalties in many markets and countries all over the world. If you're a publisher with a song that'll be recorded by another party, then you're eligible for Harry Fox Agency representation. Go to their website (HarryFoxAgency.com) for more information, as well as commission rates.

Now, to help get your name out there as well as getting access to potentially beneficial new contacts, you might want to consider joining the National Music Publishers Association (NMPA.org), the trade group that represents more than 800 music publishers. One of its missions is to protect the rights of music copyright owners, and it's been successful on many fronts to help change and enact legislation to do so.

Another good organization to join is the Alliance of Artists and Recording Companies (AARC), which is a nonprofit entity formed to distribute Audio Home Recording Act of 1992 (AHRA) royalties. The essence of the AHRA legislation is that it requires the manufacturers of digital audio recorders and blank digital discs and tapes to pay royalties to the U.S. Copyright Office for the benefit of, and distribution to, eligible artists and sound recording copyright owners. This law was enacted as a way to compensate artists and copyright owners for lost revenue due to loss of sales caused by home recording. The

Alliance of Artists and Recording Companies represents over 20,000 artists and record companies.

The Recording Industry Association of America (RIAA) is a good organization to consider joining as well. Despite what you may have heard about the RIAA being the villain in the file-sharing controversy, the truth is that the organization's main purpose is to protect artists and others in the music business from people who choose not to pay for music, services, and rights that are protected under the law. Its website and its Sound Exchange offer a lot of good information about licensing, copyrights, the industry, and the law.

Joining these organizations and gaining additional exposure is important whether you're an artist or starting your music publishing company. All of them can help get your name out there where people can see it. And the more people who see it, the better your chances of some of those people contacting you and using your songs.

Licensing and Protecting Your Work

To make money from your copyrighted masterpiece, you'll need to exploit it. This means getting it out and having it performed in public. No, I'm not just talking about someone else singing your song in a coffeehouse or bar. I'm talking about any kind of performance that requires a license for its use.

Along with licensing your work, you want your work and yourself to be protected. This means having the teeth in your licensing agreements to enforce your copyright and make as certain as you possibly can that anyone to whom your copyright is licensed complies with the terms. Be forewarned: With so many copyright pirates and infringers, for a new publisher, this can be expensive, unless you know a few tricks. Here are a couple that might be helpful.

Whenever you do any kind of licensing deal, always ask for an advance against royalties and make sure the advance is large enough to ensure that in the event the license deal doesn't pay any royalties down the road, you can be happy with just the advance. Many times, that advance is the only money you'll see.

For license agreements with royalties, always have your attorney approve any legal agreements before you sign them. For advances, accountings, and royalties, I suggest that you make sure your agreements include such clauses as quarterly accountings with statements sent to you, and reversion of all rights and loss of all advance money paid to you by the party that doesn't live up to the terms of the license agreement and fails to cure (make good within a specified period of days) any breach of that agreement.

Key Points in a Licensing Agreement

Now, let's run through some key points to include in your license agreement. First, of course, any license agreement must include the clearly stated Licensor (you/your company) and Licensee (the party who will be receiving the license from you); the date of the agreement; the name of the property (your copyrighted material/song) being licensed; and the purpose of the license being granted. The stated terms of the license agreement must include the following:

- A description of the licensed material.

- The specific grant of rights you will be giving to the licensee for its use.

- The name of the production that will be using your copyrighted material.

- The type of media in which your copyrighted material will be used.

- The license period you are granting to the Licensee.

- The day, month, and year the license begins.

- The day, month, and year the license ends.

- The territory in which the copyrighted property will be used.

- The length of the amount of material that will be used, which could be as little as a few seconds of music (for sampling) or an entire song.

- The production use, stating that your copyrighted material can be used solely within the production of the licensee and stipulating what the licensee can and cannot do with your property during the license term.

- The license fee you have agreed to accept.

- The license fee payment instructions that define when, how, and to whom the license fee will be paid.

- The license materials' effective date of use, indicating that the agreement becomes effective upon receipt of the agreed-upon license fee.

- The license warranty of rights that states that you, as the copyright owner/holder, have full power and permission to exclusively grant all rights contained in the license agreement.

- You may also want to include some kind of language (lawyer-approved, of course) that you, the licensor, will indemnify (i.e., protect against loss, damage, and injury) the licensee from any breach of warranty (i.e., this license agreement and the words contained in it) during the term of the agreement.

- The termination of agreement that gives the right to cancel the agreement in the event that a licensee breaches the agreement and fails to correct the breach within a specified time period (typically 10 days to 2 weeks).

The last page of the agreement must include spaces that indicate where you (the copyright owner/Licensor) and the Licensee (person/company obtaining the license) will sign, date, and agree to all the terms contained in the license agreement.

Always keep in mind that based on your own unique needs and copyrighted properties, your attorney will most likely want to add more contract language to these points. Keeping things simple and being protected is not as difficult as it may seem.

Finally, despite how much legal language and teeth your legal license agreements may have, someone, somewhere, will some day most likely rip you off. When it comes to copyrighted property, that is simply the cost of doing business in the entertainment world.

So what can you do? You can try and find them, and once you do, you can spend lots of money, hours, and emotional energy taking them to court and trying to shut them down. But that can be a never-ending cycle. Sure, you've got to protect your copyrights and assert your legal ownership whenever and wherever you find someone ripping you off, but you've got to be smart and pick your court battles carefully.

The vice-president of legal affairs at one of the world's biggest movie studios told me once that every day, someone, somewhere, is ripping off the studio's films and bootlegging them. I asked her what they did about it. She said that even for a company like hers, with billions of dollars in assets and a huge legal team (both in-house and outside), it's simply not worth the time and expense to go after every little mom-and-pop operation that puts up a dummy address and runs duplicators in the back room of an office.

Her advice was to go after the biggest fish first—those who are the biggest infringers, and those who have the deepest pockets and have the ability to pay big damages, regardless of whether settlement occurs inside or outside the courtroom. Because the entertainment business is such a small, interconnected world, word can travel fast once it gets out that not only are you going after, suing, and shutting down infringers, but those found guilty must pay heavy damages. And once the word is out, many would-be copyright infringers will think twice about stealing from you.

Yes, having the law on your side is a good thing. And for many of you, so will having your own publishing and licensing business. But like all good things in life, it comes with a price. First, you've got to be disciplined enough to take care of the details when it comes to the business of You, Inc. You've got to have a good team. You need to be on solid ground financially with sufficient money that can sustain your new business. You need to be protected with the right kinds of agreements that allow you to seek out and enter into the best deals you can, all the while being mindful that people who use your copyrighted property must abide by the terms of your agreements or else you're going after them.

Whatever your publishing and licensing goals may be, if you follow the guidelines in this chapter, you'll always be one step ahead and smiling all the way to the bank.

PART 4

Marketing, Selling, and Distributing Your Music All Over the World: Tapping into the Big Money Potential of Niche Markets, the Internet, and Webcasting

Lesson 13
Premiering Your Music: Three Steps to Broadcasting and Selling Your Music to a Global Audience

N ow it's time to have some fun. I'm going to tell you what you need to do to get on the same Internet playing field as the major labels. And here's how we level that playing field. They've got a domain name. You'll have a domain name. They've got a website. You'll have a website. They use the Internet to broadcast their music. You'll use the Internet to broadcast your music. Follow the three steps in this lesson and you can be up and running before you know it, getting your music to listeners all over the world.

For now, let's talk about how the labels use the Internet to broadcast music. It's well known just how slow the labels were to jump into Internet music distribution. Piracy and downloads really caught them off guard. One of the first ways labels began using the Web was by putting bios, photos, and tour information for their artists on the label's main website, with links (where applicable) to each artist's own website. Many also included links to legitimate (read: not pre-legit Napster) music download sites.

As mentioned in Lesson 2, some artists and bands are using the Internet to create an audience, interest, and buzz (perhaps even worldwide) by allowing free downloads of their music. If you were to go this route, you could, for example, send MP3s of your music to Web radio stations (go to any search engine and type in "Internet radio stations" for a listing of sites). Once you get your music to chart on such sites as MP3.com and Amp3.com, you can see what kind of global audience could build from such exposure. However, be sure to have a link to your own website (which we're going to show you how to set up) and make sure CDs are available for those new listeners who'd like to buy them.

David Bowie was one of the first established artists to embrace the Internet and its power for music distribution big time. Besides offering his music for sale on his website, Bowie has offered free songs online from his live shows and sneak previews of upcoming albums. He has even run a contest giving fans the opportunity to write lyrics for his songs.

And make no mistake. The enormous potential of the Internet for promoting and distributing music is just beginning to be tapped. So what you need to do is get your name and your music out there by choosing a cool domain name, setting up your own site, and, ultimately, broadcasting your music to listeners all over the world.

Step One: Get a Domain Name

Before you create your website, you're going to need an address. In the world of the Internet, this address is called a domain name. Each day, thousands of domain names are registered all over the world. The good names—maybe the very one you'd like—are going quickly.

Many businesses use their business names as their domain names because the name recognition makes them easy for people to remember. If you're a solo artist or in a band, you might want to try using your name or the band's name for your website address. The bad news is that if you haven't already registered your domain name, it may already be taken. The good news is that even though the .com-ending addresses were gobbled up quickly, under the appropriate circumstances, you can now register your favorite name with a different ending. In fact, getting a domain name has never been easier. Type in the words "domain name" into any search engine and you'll get hundreds, if not thousands, of results. The process is pretty much the same from site to site. Here's how it works.

When you type in the name you want in the site's domain name search box, it searches its database to see if the name's available. The search results also indicate the different dot endings available for that name. Once you find a name that's available, you choose which available dot ending you'd like (org, biz, com, etc.). There are over a hundred possibilities, but some are restricted, as discussed below.

After you've chosen your domain name and dot endings, you then choose how long you want the registration of that name to be in effect. Some people opt for only a 1- or 2-year term because they aren't sure that, down the road, they'll want to keep the name they've chosen. I suggest that if you're lucky enough to find that your name or names of choice are available, you'd be wise to lock it in for as long as you can. When I found that my name was available,

I initially registered it for 1 year. But before the registration expired, I took advantage of a bargain-price package deal that allowed me to lock up my name for another 9 years before I would have to renew the registration.

After you choose your domain name, dot endings, and length of term, you fill out a registration that asks for your name, address, contact information, etc. Easy stuff. The final step is payment, and a credit card is the way to go. You can register a domain name so cheaply now (and it can cost you even less if you choose more than one). You should do all this quickly because the name you want can be snatched up by someone else in an instant.

I've just walked you through the process of finding and registering a domain name. If you're like me, though, you probably have a few questions. I asked Domain Name Expert Andy Broadaway to give you some answers.

What exactly is a domain name? To understand what a domain name is, you need to know some basic World Wide Web (Internet) terminology. A domain name is part of the Internet domain name system, which is the system that assigns a 32-bit number, or Internet Protocol (IP) address, to every computer logging on to the Internet. If you are simply using your computer to browse the Web or to access your e-mail service, your computer probably does not have a static (permanent) IP. The IPs of most host computers are static. Obviously, it would be ridiculously unwieldy to require you to store and/or remember numerical IPs for websites you want to access, so every host computer's IP is mapped to a domain name, the more or less user-friendly string of letters and dots you type in when you want to go to a site. All domain names have a TLD (top-level domain) part and an SLD (second-level domain) part.

What do you mean by "host" computer? The definition of "host" varies depending on the circumstances, but for our purposes, a host computer is any computer that houses, serves, and maintains one or more websites.

What is a TLD? A TLD is that part of the domain name that identifies the type of entity being named. There are some restrictions on the use of certain TLDs. There are also ccTLDs (country-code TLDs), which indicate the country in which that entity is located, for example, .bz (Belize), .ca (Canada), .dk (Denmark), .ec (Ecuador), .ie (Republic of Ireland), .uk (United Kingdom), .us (United States), and .zw (Zimbabwe). The number of TLDs available is limited (currently about 100). A few of the most well-known unrestricted TLDs are as follows:

> **.com** ("commercial") is the most common extension for domain names; it often represents companies or for-profit organizations. Most personal websites also use this extension.

> **.net** generally represents Internet Service Providers (ISPs).

> **.org** usually represents nonprofit organizations or groups.

> **.biz** ("business") is reserved for use by businesses.

> **.info** can be for either businesses or individuals. Usage is unrestricted, but a .info TLD indicates that the website primarily is informative.

> **.ws** (website) is an all-around, universally available top-level domain.

Some restricted TLDs—meaning that you cannot choose one of them unless you can prove you have the right to it—are .aero, .biz, .edu, .mil, .museum, .name, and .pro. The .name TLD is available strictly for use by individuals, .edu is reserved for educational entities such as universities or high schools, .mil can be used only by the U.S. military, and .pro is currently reserved for certified doctors, lawyers, and accountants.

What is an SLD? Located immediately after www. or http://, the SLD is the "readable" part of the domain name. A second-level domain name is entirely defined by the registrant, and may or may not be some form of an organization's or businesses' brand name. For example, in www.cnn.com "cnn" (Cable News Networks) is an SLD. There can be more than one part to an SLD, for example, www.sportsillustrated.cnn.com, where "sportsillustrated" is a subdomain.

What does it mean to register a domain name? The Internet domain name system consists of a directory, organized hierarchically, of all the IP/domain names and their corresponding computers registered to particular companies and persons using the Internet. When you register a domain name and designate an Internet host (whether it is your own computer or one of the many, many host computers out there), that name will be associated with the host during the period the registration is in effect.

What if I haven't designated a host? You can register as many names as you like without designating a host. However, you cannot build a website around any of those names. They are considered "parked." If you aren't yet ready to go to the expense of setting up and maintaining a website, but don't want anyone else out there to register the name you want, go ahead and register and park the name or names you have in mind. For the same reason, many people also register and park several variations of their company names, effectively preventing anyone else from using them. If this option is chosen, users typing in the name will be directed to a temporary one-page site that says "under construction," "coming soon," or "for sale," according to circumstances.

What can I do if the domain name I want is unavailable? If the domain name you requested is already taken, you will be presented with reasonable alternatives that are available. If you have requested the name Mybusinessname.

com, and that name is already taken, you might be offered the alternatives Mybusinessname.info or Mybusinessname.ws. Or you could start over again and search for a different SLD with the .com extension.

Can I cancel a domain-name registration? Any reputable domain-name registration service will let you cancel your registration. On Hamiltondomains.com you can perform this function from the Manage My Account section of the site. Click on Domain Names, log in, and select from the list the domain you wish to cancel. Next, click Cancel Domains and confirm the cancellation by clicking the Yes, Cancel Domain(s) Now button. Note that canceling a domain-name registration is a permanent action and you cannot undo this action, although you may reregister the same domain later for a new registration fee.

I just paid for a domain name and have designated a host. Can people access my website right away? No. You generally need to allow 2 to 3 business days after purchase before anyone anywhere in the world will be able to access your site by typing in the name.

What does it mean to forward a domain name? Suppose you have a free home page from your Internet service provider, but its address is long and complicated, for example, www.yourserviceprovider/web/users/yourname. You can use one of the registration sites to register Yourname.com (or, if .com is taken, Yourname.biz or Yourname.ws) and sign up for the (free or nominally priced) forwarding service. Then when people type in yourname.com on the address line, they will automatically be redirected to the already existing site. They will, however, see the longer name on the address bar. You can also "forward with masking," which means that the address the user types in, not the destination address, is the one that stays in the browser's address bar.

How do I find my domain name's expiration date? All domain name registration services have a "Whois" lookup capability that allows you to access all information pertaining to your account, including the expiration date or dates of all your domain names.

Will my name and contact information be made publicly available? Information about who is responsible for domain names is publicly available to allow rapid resolution of technical problems, and to permit enforcement of consumer protection, trademark, and other laws. The registrar will make this information available to the public on a Whois site. It is, however, possible to register a domain in the name of a third party, as long as the third party agrees to accept responsibility. Consult your registrar for further details.

How do I find out who owns a domain name? If you register your name and you select one that is already taken, a link (such as Already Taken, Click Here for Info) to the Whois function should appear. You will then be able to look up the contact details of that domain's owner.

What can I do if I have misspelled my domain name? Your domain name cannot be changed after you complete the registration. You will have to register the correctly spelled name and pay the requisite fee.

Step Two: Get a Website

Okay, now that you've chosen and registered your domain name, you're going to need a place to use it: your own website. Didn't I tell you I'd turn you into a businessperson before you were finished with this book! You're doing great.

I'm going to assume (and pardon me if I'm wrong) that you don't have any hands-on experience with HTML (hypertext markup language—the codes used to mark website text so that it has the look the designers want) or website design. I'm also going to assume you want a great-looking site, but are underwhelmed at the thought of paying a website designer big bucks to create one. Wouldn't it be wonderful if you could easily and quickly design your own website and have the ability to change the design, look, and feel of that site as often as you'd like? How about putting files of your own music on there for people to hear? And what if you could do that for under $10 a month?

You can! From GoDaddy.com to hundreds of others, creating a great-looking Website where you can literally go from zero-to-online in minutes is only a Google click search away. Read on.

Step Three: Begin Broadcasting Your Music

Ever dreamed of hearing your music on radio? What about hearing your music on your radio station? A few years ago, unless you had millions of dollars, having your own radio station was just that—a dream. Ah, but fast-forward to the twenty-first century. All you need is your home computer and, my friend, you can have your own radio station and begin broadcasting your words and, music tonight!

Many record labels and artists already run their own Internet radio stations. It's all about getting the word out, and with the Internet increasing in power and popularity each day, having your own Internet radio station takes you a giant step beyond duplicating promo CDs and flyers that get tossed in the trash—especially if you not only use it for your music, but also give listeners other great information, like artist interviews.

Once you have your own radio station on the Internet—and you can have it in under 10 minutes—you'll be able to broadcast your words and music to a potential audience of more than 500 million people worldwide. In the United States alone, it's estimated that more than 77 million people listen to Internet radio stations. Your station and music can be one of them. If you follow the quick and simple tips in this lesson, you can be on the air before you know it.

You might be thinking: What kinds of music are people broadcasting on their stations? How about alternative, ambient, Asian, blues, Christian, classical, classic rock, comedy, country, dance, downtempo, drum 'n' bass, dub, experimental, folk, funk, Goth, government, hard, house, hip-hop, holiday, house indie, rock industrial, international, Irish, jazz, jungle, Latin, metal, new age, oldies, pop, punk, R&B, rap, reality, reggae, religious, rock, soundtracks, swing, talk, techno, trance, UK, garage, Western, world, '50s, '60s, '70s, '80s, '90s. And the list goes on, as new styles constantly evolve.

So how do you do it? You begin by hooking up with a company that specializes in personal Internet broadcasting. There's a big difference between that kind of company and websites that simply broadcast other people's music over the Internet. Those are the sites that only allow you to be a listener and not a broadcaster. A site called Live365.com is different.

Billed as "The World's Largest Internet Radio Network," Live365 provides everything necessary to choose the best kind of Internet radio station for your needs. It:

- Helps you upload your tracks (via CD or MP3 format), format your music, and put your music and/or words on your station.

- Places you in a directory so that any of their more than 3 million listeners can tune in to your station.

- Provides you with software so you can send your home broadcast out live directly from your own computer. You can talk into the mic, play tracks on the fly, or relay another broadcast.

- Gives you lots of bandwidth and storage capacity on the Live365 servers and provides a central hub where your station will be based and from which you can play your words and music to a worldwide audience 24 hours a day.

Live365 offers several different packages, which I'll get to shortly, but if you're new to the world of Internet broadcasting, you need to answer some basic questions about your intended audience and what you want to do.

- How many listeners do you want to reach? (The monthly cost of your station will be tied in to the number of listeners that will be able to tune in to your station at the same time.)

- What kind of broadcasts do you want to do: tracks in a fixed playlist that are available 24/7 even when you're not online, streaming in real time, or rebroadcast of an existing audio stream?

- Do you want to sell advertising or otherwise make money from your station, or do you want to broadcast ad-free?

Personally, I'm into doing things in a top-shelf professional way, but also into doing them (whenever possible) on a budget that saves me money. And I want lots of options. For Internet broadcasting, I want the setup to be fast and easy. I want to broadcast 24 hours a day. I want there to be enough bandwidth (and not have to pay for extra bandwidth) and storage on servers for all of my content (with plenty of room to spare). I don't want to pay for any Internet connections or have to download anything whenever I broadcast.

I want to be the one who is responsible for my station, and I don't want to pay server-licensing fees or even pay to have someone else broadcast my words and music. I don't want to be locked into the same agreement for a fixed period of time. I want to be able to adjust my station—reduce or increase its options, features, and size—whenever I want. And I want to be able to broadcast my words and music either in real time or in an archived loop. What you're about to learn will allow you to do all of those things.

Personalize your music and message. In the music world, not only do you need great songs and a great sound, you also need a great image. You've got to give people something that'll make them want to remember you. One of the things I like about what Live365 does is that they'll build a special "tuner" (or pop-up Player Window) with your own customized look and feel. The Player Window launches directly from your website, so visitors never have to leave it in order to listen to your broadcast.

Another feature they offer (for free) is to include your Internet radio station in their directory. This could be a big deal for your music. Live365 tells me their directory is the Internet's largest and they have millions of visitors—from more than 100 countries—who use it each month. Whenever one of those millions of listeners sees your name and chooses it, your Internet station's broadcast will play through the standard Live365 Player Window right there on the spot.

You can also program tracks from Live365's central Music Library. When artists and labels add music to this "record pool," Live365 broadcasters can easily find, preview, and add these tracks directly into their playlists. This is a great way to cross-promote your music with a lot of people.

Know who's listening to your music. The major labels are known for doing lots of research. Before they sign any new artist or group, they already know what market the new act will attract and how big it will be. It's all about minimizing loss and maximizing exposure and profit—quickly. As a smart Internet broadcaster, you need to have the same kinds of feedback tools at your disposal.

With your station on Live365, you have access to a special customized partner Web page that contains accurate and up-to-date listener data specifically for your broadcast. For example, it tells you:

How many listeners you had yesterday

How many listeners you had last month

How long each person listened

And it provides the information in printable graphs.

In addition, you get valuable feedback from listeners. Through the Live365 interface, listeners can click on a link to purchase a track, get information about a track, add a track to their wish list, and rate a track thumbs-up or thumbs-down. You can also get "live" (e.g. in real time) statistics for artists and labels on these active, real-time responses, as well as the number of overall "plays" and the number of broadcasters who have added your track by choosing it from the Library. Having this information at your fingertips allows you to test tracks with a live audience before spending lots of promotional dollars. It helps you position your music and marketing efforts much more effectively as well.

Another powerful marketing tool you'll have available is a profile of all broadcasters who've included tracks from the Library and all listeners who've heard or actively responded to (e.g. wish-listed) a track. This information—which can be provided on a geographic or demographic basis—gives you insight into audience tastes. It tells you what kinds of music are increasing or decreasing in popularity at any given moment.

You can also get data as to which music genres are most popular among the broadcasters and listeners, and which ones like (or dislike) a track. And you have access to information about the most popular tracks on all stations that play a particular track or artist. This information gives you, the artist, and your label valuable insight into what other kinds of music fans enjoy.

Finally, you can take advantage of having a message board that can launch directly from your own customized Player Window on your station. You'll see message boards on a lot of websites and for good reason. You can use them to discuss current issues, to announce events and news, and to receive feedback from your listeners. All of this helps you fine-tune and craft your music and message for your target audience.

Learn how to promote your music. The old line about any kind of publicity being good publicity is so true. With so many artists and songs today, you need to keep your music and message fresh and out there making some noise.

One of the ways to do this with your own Internet radio station is by using targeted e-mail promotions. Live365 features artist and label releases in regular e-mail newsletters that are sent to over 600,000 music fans. These newsletters can be targeted based on genre preferences, demographics, geographic location, or other criteria.

Another promotional vehicle is targeted advertising. Besides having your songs available for anyone to hear in their personal Music Library, you can also use audio and visual ads which can be placed on other Live365 stations by genre or geographic region. A clip of a track of your music can be included to promote the song to broadcasters and listeners. Trading ad space with other Live365 broadcasters is a terrific way to cross-promote each other's music.

Select the broadcast package best suited to your needs. Let's talk about how you're going to send your music out over the airwaves. Live365 gives you a number of broadcast packages to choose from:

- *On-Demand Audio.* You can offer archived content (programs, speeches, announcements, interviews, and more) to listeners on an "as demanded" basis with On-Demand Audio. Your listeners will be able to tune in to this content from the beginning of each discrete audio track or recording.

- *Studio365-Live.* You can create a live broadcast from your computer in minutes with Studio365-Live. You can broadcast live to the world speeches, musical selections, and anything else you can think of.

- *Studio365-Basic.* You can create maintenance-free broadcasts by storing your content on the Live365 servers with Studio365-Basic. Once you've uploaded your audio content, you no longer need to be online to have your station up and running.

- *Relay Broadcast.* Finally, you can take your current live signal (one you're already broadcasting on the airwaves or on the Internet) and with Relay Broadcast, send that broadcast to more listeners by accessing the world's largest directory of Internet radio and using Live365's Relay channel. All you need is Live365's proprietary broadcasting software, a computer, and an Internet connection (ISDN or better recommended). The Relay broadcasting solution is recommended for radio stations or other groups who are already broadcasting.

Create your Internet radio station. Once you choose the broadcast package that fits your budget and needs, all that's left is to create your new Internet radio station. This is where it gets exciting. Go to Live365.com and follow their quick and easy steps on how to do it, and you'll see just what I mean.

Questions about Internet broadcasting. When it comes to something so new as Web broadcasting and having your own Internet radio station, I'm willing to bet you've got a bunch of questions. I asked Steve Chang at Live365 to give me their most frequently asked questions and, of course, their answers.

Q: *Can I have a station that plays only songs from one, or a few, of my favorite artists?*

A: Generally, no. With the sole exception of Internet broadcasts that exclusively include recordings in which you own all copyrights (such as recordings featuring your performance or possibly the performance of a band in which you are a member), only Internet broadcasts that are eligible for compulsory licenses may be posted on the Live365.com website.

One key rule relates to the number of songs from a particular artist that may be included in an eligible Internet broadcast. In general, in any 3-hour period, you should not intentionally program more than three songs (and not more than two songs in a row) from the same recording (or album); or more than four songs (and not more than three songs in a row) from the same recording artist or anthology/box set. Because of this rule, you cannot legally have a program that plays only music from one artist or a small number of artists.

Q: *Is there a way I can link my broadcast to my Web page?*
A: There are a few different ways to launch your station from a Web page. Check out our Launch Examples on Live365.com for examples and instructions.

Q: *Can I broadcast music from CDs I have purchased?*
A: Generally, yes. So long as the recordings that you play in your programs are authorized (that is, created originally by the band or record label that owns the copyright), and are not unlawful copies, they may be included in your program without further permission or payment.

This is because Live365.com has taken care of, or is currently in the process of taking care of, all U.S. musical composition performance royalties through its licenses with ASCAP, BMI, and

SESAC, and has taken care of U.S. sound recording performance royalties by complying with the terms of recent legislation enacted by Congress.

You should be aware, however, that some songs may be written by writers who are not affiliated with ASCAP, BMI, or SESAC (including, for example, many songs written by local and international songwriters for albums that are not released by a "major" label in the United States).

Such songs are not covered by Live365-com's blanket licenses, and you would need direct permission from the writers (or copyright owners) of such songs before including them in your programs. Generally, the liner notes of your CDs will indicate in small print whether the songwriters are affiliated with ASCAP, BMI, or SESAC.

You may only broadcast sound recordings that are authorized for performance in the United States.

Q: *Do DMCA (Digital Millennium Copyright Act) rules apply to me if I live outside the United States?*

A: The rules contained in the DMCA and on Live365.com apply to all users generating Internet broadcasts for transmission via the Live365.com website, no matter what country you live in.

However, if you reside outside of the United States, other rules and regulations might also apply to programs that you generate. You should consult a local music organization (such as a performing rights organization) in your country and/or an attorney to determine whether any such rules might apply to you.

Q: *Can I broadcast music from MP3 files that I have downloaded?*

A: It depends on whether the MP3 files are legal or unauthorized.

Currently, most recordings from major bands available for download on the Internet in MP3 format are not authorized. To the extent that the band's record label (or the band itself, if it controls its copyrights) has not made the recordings available, they probably are unauthorized.

You can usually tell by the type of site from which you downloaded the files. FTP sites, personal websites, etc., tend not to be sources of authorized files, while sites operated by the record labels and major Internet retailers tend to offer only authorized files.

As is true with lawful copies of CDs that you own, legitimately acquired MP3 files may be included in your programs. This is generally true whether you obtained such MP3 files for free or for a charge. On the other hand, if the MP3 files are unauthorized, you cannot lawfully include them in your programs, whether you paid for them or not.

Q: *Can I transmit certain special programs I've created more than once?*
A: Yes, but subject to certain rules. The DMCA specifies that rebroadcasts of identifiable programs in which recordings are played in a predetermined order (such as published chart countdowns, etc.) and which are preannounced in advance (such as by telling listeners that the program airs at certain times) may be performed at scheduled times. Programs of less than 1 hour may be performed no more than three times in a 2-week period, and programs longer than 1 hour may be performed no more than four times in any 2-week period.

Q: *Can I let listeners know in advance what songs will be played in my programs?*

A: Generally, no. Although you may announce a song right before it is about to be played, as well as after it is played, you should not make available, either during your program or in print (or e-mail) form, advance program guides, nor should you use other means to preannounce when particular songs will be played.

This rule applies regardless of whether you list the songs that will be played in the particular order in which they will be played. In other words, it is not permitted to list in advance the songs that are included in your programs in any manner.

Q: *Can I include bootleg recordings in my programs?*
A: Generally, no. The only recordings that may be included in Internet broadcasts are ones that are authorized (for example, ones that you purchased from a store). Even if a particular band allows bootleg recordings to be made of its concerts, you should not rely on this fact alone to suggest that you can include such recordings in your programs.

The reason is that, if the band has a recording agreement with a record label, the record label may be able to prevent you from exploiting any recordings you made, despite the band's explicit or implicit authorization of your making a recording in the first place.

Q: *If I am based outside the United States, am I subject to any additional requirements to protect against litigation?*
A: The legal issues involving Webcasters outside the United States are evolving and there are at present a number of uncertainties. To some extent, the issue may depend on an analysis of the

specific facts involved. You should follow our rules to ensure compliance with respect to your stream as it is transmitted from Live365 servers in the United States.

However, with regard to any transmissions from your own website in any country other than the United States or via any other servers besides ours in the United States, then you should look into any requirements by the performing rights organization(s) of that particular country.

It is our understanding that the performing rights organizations in the United States generally have reciprocity agreements with performing rights organizations of many other countries. Therefore, if these agreements are in place with performing rights organizations in the United States, they will make allocation payments to the other country's performing rights organization(s).

Please keep in mind that there are international issues that are still being discussed among the performing rights organizations and among organizations representing record companies in different countries. To the extent that a performing rights organization of a particular country has jurisdiction, then you need to abide by its rules. You should direct these inquiries to the appropriate U.S. performing rights organization or the particular country's performing rights organization for information on how payments are allocated.

We cannot assume responsibility for compliance with any applicable laws or regulations outside the United States, but we are willing to try to assist Webcasters in obtaining information that may be helpful.

Q: *What speed is best for encoding my music for my broadcast?*
A: Keep in mind that your broadcast bit rate cannot be higher
than the connection speed of your listener. For example, if your
listeners have a 56K connection, you will want to encode your
music at a lower rate than 56K to allow the music to play
without skipping.

Q: *Do the licensing guidelines also apply if my station only plays my
originally created music and my performance of such music?*
A: Ordinarily, you must abide by the rules as stated in the Digital
Millennium Copyright Act. However, if you own the copyrights
in both the music and in all sound recordings embodying the
performance of such music, you would not need to comply with
all the rules that would otherwise be applicable. In addition, you
must still abide by our User's Agreement, Terms of Use, and other
guidelines set forth by Live365.com. Please keep in mind that we
do require proper documentation from you.

If you are an independent artist and wish to create an
Internet radio station featuring your own music, you can do so by
forwarding to us written consent from you, as long as you are the
sole owner of the copyrights in both the music and in all sound
recordings embodying the performance of such music.

If you wish to create an independent artist Internet radio
station that features music owned and/or controlled by you,
please send us a notice stating that you are in fact the artist being
featured and that you own all rights in the music and in all sound
recordings embodying the performance of such music (and that
no third party, including any record company or other party, owns

any such rights) on your Internet radio station. Please provide your DJ name and description of your Internet radio station as well so that we may stamp it as an "independent" station.

If, however, you are featuring someone else's music on your Internet radio station on our site, you must forward to us written consent from the artist and/or artists, and any third parties involved (including record companies) that own any of the copyrights in the music or in any of the sound recordings embodying the performance of such music.

Promoting and selling your music and website. Okay, so you've got a cool-sounding domain name, you've created a great-looking website, and you've got a kick-ass radio station ready to broadcast. Way to go! The next step is promoting your music and website, and contrary to all the myths you may have heard, you're not going to need a lot of money to do it.

In the history of business, great wealth and opportunity have gone hand in hand with great ideas. Every invention or great business first began as an idea in someone's mind, so you're going to use some creative ingenuity to open doors. What follows are some tips that'll help.

Use search engines and metatags to direct traffic to your site. You just read about the search engine submission services you can use that'll get you listed on the Internet's biggest search engines. Use them and metatags (i.e., words or phrases to use in your search engine submission description that'll direct people who type in that search word to see your site listed as a search result)—lots and lots of metatags—to get your website listed and seen by as many people as possible.

Create tie-ins with other sites and companies. A great way to get your name and music out there in a big way is to be associated with other websites and companies you like. And they don't need to be music-related companies. Any company that has customers can be a terrific place to find new ears and eyes.

In exchange for providing music to an individual or a company, ask them to include a link on their site that says "Click here to buy Mymusic." That link will take them to your site where you'll, of course, have plenty of your music available (in many different formats) from which to choose.

Be flexible on the price or deal you're looking for. Start by offering free or reduced-rate music to promote your music and website on other sites. As the demand for your music grows, you can always revisit the terms of your agreement.

Associate yourself with a powerful brand. Associating with a powerful brand can open doors for you and your music in a hurry. People go after brand names they're familiar with before they choose lesser-known names. Having you and your music associated with a brand-name company or individual not only gives you instant clout, it also gives you a powerful reference and door-opener to other companies who'll now see you as a major player worthy of playing with the big boys (or girls).

Do deals with other websites. The number of indexed pages on the Web now total more than 8 billion. And the number of Websites total more than 360 million. It's huge, and more new sites are coming online each day. And guess what? Many of them need music content. Bingo! Find the ones you like and do a deal with them to provide musical content for a fee, a trade for promotion and association with them, or a combination of the two.

Not only should you seek out the entertainment providers, companies that specialize in visual content (music and visuals are a powerful pair), but you should consider companies that most people wouldn't associate with a need for music to promote their business—florists, card companies, even auto parts manufacturers.

The Internet is filled with great places to hear MP3s. Make MP3.com the first place to make your music available after you have got your own site up and running.

Sell your music on the Internet. First, set up Amazon.com link. It takes only seconds to do. Simply go to Amazon.com and click on the "become an associate" link and they'll walk you through the setup. As you and millions all over the world know, amazon.com is the place people go for books and music, and having your music for sale on amazon.com will give you presence in front of the eyes of millions. You'll also get a commission on every sale if someone else (e.g. a site you have linked with that directs its customers to Amazon) sells your music. Amazon.com will also buy your CDs from you—the new music business owner of your own record label—directly.

Don't limit yourself to Amazon. Linking with online booksellers or music sellers is easy to do. And the big bonus is, those retailers who may have turned you down in the past when you've wanted them to sell your records in their stores probably won't this time. Why? Because all they have to do is include your name and CD name on their website list. There's no warehousing, pre-order, or out-of-pocket expenses for them. And you get to be included with all the other major label artists on their site.

Don't forget eBay. Write a great description of you, the artist, and your music, and put your Web address/link in your ad copy that'll direct eBay buyers to your site to hear a free sample of the CD. Include a nice-looking picture of the front and back of the CD cover artwork, include any glowing reviews, price your CD below the cost of others, and get ready to start taking orders!

Sell all forms of your music on your site. Give consumers the widest variety of ways to hear your music as possible. Of course, when you're first starting out, funds might be tight and the best you can do might be a CD and MP3 or other music file download for a price. That's fine. Even though CDs are up there at the top as the most preferred way to purchase music, downloads (legal downloads) are skyrocketing in popularity.

The other thing you need to think about is having your sheet music available in electronic form that readers can download and print themselves. All you have to do is create the written version once and put it on your site, where it can be downloaded unlimited times by anyone who pays a fee.

Cool ways to record, send, and receive music from anyone, anywhere, anytime. You're going to like having your own Internet radio station. Whenever you want, you'll be able to broadcast your music as often and as long as you want. But what if you want to connect and record with other musicians without being in the same room, or even the same city, at the same time? What about if they're in another country halfway around the world? In the new music business, your dream has come true.

I want you to check out the Website Indabamusic.com. Lots of pros in the business use them, and it could be a great way for you hook your music and dreams up with others.

Now let's talk about other ways you can share your music with others who may live down the street or halfway around the world.

The first method is the old tried-and-true way to do it: sending e-mail files to each other that have audio files attached to them. Lots of people do it, so it's got to be working on some level for those folks. While there are quite a few programs that'll help you convert your recorded audio to various Internet audio file formats, a lot of people like to use RealAudio.com. Real Audio helps convert music files to WAV files, which are super easy to transfer. This is a good way to jump into audio file transferring. Another way is by using Advanced Audio Coding (AAC), an audio codec which, when compressed at 128 kpbs, delivers audio quality very close to that of uncompressed CD audio.

You might also choose to do it the way the pros do it.

First, check out a company called "ednet" (at Ednet.net/audio/index.html).

Think of ednet as the way for you to hook up with and record with talent (be they artists, producers, clients, etc.) from anywhere in the world and still be able to deliver top-level performance quality from wherever you are. *Lots* of major recording artists, songwriters and producers use ednet.

When I went to California to interview Bob Clearmountain, he took me on a tour of his amazing studio before we did our interview. Of course he had the best gear you could imagine, but he also had something else: DolbyFax. You might be wondering what the heck a DolbyFax is. It's a device that receives and sends CD-quality audio in real time (with immediate confirmation of audio delivery) by means of standard ISDN phone lines. The basic system allows users to send and receive two discrete 20-kHz bandwidth audio channels in both directions simultaneously, with the option of sending and receiving up to eight audio channels if higher-end versions are used.

Bob told me that by using ISDN (integrated services digital network) lines and the DolbyFax, he's able to receive music from anywhere in the world and mix it right in his studio in California. He's also able to send mixes back to his clients and he never has to leave his home studio. I like the sound of that.

I think you'll find it helpful to understand how an ISDN line and DolbyFax work together. An ISDN is a digital phone line that is able to simultaneously transmit and receive data across the world. It carries voice and data over B Channels (e.g., bearer channels) at between 56 and 64 kilobits (kbs) per second. There can also be a D Channel (e.g. data channel) that handles signals at 16 kbs or 64 kbs. And ISDN uses two kinds of service: primary rate interface (PRI) and basic rate interface (BRI). Primary rate interface is designed for higher-end usage, while BRI offers two channels at 64 kbs and one D Channel at 16 kbs, giving the user 144 kbs.

Many Internet service providers and phone companies offer ISDN service. Typically, your home (or studio) needs to be within a certain distance to a phone company's main office in order to get the cheapest rates. For some providers, the farther away your location is, the more expensive the service can be, due to the need for repeaters to carry the signal. When using ISDN and ISDN products, both the sender and receiver need to have ISDN routers and ISDN modems.

Because DolbyFax uses ISDN lines as its method of transmitting audio data, it can send and receive much more quickly and efficiently than is possible with DSL, cable, and dial-up services. With DolbyFax (and other, similar products, such as Telos Zephyr, APT Milano, and CCS/Musicam Prima), you can send and receive overdubs, work on scores for TV and movies, record and mix music, and co-create musical ideas with anyone, anywhere, anytime.

APPENDIX

Appendix A
Special Report: Capturing Niche Markets
Producing & Selling Music for Niche Markets: Little-Known
Avenues of Music Opportunities That Can Pay Big Rewards

One of the biggest misconceptions held by musicians is that there are only two ways to make money in the music business: playing gigs and getting a record deal. If you've played gigs, you know that they're unlikely to put a Bentley in your garage any time soon.

If you've had a record deal, you know that you're lucky to come out with the same amount of money that you went in with.

There are little-known avenues of music-selling opportunities, though, that you ought to consider. But first, you need to start thinking differently about your music.

Think Out of the Box

One of the best strategies you can use to identify and take advantage of new avenues for marketing your music is by looking at your music in different ways. Start thinking like a successful businessperson, instead of a musician who happens to sell music.

Many times we can become so passionate and emotionally close to our music that we miss many potentially great opportunities. Everywhere you go, look around and ask yourself "What are some other ways for me to sell my music?"

We get the answers we need that can help change our lives, by asking our-selves questions. The better the question the better the answer. And it's by act-ing on those answers that helps guide us to and along the path we need to take.

Ask others who aren't musicians where they would buy music. Look at other businesses and ask if they could offer your music with their product. Perhaps it's the new pizza delivery business that gives away a download or CD for any order over $20. Perhaps it's the dry cleaner that gives away holiday music downloads and CDs in December to his or her customers.

The possibilities are endless and so can be your success if you dream it, open your eyes to the possibilities, and listen to the inner voice that's always guiding you.

Begin at once to act on the message and inspiration you receive and keep acting on it until you achieve it. To get the ball rolling, let's look at some potentially big markets for all kinds of music.

Niche market #1: mood music. People love rock, rap, country, hip-hop, jazz, blues, R&B, classical, pop music. They also love mood music. Time to pay attention. Creating mood music can be potentially lucrative and open new markets for your music.

So what kinds of mood music and markets are we talking about? Some of the more popular types include:

• Romantic Jazz • After-Dinner Music
• Relaxing Sounds of the Sea • Gregorian Chant • Relaxation
• Meditation • Sleep • Stress • Thinking • Learning
• Sounds of Nature • Sounds of Weather

So how do you make a music download album/CD of, say, the weather? I've heard a variety of recordings of weather and nature that had the sounds of rain and the rumble of thunderstorms mixed in the forefront, with lush sounding synth pads, percussion, flutes, guitar, keyboard, the voices of "ooh's, ah's" or Native Indian or other chants, as the background. There are no limits to style, instrumentation, or voice you can use.

Check your music collection. What kinds of mood music do you already have? Ask yourself why you bought it? Was it to have background music for a romantic occasion or party? Was it to have relaxing instrumental music for those times you don't want to hear lyrics?

People are always looking for great music that'll help put them in the mood for whatever they like to do. Your goal is to create that kind of music in ways that are fresh and different from what's being offered now. In a moment, I'll tell you where you can market it.

Niche market #2: genre & ethnic music. Let's talk ethnic and genres. Whereas mood music can use different genres and styles to help create mood, genres (and the many flavors of genres that ethnic music can use) are actually the styles of music people enjoy listening to on a regular basis.

Putting together a download/album/CD of your favorite genres that influence you as a musician and listener can be a fun way to stretch your creativity and add more bank to your bank account. Some of the more popular genres include:

• Folk • Fiddle • Bluegrass • Ragtime • Tango • Polka • Waltz
• Jazz • Big Band • Swing • World Beat • Barbershop • Samba
• Easy Listening • Rock and Roll • Hard Rock • Metal • Pop
• Reggae • Country • Blues • R&B • Soul • Ska • Latin
• Hip-Hop • Trance • Industrial • Rap • Classical • Orchestral
• Choir • Chamber • Strings • Wind • Percussion • Salsa
• Marching Band • Baroque • Gospel • Christian • Religious
• Cuban • African • Afro-Pop • Asian • Tibetan • Celtic

• Latin • BBQ (Just kidding and checking to make sure you're
following me) • Ambient/Digital • Funk • Rai • Rumba
• Dance • Disco • Fusion • Sephardic • Merengue • Children's
• Flamenco • Opera • Theater • Ragtime • Reggae • Tango
• Christmas/Holiday • New Age • Mambo • Chanson • Fado
• Gamelan • Indian • Klezmer • Liedermacher • Hawaiian
• And the list goes on....

So, I have a question.

Can you think of any way you can take mood, genre, and ethnic music
and put them all together in a download/album/CD and sell it to a non-retail
store type of business? I'll give you some ideas.

Niche market #3: restaurants. According to the National Restaurant
Association (Restaurant.org), there are more than 870,000 restaurants in the
United States that do over $400 billion (with a B) in sales a year. Hello! And,
more than four out of ten people eat out each day, with takeout and delivery
accounting for more than 50 percent of restaurant traffic. And, of all the days
people like to eat out, Saturday is the most popular. AND... more than 50 percent of us visit restaurants on our birthdays, but Mother's Day and Valentine's
Day are the number two and three most popular occasions to eat out.

What in the world could all of this possibly mean for you, the musician,
looking to create new markets for your music? How about numerous possibilities for creating mood/genre/ethnic music for the different kinds of restaurant in your town?

I'll bet if you look in the phone book under "Restaurants," you'll see lots
of them. And think about it: a large number of restaurants are always playing
background music that complements their style of cuisine and clientele. Time
to start dining out and taking notes.

Niche market #4: massage therapy centers. Have you ever received a massage? Besides how great it made you feel, did you also notice if there was any low volume background music playing while you were off in never-never land? I'm willing to bet there was.

For the most part, massage therapists go out of their way to create a tranquil and relaxing environment. In addition to the soothing sounds of the little rock waterfall, fragrant smells, and low lighting, many will play mood music (that can be of different genres and quite ethnic).

Strategy: book a massage and relax your way into a few great ideas that will take your music into lots of other rooms of relaxation.

For a listing of more than 52,000 licensed massage therapists in 27 countries, go to AMTAmassage.org

Niche market #5: resorts & hotels. Not only do many resorts and hotels offer full amenities like massage, but they also play music throughout the hotel. This is especially true in different locations in the hotel like gyms and fitness centers, lobbies, poolside, outdoor cabanas, etc.

Pick a day and go and check out a few bigger name hotels in your area. Walk around and listen. Make notes what you hear and where. Look around and observe what you don't hear and where, as those locations could be great places for the hotel to play your background music.

Also take special note to hear how the volume and style of music changes as the day progresses into night. Hotels, like retail outlets, restaurants, and other mood music playing places, often change their playlist at certain times of the day to reflect the mood and music their clients want to be in and hear.

For a list of hotels in your area and anywhere in the world, go to any of these:

Hotels.com

Expedia.com

Orbitz.com

Lodging.com

Travelocity.com

Priceline.com

Niche market #6: TV infomercials. Okay, now that I've got you thinking off the beaten path on new kinds of music to create and markets to sell it, let's look at a few traditional music retail outlets that can be potentially big, if you've done your homework.

If you've ever seen or heard CDs for sale of theme music (i.e., *The Best Rock Hits of the '80s, The Sounds of Ireland,* or *The World's Greatest Music from Commercials*), then you heard music created for a niche market.

Turn on cable television and you'll see plenty of other kinds of theme, artist, compilation, or specialty music offered by companies like Castalian Music, Time Life (Timelife.com), and Razor & Tie Direct (Razorandtie.com). These companies keep advertising regularly because direct marketing pays. Having a great idea and using the right outlets to promote it can put big bucks in your pocket. What follows are a few ideas to get you thinking in that direction.

Niche market #7: Target, Walmart, Kmart & all the little department stores. Stores like Target (Target.com), Walmart (Walmart.com), and Kmart (Kmart.com) all sell music. Yes, they have a special section for major label artists and their records. But, they also sell music by independent artists and labels that simply do specialty music.

By specialty music I mean, offering music created for different moods or themes like Romantic Jazz or Relaxing Sounds of the Sea or many others. While getting into a major department store and discount retailer can be tough, I know people who've done it and are making more money than most major label artists.

Start by going to your local store and talking to the manager. He or she might give you the okay (or refer you to the district manager) to test-sell your music in their store. If they do and it sells, this gives you a calling card and opening to go to the next store in your area and do the same thing. This is how things can snowball into something great quickly.

Niche market #8: bookstore kiosks. Another terrific place for your music can be your neighborhood bookstore. Go to a Barnes & Noble (Bn.com) and in many stores you'll find music kiosks in addition to their music section.

Many of them are filled with mood and theme music created by independent artists and labels. They could be anything from After Dinner Jazz to Celtic Music to Saxophone Classics.

Be creative when looking at the selections and think about what kinds of music and themes they're not selling and create a CD accordingly. Talk to the store manager (who'll refer you to the district manager/buyer, if he or she can't help), get the okay, test your CD, and watch what happens.

Niche market #9: card, gift and specialty shops. The clientele in card, gift, and specialty shops tends to be more female-based, so adjust your ideas and music accordingly. Walk into each store and get a good sense of the environment and products they sell. Listen to the music (if any) they play. In card and gift shops, a lot of the music tends to be soothing and easy listening.

Specialty stores, like clothing and shoe stores, may not have any kiosks, but they may have CDs of the cool music you've been listening to in the store for sale at the check-out counter.

Among the gift, card and specialty stores out there, the biggies are Hallmark (Hallmark.com) and Spencer Gifts (Spencergifts.com) and Z Gallerie (Zgallerie.com). But you should also think of hotel and hospital gift shops too.

A huge upside to selling your music to these kinds of stores is that your music is typically sold on a non-returnable basis. You get paid and they either sell your music or will give it away.

Also, a company like Hallmark has many other divisions that could also be good outlets for your music, thereby giving you multiple opportunities within just one big company.

Pricing your CD right is very important. My suggestion is to keep it under ten dollars. You will also need to know that many of these stores and buyers will want to see a finished product and have it their hands before they will buy. Spend the time to not only cut a great sounding record, but, do a nice design and package.

Much of the gift and card business is seasonal and buyers will typically start thinking of buying for a holiday six months or so before the event, so be sure to time your ideas and pitch to the specific time and season you want your music sold. For music that isn't season time-sensitive, pretty much any time of the year should be fine.

How to get in the door. People need to know about your music. While fax, phone and e-mail are great first steps, you should consider getting some face time in front of the buyers and distributors.

A smart strategy would be to attend a gift mart or trade show held across the country throughout the year. For a list of all major trade shows go to Tsnn.com.

Another good idea would be to get your music CD featured and listed in co-op advertising catalogs that are sent out to card, gift, and specialty stores. Two companies that can help you do this are Gift Creations Concepts (Gcccatalog.com) and Ideation (Ideationgifts.com).

At the end of the day, the best place to start is locally with card, gift, and specialty shops near you. Go to them and talk to the manager and buyer for the store. Get the okay from the manager, create some great beats and melodies, and price your CD below the others on sale.

For more information about the card, gift, and specialty markets, go to:

Giftwarenews.com

Giftbeat.com

Giftsanddec.com

Market specific outlets. These aren't retail in the sense of having a store in a mall or selling an item that you can put in a shopping bag; however, they are businesses that sell a product or service and can be a great market for your music. Each one is different in their clientele and needs, so adjust your plan accordingly. Let's begin with realtors.

Niche market #10: Realtors. Here's a strategy you may not have thought of: selling CDs to realtors. You might be thinking it sounds silly (after all, what would they buy?) and there couldn't be that big a market. But you'd be wrong—as in "selling more than 20,000 CDs to them" wrong.

I know a man who has a gift specialty company. One of his biggest clients is realtors. Now, realtors are always thinking of unique ways they can stand out from all the other realtors and be remembered (and hopefully referred to friends) the next time their client or client's friends buy or sell a home. One of the ways they stand out is by giving their clients and referrals gifts that show appreciation.

Some years ago, this gift specialty company entrepreneur offered his realtor clients an instrumental CD of theme music. He contracted a local composer who arranged and performed most of the instrumentation and hired a horn player for the parts the composer's music software couldn'tcover. (Note: This was some time ago before having the great sounding music software tools available to you right now.)

They filled the CD with 10 or so familiar songs and gave it a catchy title. The business owner contacted the Harry Fox Agency to get permissions and licenses for the songs, and had 500 CDs duplicated.

He priced the CD to realtors at $5.00, who in turn gave the CDs to their clients for Christmas, when they moved into a new home, or any other occasion. The clients loved them, the realtors loved them, and the man loved them—he's already sold more than 20,000! There's no reason you couldn't do something similar.

For a listing of realtors and offices in the United States and worldwide, go to the following:

> Realtor.com
> Coldwellbanker.com
> Century21.com
> Remax.com

Niche market #11: auto dealers. This is a potentially terrific outlet to create great music and sell it. Think of it: how many auto dealers are in your town? In your city? In your state? Now think of how many different kinds of dealers there are. You've got import dealers, truck dealers, new car dealers, and used car dealers (even though many dealerships offer all the above).

Now consider how many people buy a car or truck each day, each week, each year. The numbers are huge. So what does all that mean for you looking for another market to sell your music? Potentially, big opportunities.

I know of a music production company in one of the bigger southern cities that specializes in niche market music and one of their clients is a luxury carmaker. This music company sells themed CDs (i.e., cool jazz, classical, etc.) to the automaker and its dealerships, who in turn sell the CDs in their dealerships and give them away if someone takes a test drive or buys a car.

The music company, will typically create/compile two or three different CDs a year (to keep content and theme fresh), and the company and their CDs are a huge success.

Why not take that similar strategy to the dealers in your town? If one dealer sells Jeeps and imports to the younger crowd that may be into hip-hop, rap, metal, or more edgy music, create a CD (even an instrumental one of all originals if you don't want to do cover songs and get clearances and licenses from the Harry Fox Agency) targeted to that dealer's clientele.

Keep your costs low so you can sell it to the dealer on the cheap. Get your foot (and music) in the door with just one dealer, and you're on your way to creating a potentially great niche music market.

For a list of auto dealers, go to Nada.org and Autoworld.com

Niche market #12: background music for commercial & public service advertising. Very lucrative markets, if you can get that first break. Lots of advertising agencies use established companies who have created music for their ad campaigns in the past. However, each of those jingle music companies started at the same place—having never written or placed music for a public service announcement, or commercial radio/television advertisement. So take heart. Advertising companies are always looking for the next great sound and song. Just look at what Mitsubishi did with music to sell an image, a vibe, and lots of cars.

Advertising agencies typically want 20–30 second samples of lots of different styles to see what kind of "range" you have. Put at least 20 samples of different music styles on a CD.

Send each of the ad agencies a one-page letter asking permission to send a sample CD of your music. Once you get permission, include at least five copies of the CD for the ad agency creatives/producers.

Always include a self-addressed stamped envelope for their reply and an e-mail address and phone number. You could have an e-mail reply sooner than you think! For a listing of and web addresses for the world's biggest ad agencies, go to Siu.edu/~aaf/agency.html.

Niche market #13: background & theme music for video games. Millions of people buy and play video games. Besides the amazing graphics, people want cool background and theme music. Video game creators know how expensive it is to license hit music from big name artists. That's why many of them use composers who can create original music for their games.

Different games with different themes and audiences need different music, and each game needs its own theme. Not only that, many games can have multiple original pieces of music contained on the same game. This can be a huge opportunity for you and your music.

I suggest that you find the game(s) you like, find out who created, manufactured, and distributed it, and then contact them. Use a similar contact/submit/follow-up technique that I just told you about to use for the independent film, video, and television companies. Many of these game creation companies are based in Asia (especially Japan), so use the power of the Internet to research who they are and contact them.

For a listing of video game companies, publishers and studios, go to Gdse.com

Niche market #14: soundtrack music for independent films, video, and television companies. I know a lot of people who have their sights set on breaking into writing music for the film and television business. It can be a challenging nut to crack, but it's far from impossible; so if that's what you dream of, then go for, it because you can do it.

The big league entertainment industry is a close-knit community, and while you need talent and good ideas, it also helps big time if you have contacts. You know, the friend of a friend who makes the call on your behalf or gets you a meeting and audience with Mr./Ms. Studio Head. It can be done, as the top composers for movies and television all started with no shows or credits on their résumés.

My advice is to seek the lesser-known and lesser-knocked-on doors of independent film, video, and television companies. And don't forget the cable networks. With hundreds of channels and 24/7/365 broadcasting, there's so much content, and so much need to fill it with great (okay, we can debate how great it is) musical background that you could very well find your music on film or television before you know it.

Always keep in mind the protocol of submission and making contact:

- Begin with either a phone call or e-mail.

- Be brief, be concise, be enthusiastic, don't over-promise or hype, and always ask for permission to send a sample (only brief clips of 20–50 seconds each and never entire songs) of your work.

- Once you're given the go-ahead to submit samples, follow-up within 24 hours (always strike when you're still fresh in their minds) with a PR package that includes: a 1–2 page letter that thanks them and gives a synopsis of your best reviews/history/experiences and samples of your work.

- They'll only give your package (music and résumé) a few minutes' consideration at best, so make your time in front of their eyes and ears as crisp, clean, clear, and concise as you can. Make them want to know and hear more.

- Follow-up one week later by contacting them with a letter,
  e-mail, or fax to find out if they've had a chance to look over
  written materials and listen to your music. If they answer no,
  ask them when they expect to. If they answer yes, ask for
  their feedback.

Niche market #15: soundtrack music for video & DVD distributors.
Video and DVD distributors are a good place to look if you want to do music
for videos and DVDs. Many people think it's just the major movie studios that
do all the music for their videos, but you'd be surprised at the market for music
for special project releases.

Many video distributors enter into deals with major movie studios to release boxed sets, one-offs, combined packages, and special edition releases for
videos that may have sold well years ago, but need a new theme, new look, and
great packaging to sell to a whole new audience. This is perfect opportunity
for you to pitch them and your music to be a part of their upcoming projects.

For a listing of names and web addresses for the world's biggest video
distributors, go to Dvdverdict.com/studioinfo/index.shtml.

Niche market #16: website content. Another potentially huge interactive
music market is websites. Specifically, providing music content in unique ways
designed to keep the web surfer interested in the site. This can be as simple
as having music playing as soon as the website visitor enters the site, to more
in-depth music usage as having different clips of sounds, beats, and songs play
each time they go to a different page or section of the site.

Niche market #17: collaborations via independent music e-newsletters.
A lot of people I know are impressed with a freebie e-newsletter that arrives
in their e-mail boxes each month called "The Indie Contact Newsletter." It
includes listings of contacts, places to get reviews, overseas venues, and music

publications looking for new talent. One tip or lead could open one door that opens another door that opens another door. Go to Indiebible.com.

Keeping the Dream Alive and the Big Goal in Mind

When first starting out, expect to be rejected. It happens to everyone. And don't take it personally. Even though your music could be the biggest breath of fresh air to come along to these stores, advertising agencies, and studios in years, they like working with people they know and who are dependable in delivering on time and without problem.

You will get a break. While you're waiting for it, use each "no" and "try us again later" to refine your music and message so that it's razor-sharp and kicks anyone's butt who hears it.

You know, it's so easy to get in the habit and rut of thinking that you'll do and learn a little today, and tomorrow... *that's* the day you'll take action to make your musical dreams come true. But look back on your life and how quickly the last year has passed. Are you any closer to your dreams?

Always remember that today is the tomorrow you thought about yesterday. Quit being a spectator and get in the game and get started now. Live by the motto "I dream it and I become it!"

Let me leave you with some words of wisdom that I hope will inspire you to follow your passion and music dreams.

> Always remember that in the new music business, there are no
> hard-and-fast rules on how to promote, distribute, and record
> your music. It's now cheaper than ever for you to get the biggest
> musical and business bang for the buck. So take advantage of it.
> Do all of this and don't be surprised one year from now, when
> you look back at what you've done, at just how much your
> music/business life has changed for the better!

Appendix B
Lessons of Inspiration

Inspiration. We all want it. We all need it. When we look for it, it can be very elusive. But often it's just when we are not looking anymore—when we've given up—that it finds us. In fact, the possibilities for inspiration are always there, awaiting our discovery. All we need to do is open ourselves and lives to those possibilities. Life is the greatest of teachers, and, if we are open to learning, will teach us what we need to know at just the right time.

Throughout my life, I've been fortunate to have had many experiences that helped shape who I am. Some of the lessons I learned were taught to me by people I admired. Most were learned from people I didn't know. And many of the lessons have lasted a lifetime. You're about to read a few of those lifetime lessons that I think will put a big smile on your face.

Your life and your talent are gifts of amazing power and potential. With music, you have the power to change people's lives in a big way. You have the power to inspire. Always remember that. Now, let me be the one who inspires you.

Learning from Greatness: The Tommy Tedesco Story

For as long as I can remember, whenever I'd pick up one of the guitar magazines on the stands, one guy's name seemed to always be in it. His monthly column in *Guitar Player* magazine was a reader favorite. He was referred to by studio players and other great guitar players as The King of Studio Musicians. He was a master of many styles. He had the ability to read music like no other studio guitarist. On top of all that, he was one of the most likable human beings you would ever want to meet. His name was Tommy Tedesco. I always wondered what it would be like if I could meet and talk to him.

The first time I came to California was in 1988, and after arriving in Los Angeles, I called the Musician's Union, told them I wanted to contact Tommy Tedesco, and asked if they could give me his number. They did and I called him. The conversation was like one that I might have had with an old friend, and at the end of it, he invited me to visit him the following Thursday.

Thursday couldn't come fast enough. With map in hand, I started out (2 hours early; it was only a 45-minute drive) to meet the man in person and at his house. I couldn't believe it was about to happen.

After getting lost only twice (hey, it was my first time in Los Angeles), I found his home (it was gorgeous) and with 30 minutes to spare I headed to a nearby 7-Eleven for some water (dry mouth and nervous, you know) and a pit stop. At 12:55 I pulled up to Tommy's house and walked up and rang the doorbell. I introduced myself to the woman who answered the door, and she told me that Mr. Tedesco would be right down.

I sat down on a massive sofa in the living room, next to a flamenco guitar. I got up when I saw a man with black hair and glasses, wearing an oversized shirt, shorts, and sandals, walk into the room. I was smiling from ear to ear because the man was Tommy Tedesco.

Tommy [holding out his hand with a smile]: Hi Bob. I'm Tommy. Welcome to California and Los Angeles.

Me: Thank you. Thank you. I really appreciate you inviting me to your home and to meet you.

Tommy: So, tell me about you.

Me [not wanting to bore him with all the details]: Well, I was born and raised in St. Louis and I've always wanted to come out to California and Los Angeles. I think I wanted to see what it would be like to be around such great players, learn from them, and be inspired by them. I always wondered what that might do to help me become a better player.

Tommy: Well, there are lots of great players out here.

Me: Yeah, and you're certainly one of the best.

Tommy: That's very kind of you to say and I appreciate that, but I'm just a lucky guy who can play a few different styles, read music okay, and people are nice enough to call me when they think I can help them.

Me [thinking this is a very humble statement from the man whom so many in the business for years have said was the best studio musician in Los Angeles, if not anywhere in the world]: Oh, I think it's more than that, Tommy. You're such a great player and the stories are legend of you being able to read incredibly difficult pieces of music like movie scores, classical and orchestral parts, and the Frank Zappa stuff...

Tommy [laughs]: ...Good ol' Frank. Yeah, that was fun.

Me: With so many great players out there, can you give me any advice on how I can become a great player too?

[Tommy got up from where he was sitting and walked over and picked up the flamenco guitar sitting next to me on the couch. He walked back over to where he had been sitting with the guitar in his hands.]

Tommy: What do you see here?

Me: It's a guitar.

Tommy: And do I have three arms and twenty fingers?

Me [laughs]: No, you have two arms and ten fingers.

Tommy: That's right, just like you. [He begins to play a few notes.]

You see there are lots of people who can play like this. [He rips into some cool-sounding rock riffs.]. There are also lots of people who can play like this. [He effortlessly switches to finger-tapping Van Halen–like leads.]

And there are lots of people who can play like this. [He quickly switches to pop and country and Chet Atkins–style finger-picking.] And there are many people who can play like this. [He starts playing straight-ahead and bebop jazz lines.]

Me: Wow! [By now I'm shaking my head in amazement.]

Tommy: But… there are very few who can play like this. [He begins to play lightning-fast finger-picked brilliant flamenco melodies that sound uniquely his own. Then he stopped playing, and looked at me.]

Tommy: And that's why my phone always rings.

[I was speechless, realizing I had just been taught a very important lesson.]

Tommy: You don't need to play everything I just played to be a great player. You don't need to read music to be a great player. You don't need to live in Los Angeles, New York, Nashville, or anywhere else to be a great player. You don't need to copy other people or try to play like anyone else. You've simply got to let what's inside your heart [tapping his chest]—whatever it may be—come out through your fingers, and keep letting the music inside of you come out. When that happens, you will have become a great player.

I have never forgotten Tommy and the lesson he taught me on that fateful Thursday afternoon in his living room. Sadly, he passed away a few years later and much too soon. He was a guy who didn't know me from Adam, yet he invited me into his home and gave of himself to help me. I learned later that throughout his life, he helped many, many people without ever asking for anything in return.

I've carried this lesson and experience around inside of me for many years. And now, looking back, I realize Tommy wasn't talking to me that day; he was talking to you, me, and to all of us. Be true and stay true to your music, he would say. And when you do, you will be walking with Tommy on the road to musical greatness.

On Selling Your Creative Ideas to Noncreative People

I want to tell you a little story about dealing with noncreative people. There's no doubt you're going to come across them on your musical journey (probably you already have), and they can zap the energy and passion right out of you unless you know where they're coming from and how to train them to be receptive to your creative ideas.

The world is full of so-called noncreative people who really are creative, but have closed their creative minds in order that they may fit in with all the other noncreative people they work with. They like things predictable, they tend to be conservative, they don't like taking chances and gambling on new and untested ideas, and they want everything spelled out for them.

You give them an idea and they absolutely love it until someone they work with tells them they don't. More often than not, they have little creative or marketing vision and will depend on you to convince them why your ideas are right (even if you're a well-known authority in your field). They want you to tell them—over and over again—why they should believe in and accept what you are telling them.

Don't expect them to see things you may have overlooked or not realized about how your great ideas could be promoted in other ways besides those you give them. Rarely will that happen. Typically, they go with what you tell them and that's it. And for heaven sakes, don't mention anything that gives them a reason to shoot down your ideas.

Too often, I've seen how an artist's passing comment about his or her song or idea that had maybe a hint of negativity about it can be seized on by the noncreative types. They are always looking for any red flag or potential problem (however far from reality), and they'll turn that comment into just the red flag they need to change your idea to something different, use your words against you to give them a better deal or more favorable terms in their favor, or shoot down the idea altogether.

My friends, the music and creative business world we live in is populated by bean-counters who sit inside the four walls of their headquarters and insulate themselves from the people outside. They say they want what's fresh and what's new, but what they do is seek out the predictable. If so-and-so had a hit song last month with that vibrato-ish funk vibe in the background going on, then they want that on such-and-such's new record too. As the old saying goes, "Imitation is the sincerest form of a lack of imagination."

So what's a creative maverick and visionary like yourself to do? Here are a few tips.

Come up with lots of ideas, but keep them within a consistent theme. The noncreatives love to pick from multiple options, and may not notice that all of the ones you are giving them have a common thread, so whatever one they pick is something you can live with.

Give them lots of ways to promote your projects. The more ways you give them (read: ways that won't cost them any money), the better. And take all their complaints—that they have little or no budgets for projects, that business is down and they're scaling back right now, that the market has changed, blah, blah, blah—with a grain of salt. They're still in business, so someone, somewhere, is still spending money. If you come up with good ways to promote your ideas (co-op advertising, promo tie-ins with other businesses, etc.), watch how quickly they find a few extra pennies for your project.

Be ready to give them some real-world education. You'd shake your head at how many people out there have reached positions of power, decision, and influence without having a clue as to what people really want. They make decisions based on what other people, focus groups, trend analysts, and research tell them, and they have the paper to CTA (cover their asses).

So, why then, with all that powerful information, do music and publishing companies lose big dollars year after year? One huge reason is that they've lost touch with the emotional side of things, and it's the emotional that drives people to buy music, dance to music, play music, and love music.

My advice is think like a businessperson when you give them ideas, but always do so with one hand still on the pulse of your heart.

On How to Make Yourself Wanted

We live in a world where people with great talent are often emulated and sought after—up to a point. If we see them too often or hear them too much, their value decreases, as does our desire for them. Some years ago, before moving to Los Angeles, I had the pleasure of meeting and becoming friends with a gentleman named Reg Park from South Africa.

Park was one of the legends of bodybuilding, having been a Mr. Universe, a star in some of the *Hercules* movies (the other being Steve Reeves), and a friend of Arnold Schwarzenegger. He was wise in the ways of fame, fortune, and human nature and offered me some advice on a decision I was about to make: whether and when I should move to Los Angeles.

In the course of a year, I had traveled many times to Los Angeles to do interviews and write articles for magazine publisher Joe Weider, whose magazines included *Muscle and Fitness, Shape, Flex, Men's Fitness,* and a number of other publications. And each time I was there, Joe would ask what it would take for me to move to Los Angeles and write for his magazines full-time.

I'll admit what with all the phone calls, lunches and dinners, and private meetings at Joe's exclusive home, the attention that the icon of fitness was paying to me was a little overwhelming. While the money he was offering was good, I felt there needed to be a little more guarantee of opportunity before I pulled up stakes and moved from my little town in the Midwest to the big city of Los Angeles.

So I spoke to Reg about it. I told him that I felt the opportunity to learn the magazine publishing business and work for the legendary Joe Weider in Los Angeles could be a once-in-a-lifetime opportunity, but I wanted the timing to be right.

Here's what he said first: "One of the reasons you're in demand is because you're reclusive. You have your own business. You live in a little town 1,600 miles away from L.A. You have something they want but can't seem to get. That fact, along with the thought that someone else, some other magazine, could take you, keeps your phone ringing and you on those junkets to Los Angeles."

He wound up with the following advice.

"There is no reason for you not to stay right where you are and double your effort to become excellent at the work you do. With each passing month that your writing and articles get better and better, Joe's desire to have you out there working for him will intensify. Be aloof. Be admiring and respectful, but don't be overtaken by awe and by the legend of Joe Weider. And don't become too common—either in the frequency or in the tone of your conversations and appearance. If you do, your value will decrease in their eyes and it's the first step to becoming quickly forgotten."

I took his advice.

Soon thereafter, Joe was sending me to many parts around the world on behalf of him and his magazines. A few months later, along with a good salary, he offered me incentives that I just couldn't turn down. I made the move and it turned out to be an incredibly positive, life-changing decision. It also taught me an important lesson about music and the people who make it.

Perception is reality. Many times, people treat us the way we train them to treat us. And they can judge our music—not so much based on the reality of how good it is—but on their perceptions of how, who, and where it is made.

You can record music in Los Angeles and it can be great. Yet you can record that same music in London or some exotic locale, and people will think—because of the mystery of where, how, and who recorded the music—that your music is twice as good. Never forget this lesson.

We cherish and value that which we don't have, for we think what we don't have is certainly more desirable than what we do. That's human nature. It's "the grass is always greener on the other side" story. My advice is to use that to your musical advantage.

Let your music trickle out and start a buzz among people. Be elusive. Be mysterious. Never reveal too much of yourself, your talent, or your craft too quickly. Keep your cards and your music close to your vest. Give out only small bits at a time and keep people hungry to hear more and know more about you. Then wait patiently for the right people and circumstances to appear. When they do, that will be the perfect time to strike.

Shattering the Myth of the Must-Have Music Town:
The Studio on Music Row

Many years ago, I worked for an FM radio station that shared the top floor with a recording studio on the famous Music Row in Nashville. Often after work, I'd walk down to the studio and listen to who and what they were recording that day. Each week, studio musicians' cases filled the hall just off the elevator, and it was always a treat to see who was recording.

One evening after work, I was getting ready to catch the elevator down to the parking lot and head home when the studio owner waved his arm in the control room and motioned for me to come in and listen to a record he had just finished recording. He was alone, and the two of us sat down with a couple of cold beers as he rolled tape.

This new artist had a good sound, but I was particularly impressed at the quality of the recording. There was great depth and separation. The sound was full, clean, and very dynamic. I wanted to know more about how he got that sound.

"I really like the sound of this," I commented. "What did you do to get it?"

"Well, we got some new microphones," he said, as he held one up and handed it to me to see. "Then we did a little experimenting and changed some of the sound deflection and absorbing panels in the studio and that made all the difference."

It was his response to what I said next that was about to shatter one of the biggest myths I had believed for years about music.

"Well, listening to what you just played me just goes to show why it's so important to live in a music city and be around all the great studios that can get this kind of sound," I ventured.

He held out his hand as I gave the microphone back to him and he got up and said, "Come with me for a minute."

As we walked into one of the main recording rooms, we stopped and he asked, "Tell me what you see in here."

I looked around for a moment and said, "I see mic stands, direct boxes, headphones, some guitar cables, chairs, sound baffles, and…"

He interrupted. "Do you see anything secret in here that you've never seen in any other studio you've ever been in?"

"No," I said. "Not really."

"Of course you don't. What you see in here are four walls, a ceiling, a floor, and equipment that you or anyone, anywhere, can go out tomorrow and buy. Equipment that you can put anywhere you want and get 'that magic sound' you heard in the control room. And you don't need to live in a 'music city' to do it."

I was stunned.

He went on. "A studio is simply four walls with equipment. Anyone who's got four walls and the same equipment and a little smarts can get the same sound whether they're doing it in Nashville or Whistlestop, North Dakota."

After looking around again and making sure I hadn't missed any secret gear he was hiding, I said, "You know, you're right. Anyone can do this anywhere, can't they?"

With a big smile on his face and chuckle he replied. "Yeah, but few believe it and that's one of the reasons why Nashville is 'Music City USA.' And you know what? Next month, like they do every month and have done for years, cars filled with people and their dreams will make the drive down Highway 40 and turn into Music Row so they can get that 'magical sound.'"

I never forgot that night, that man, that studio, and that time in my life. Whoever you are, wherever you are, you can create your music and your dreams anywhere your heart leads you, and you don't need to live in a big music city to do it.

On What Inspires Greatness

I'd like to tell you two stories about what I learned from two of the best jazz guitarists to ever play the instrument. It's about how true greatness can't be taught, but is inspired from within.

Early on in my guitar-playing years, I had the good fortune to study with Herb Ellis and Barney Kessel. At the time, I didn't know very much about either of them or jazz, but thought the education and experience would be valuable. It turned out to be valuable in ways I never imagined.

The Herb Ellis experience was a one-week master class, in which Herb taught a very small group of people about playing jazz guitar. We even got a chance to play one-on-one with him. Of course, being the young, naive guy I was, I wasn't ready to start thinking like a jazz player and it wouldn't be until years later that what I learned could be heard in my playing.

Watching someone of Herb's caliber and ability play was humbling. He used no effects and the only thing between him and his amp was a guitar cord. He wasn't a brilliant finger picker, but he could make his left fingers dance and his right hand and pick race across the strings with pinpoint accuracy and speed.

Watching him play was like watching someone enter into a completely different zone. His eyes were closed and his mouth open as he hummed the notes he was playing. Herb was oblivious to anyone and everything around him. Only when Herb was finished playing would he open his eyes and return to earth.

He also had no idea what he had just played. When people watching him asked him to show us again such-and-such "cool lick," he couldn't. We soon figured out that he never played the same song the same way twice, and we stopped asking him to show us stuff and started watching and listening to what greatness was all about.

While I learned a lot, the biggest lesson I learned didn't have anything specific to do with making music. On the last day of class, Herb told us to get a book called *Psycho Cybernetics*, by Maxwell Maltz. He said the book had really changed his life, and he believed that it would change ours.

I bought the book, and once I started reading it, I couldn't put it down. The author, a famous plastic surgeon in New York City, wrote about his surprising discovery that people who had come in hoping that a changed appearance would lead to a changed life were, for the most part, doomed to disappointment. No matter how successful the procedures had been, the lives of these people were the same as before, as if nothing had ever happened.

Dr. Maltz wanted to know why. He discovered that often the beliefs we have about ourselves—our self-images—which we have accepted as truth, are wrong. Yet even though they are wrong, they may guide and direct every action we take or don't take. And many times they lead us in the wrong direction, especially when the self-image is a negative one.

Maltz says that if we can change our self-images—and plastic surgery won't do it—we can change our lives. If we can imagine, then believe in, then truly accept a positive self-image, one that includes our ability to fulfill whatever dreams we have, the job of our brains ("servomechanisms," as Maltz calls them) is to make that self-image a reality. It's really a variation of the old adage, Be careful what you wish for because you're likely to get it. Powerful stuff. It changed my life. It may change yours.

Another person I took a master class with was jazz guitar great Barney Kessel. Barney was not only a legendary player but he, like Ellis, was a great human being who understood life in more than musical terms. Yet it was how he thought as a musician that fascinated me.

During a performance, he had just played a brilliant rendition of a jazz standard tune and when he was asked about why he used a certain chord or phrase for a certain part of the song, he paused and said, "I was imagining myself surrounded by a B major seventh. Everything I played sounded good to my ear and connected to that B major seventh."

That stunned me. Remember, I was still the young wet-behind-the-ears guitar player who wasn't ready for all the heady jazz stuff yet. Still, his approach was inspiring. After that, when I played I would close my eyes and become wrapped up in the music, imagining whatever chord I wanted to play as being all around me. The possibilities were limitless. No longer would I have to keep going back to the same old safe positions, notes, licks, riffs, and runs. I could begin thinking differently, getting results and sounds that would be interesting, different, fresh, fun, and exciting!

Barney Kessel and Herb Ellis became great not because they played the coolest stuff. They were great because they always let what was inside of them be their most important inspiration.

On Getting to Where You Want to Go and Surprising Ways It Can Inspire You

I don't come from a musical family nor did I, when I was 18, have connections to anyone who did. I didn't live in a "music city" (not that it matters today, but some years ago it was a different story) or have any idea which of those magical metropolises would be best for me to move to.

I had to reject New York and Los Angeles because the cost of living in those cities was just too high. Nashville, however, was less than 350 miles from my hometown in St. Louis, it was smaller and cheaper than Los Angeles and New York, and it reminded me a lot of the area where I was raised. And it had lots of music going on, albeit mostly country, but still a good place, I thought, to jump in and get my feet wet musically.

After graduating from college, I moved to Nashville. On my second day in town, I went to the CMA (Country Music Association) office on Music Row to apply for any kind of job they might have. The receptionist was one of the best examples of southern hospitality I had ever met. She asked all kinds of questions about me and where I was from and why I had moved to Nashville. After quizzing me in detail, she informed me that there were no openings at the CMA at the present time, but to stay seated while she made a couple of calls.

As I sat there in the lobby, paging through magazines and watching her talk on the phone, she signaled me over to her desk. She then handed me a name and phone number on a piece of paper and said, "Go see S— at RCA Records. She knows you're on your way."

The record label's office was just around the corner, so I high-tailed it over there pronto. I was met at the front door by the receptionist, and I told her who I was and who I was supposed to see.

A few minutes later S— ushered me into her office. She too, was wonderfully kind as she listened to me describe my background and love for music and explain my wanting to work in the music business. She told me that the only entry-level position was a job in the mailroom. I didn't care what it was. It was a job working for a major record label and as long it was in the music business that was all that mattered.

Within a matter of weeks, I was already doing more than delivering mail to everyone at the label. (Watching how A&R, promotions, the president, and all the other people worked was a priceless education.) I was also taking master tapes and lacquers (this was before digital hit big) to the record pressing plants.

Furthermore, I was meeting the record label's recording artists (artists I had heard on radio and watched on TV for years) and making contacts like you wouldn't believe. Even riding the elevator was an adventure. When the doors opened on any given floor, I never knew which major label recording star might be getting in that little elevator car with me.

I also began doing a few demo sessions here and there and getting my feet wet in the studios.

And I was learning some amazing lessons in how to listen to a record as well. One of the friends I made was a quality-control man who vetted the records that were ready for radio release and pressing before they were sent out.

It seems like only yesterday that I was sitting in his office watching him check a test pressing. After cranking up the music equipment in his office, he'd sit down at his desk, close his eyes, and listen. "No, the grooves are too wide [or too close] on this," he might say. Or "there's too much distortion in the groove." Or "Have them set the lathe at x and recut." I was listening to exactly what he was listening to, but thinking all the time, "How in the world can he hear that?"

The ears this guy had were incredible, and it was a fantastic learning experience to watch him work his magic on the records that left the Nashville office—and explain just how he did it.

Yet, while the RCA experience was wonderful, perhaps the best decision I made during those early years in Nashville was to go to work for Studio Instrument Rentals (SIR). I met more music people in less than 6 months at SIR than I would have in 6 years on my own. Let me tell you about it.

At that time in Nashville, SIR—like many companies in the bigger music cities—provided cartage (i.e., picking up and delivering music equipment to studios), and also rented music equipment and rehearsal rooms by the hour, day, or week. My duties included picking up, delivering, and setting up studio musician clients' gear for demo and recording sessions in the studios, plus booking rehearsal rooms and dates with clients and setting up sound systems for them. Many of these clients were major label recording artists who would rent the rooms to rehearse either before going into the studio to record a new record or before embarking on a concert tour.

And while the job didn't pay much, I worked every available hour I could—some nights even sleeping at SIR on the sofa in one of the rehearsal rooms—just so I could get a chance to work early and late for anyone and everyone. And it paid off.

One day, the manager at SIR told me that a group of big names had just rented the biggest rehearsal room for the week and he wanted to know if I wanted to mix sound for them while they were there. It was a no-brainer.

The next day, as I was setting up mic, running cables, and checking the system, who walks in but Chet Atkins, The Everly Brothers, Mark Knopfler (who was then lead singer and guitarist of Dire Straits), Emmylou Harris, drumming legend Larrie London, and many others, all of whom were gathered together for the Cinemax Television special starring Chet Atkins and Friends. It was heaven.

One night after everyone had left and I was shutting all the equipment down, I noticed that everyone had closed his or her guitar case except Chet Atkins. Well, being a guitar player, I couldn't let Chet's magical Gibson nylon string just sit there all by itself in the cold air. As I walked over to close the lid on the case, I thought about how beautiful the instrument was and how Chet could coax the sweetest sounds from its mellowed wood as he finger-picked those nylon strings.

I knelt down, reached my hand inside the case, picked up and held the guitar (like a jeweler holding a rare gem), and put my fingers on its frets and strings and began playing. I swear, for those 30 seconds, I sounded like Chet Atkins. And what a shame it was that there was no one in that rehearsal room on that late night in downtown Nashville to hear me.

Ah, but any regrets were quickly forgotten as I gently placed Chet's guitar back in its case and closed the lid. I had touched and played the guitar of one of the greatest musicians who would ever play the instrument. It was an inspiration to me then, and now—many, many years later—the memory still brings a big smile to my face.

The next day, I came back to the rehearsal room hoping that Chet wouldn't find out (he didn't) that my fingers—and not his—had been the last to touch his guitar. Little did I know that something very cool was about to happen.

The Cinemax TV show taping was only one day away and Mark Knopfler wasn't happy with the sounds he was getting from any of the amps he was using. During a break, I went to him and said that I had an amp that I thought he might like and if he wanted, I'd be happy (make that thrilled) to let him use it. He told me to bring it in.

So I rushed home at lunchtime and packed up my Mesa Boogie, brought it back to SIR, and plugged it in. Later, after Mark had listened to a few notes come from it, he looked over at me, smiled, and said, "Thanks, Bob, I'll use it for the show."

The show was taped at Vanderbilt University. On that day, like all the days leading up to it, I was in a dream world, where I was hanging out with musical legends and watching a once-in-a-lifetime event take place. The show, in a word, was a smash.

After the show, as I was packing up my amp, Mark and some of the other stars of the show asked me to come with them to the after-show party at one of Chet's favorite restaurants in Franklin (about 30 minutes south of Nashville). Would there be no end to this musical dream? I sure hoped not. One hour later, there we all were. The restaurant was all ours and the food—catfish, BBQ, sweet tea, and good ol' fashioned southern cooking—was perfect.

So there I was, a young guy from a little town of 15,000 people outside of St. Louis who had just finished working with many of the music legends he grew up listening to, sitting at the same table with those legends: all the musicians I mentioned earlier, plus Michael McDonald, solo artist and former lead singer for the Doobie Brothers, David Pack, producer and lead singer of the group Ambrosia, and many others.

But the famous artists at the table that night weren't the larger-than-life icons that so many people and the press made them out to be. They were people like you and me. People from everyday towns who had humble everyday backgrounds and beginnings. They were born with a gift, a talent, and a desire to play music, to touch people's hearts and lives with that music. And it seemed to me that they would have been just as happy doing it in their local clubs as they were in front of millions.

And once the bright lights had dimmed, the applause had faded away, and the audience had left the building, these legends were who they always had been: ordinary people with extraordinary dreams who let their music come out and take them down the road we call greatness. And for one magical summer night in Nashville, they invited me to become one of them and showed me just how much we all have in common.

Appendix C
Dealing with People in the Real World

This is a good time to give you a quick lesson in dealing with people in the real world.

You can have the most amazing talent, song and sound, but unless you know how to treat and deal with others, then you're going to run into unnecessary roadblocks and obstacles to your success.

You see, the decision makers, the gatekeepers, the promise makers, the clients, and the money givers are all people. Once you hit the streets to "do business" and interact with the dynamics of people in business—whether you send an e-mail, Twitter, IM, text, pick up the phone, send a fax or FedEx, or meet that potential business contact who might be able to help you—the whole playing field completely changes, and if you want more success, you'd better know a few good rules.

They Never Told Me It Would Be Like This

Once they get serious about their music and trying to break into the business and become successful, many people are surprised at just how much they need to bust their butts to find the right people who can help them. Don't get me wrong; there are lots of people out there right now who can potentially help you, and who will happily help you find ways to make great money (for them and you), but they need to know about you. They need to know that you're around and looking for them. And then, once you've connected with them, you've got to close the deal and get them to say yes to trusting their time, efforts and contacts to you.

Know Thyself (and Others!)

Have you ever asked yourself why you play music and love doing so? If you've got a good answer to that question, then you've found one of the many answers to why other people do it too. Truth be told, you and other people who play music (or want to) have a lot in common. It doesn't matter the reasons why you write, sing or play music. All that matters is the end result—to change your life (and the lives of those who listen to your music) for the better in some way. That is a powerful connection right from the start.

The Flowchart of the Music Business and Life

Have you ever noticed how when your goal is achieved or you get great news, many other people also benefit as well?

You get your music recorded and you're out at a party or talking to someone when the subject of music comes up. You tell him that you just recorded your album and he tells you that's so weird, because he's loves listening and looking for new music to listen to.

It happens all the time.

The message is: You don't have to know all the answers or know every road you'll take to your goal beforehand. Stay open to the possibilities of what's out there, and let the natural flow of people and life find its way to you and yours.

You're going to enjoy the ride.

Okay, I Pick You!

One of the biggest mistakes that people make in business (and in their personal lives) is choosing the wrong people in their lives. Too often, the hangups of people with bad attitudes and ideas or overwhelming insecurities can become your handcuffs as their negativity seeps into your thinking and beliefs.

Start looking at your life like it's a major league pro team.

The teams that win the biggest honors and enjoy the greatest success are those that have the best players and the best management. Pretend you're the owner of your own major league team, and with a careful eye, start choosing the best supporting cast of people who will empower you personally and professionally. You're looking to fill your roster with those who will protect and encourage you and who genuinely believe in you and your dreams.

With them, the sky will be your limit.

Make Yourself "Most Wanted"

You can have the most amazing talent, but if people don't connect with you and you aren't giving them what they want, then all you'll be is just another guy or gal who's a musician looking for their big break.

Go the extra mile.

Make yourself stand out. Do the things the others aren't doing, can't do, or won't do. Create your own unique brand that people will know you for.

All the greatest businesses do it, and there's no reason why you can't do it, too. Then, once you've created your brand and your unique way of doing things, refine it to perfection by the service you offer and the results you create.

Then get ready for your phone to start ringing off the hook.

The Mills Lane Expletive Fund

Some years ago, there was a pro boxing referee named Mills Lane. Years of military service had made him one tough cookie no one wanted to mess with, and a memorable character for sure. He was short and bald, and he had a no-BS attitude.

I remember an interview with him in which he talked about the ups and downs in his life—especially the financial pressures he had once faced. As someone who didn't like receiving orders and enjoyed being the one giving them, you can imagine that waiting for others (businesspeople) to make decisions that would affect his life didn't sit well with him.

That's when he decided to change things, he said. He vowed that he'd work hard, make as much money as he could, and then save and invest it. Mills Lane said he called it his "F-You Money," because if anyone offered him a business deal or opportunity that sought to take advantage of him, his experience, or his talents unfairly, he could afford to tell them no and push them to come back with a better deal. If they didn't, he had plenty of money saved, and he could walk away without a regret.

That's a great lesson.

The world of business is full of ups and downs, good times and not-so-good times, lots of money coming in and hardly any dough arriving.

So protect yourself.

Start your own Mills Lane–style savings fund. It'll help you stay in control of your destiny and weather anything the world can throw at you.

The Natural Cycles of Surges

Throughout your music career, you're going to find there will be times when your business is booming, and other times when things are kind of quiet. Don't let it worry you. It's simply the natural cycle of surges that people in all economies go through.

When times are good, people are working, home prices are rising, and folks have a little jingle in their pockets, they don't think twice about spending money on the "extras" in their lives, like looking for new artists and music. When times are tougher and the money doesn't jingle as much or as loudly, people naturally cut back on luxuries and focus on the necessities.

And that's when you have to turn their new artist/new music desires from a luxury into a necessity. You do it by giving them such good songs and performances that they don't want to be without your music. That's why even in bad times there are lots of singers, songwriters, and performers whose incomes and audience base don't change, and even grow! People want to spend money on the things that make them feel good. Give them great product and experiences unlike anyone else, and they'll keep spending that money with you.

The Power of Synch

One thing that frustrates people when it comes to business and dealing with people is that others rarely want to work on someone else's time frame. They have their own goals, objectives, and agendas, and if they have the money and you want to get some of it, then you need to learn how to make their time frame your time frame.

So, how do you do that?

Begin by creating lots of opportunities with many different people and businesses. You'll find that some of them will fall into place and happen very quickly, some will take a little longer, and a few will be long-term works in progress. Then constantly make adjustments to your future business plans by moving the various projects you have up and down, in order of importance and action, based on the daily and weekly feedback you receive. Whenever a current or future project is completed, then move all the others up the list and add new initiatives to take the place of any you finish.

Remember that life is exciting in proportion to the number of things you have to look forward to. When you have lots of projects going on, and others that will happen at some point in the near future, then you're in control of your destiny and are directing it toward a happy result.

Control the Worry Factor

In both your personal and your professional life, there'll be times when, despite your best efforts and hard work, things just won't seem to be happening and moving forward. For so long, we've been taught that it's only by "our" actions that we accomplish anything. But sometimes life has other plans.

That's when you need to relax, take a deep breath, and step back from what's going on in your life. This is the time to stop worrying and to be a little patient.

As someone who loves and is passionate about music, you'll find the people you deal with look at you as someone who has a unique depth of knowledge, talent and understanding that can help them, and if you're worried about every little thing that someone says or does, then your audience and those who can help you will know it. Your body will be there, but your head and mind will be off in a whole different place.

There's an old saying that goes, "Ninety-nine percent of the things we worry about never happen and the other one percent that do are not even worth worrying about."

Let go of the little things that have been bothering you and forget what's in the rearview mirror. All that matters is today and where you want to go tomorrow.

Make Failure a Trusted Friend

If you look at the history of men and women who achieved amazing things, you'll discover that at some point in their lives, the majority of them experienced many failures and setbacks. Instead of seeing these experiences as stopping points, they used them as valuable learning tools that became huge stepping stones on their road to success. You can do the same.

When you're starting out, and even after you've been in business for a while, there may be times when you miss out on business and potential opportunities. When that happens, look closely at the reason why. Was your timing off? Did they listen to your A-list material or was it a performance less than you know you're capable of? Was there something about your attitude and approach that turned off a fan, buyer, or business contact?

Be honest with yourself, get over your ego's being temporarily hurt, and find the answers that will help smooth out the rough edges of your approach so that you can turn any seeming failure into a great success.

Find the Trigger Points

While people may come to you so that you can be their artist, songwriter, performer, or business associate, they will also teach you one of the most valuable lessons you can learn when it comes to dealing with people.

"Why?"

The most successful people in music have the skills to know what their audience needs and why. They ask a lot of questions. They are terrific listeners to both verbal and nonverbal communication. They then go back to their creative sanctuary and create the perfect song and performance that people need at that time in their life.

Nothing stays the same in this life of ours, and that holds true for any listener you may have, so just stay fluid and flexible, listen to what they need, and give it to them.

People Will Treat You the Way You've Trained
Them to Treat You

Many of us see who we are through the eyes of other people. That is, we like to think that we know what they think of us, and we create our self- image based on what we imagine they think we are.

Sounds kind of crazy, doesn't it?

After all, we really have no idea how others truly view us, and even if we did take the time to find out (and most people don't because they are so busy thinking about everything else in their lives), we'd be surprised at how wrong our perceptions are.

Instead of spending so much of your priceless life and valuable time caring about what others think about you, simply be the person you imagine you'd like to be. Treat people with love and respect. Be a person of your word. Go the extra mile and give them more than they expect. And fill your life with all those qualities that you like and that make you feel terrific.

You'll then be living the life you imagine, and what you imagine, you will soon become.

Be the Rabbit, Not the Fox

People are a funny bunch. You could have been the best singer, songwriter or musician in your city for years with hardly anyone knowing about you, but if you do something that gets notoriety or come up with something that gets people talking, they'll flock to you.

People want to be around and work with those who are successful. They want the best giving them the best. So, how do you stop chasing them and get them to start chasing you?

Start creating a buzz.

Put that crazy dream or idea you have about a new song, sound or performance to the test. No limits! All the most-popular music ever performed or recorded started that way. Someone had a dream and told others that they had to listen to or see it and they did, and word of mouth spread like a wildfire and the phenomenon started.

You can do the same.

The New Music/New Dream Law of Resistance

So, let's talk a little more about what happens when you take your music and visionary ideas and test them on the world.

Once you test your new idea and you get the following reactions and responses, you'll know you're on to something good:

"You're crazy."

"It'll never work."

"You're lucky."

"You're a visionary."

"You're the one I want to do business with."

Mentor Me Now

Some of the best and wisest time you'll ever spend in your life is those 10 minutes with someone who's already a big success in the business or who has gone through the tough times you've been going through and become a success because of it. Being around them will change your life faster than a year of studying books. You see, even the best singers, songwriters and musicians had to start somewhere, and each of them started at the bottom. But it was what they did and how they did it that got them to the top. Take them to lunch, ask lots of questions, and then listen. Your life is about to be changed for the better because of it.

A Signed Deal Is Just the Beginning

You love composing, playing and performing music and you'd probably do it for free if you had to. But you've got your life to live, things you want to buy, and investments you want to make, so you need to get paid.

That's when you need to start thinking more like a businessperson and less like a musician.

Come up with a system that works great for you and those you do business with whereby each party knows what's expected of them and when.

I suggest using a very simple one-page agreement for every business deal you have. Be sure to have an attorney draft it for you so that you are fully protected and your agreement is valid within the laws of your state and where you do business. The agreement should spell out what you will be giving the client, and the client agrees to engage the use of your services and pay you an agreed amount at a specified time and in a specified way. And be sure the agreement states that the client understands and agrees to not hold you (and your company) liable for anything (other than breach of contract) and so on.

You've got better things to do with your life than chase down people all over town trying to get the money they owe you.

Put everything in writing, protect yourself, and everyone will know the rules and be happy.

Always Remember: It's Just Business, Not a Marriage

Let's take this dealing with people in business thing one step further. In your business life, you'll find that you need to deal with many people only once, others only a few times, and a select few (hopefully in a good way) longer. Before long, you will get to the point where you'll be able to pick and choose the clients you want to work with, and that's when it's nothing but fun.

Until then, keep your mindset in the proper perspective by understanding that you're building your business and there will be all kinds of people who will cross your path who will help you do it.

Keep the happiest people and experiences, and let go of the rest and wish them the best.

Be a 30-Second E-Mailer

One of the non-music things you can do that will make you stand out is the quickness with which you respond to e-mails and questions. Some people make the mistake of thinking that if they get an e-mail, they'll get back to it and answer it perhaps a day or so (or longer) down the road.

Big mistake.

If someone took the valuable time out of her life to think about you and e-mail you, then show her the same respect and courtesy by taking the time to reply.

And the quicker you can do it, the better.

That shows those people that they are important to you and that getting back to them is a priority. They'll remember you for it, and when it comes to them needing you for their next project or choosing between you and someone else, you've just stacked the odds in favor of them making the call to you.

Say "Thank You," and Say It Often

Here's another great way to open doors and have people remember you: Say "thank you," and say it often.

People don't have to do business with you. People don't have to call or e-mail you. People have other options.

So make yourself memorable in a good way in their minds, by thanking them for any good words they tell you and any thing they do for you—like choosing you for a great opportunity!

People want to feel loved, needed, and appreciated. Telling them "thank you" is a great way to make them feel that way.

Tough Times Are Here Only for a Short Time

We all go through tough times. It's as if life uses those adversities and tough times to wake us up and teach us the valuable lessons we need at the time so that we can learn, grow, and move to the next higher level in our life's journey.

So, whenever the business ebbs or the tough times seem to arrive in bunches, step back and give yourself a breather and some perspective.

Tough times never last too long, and soon you'll be enjoying those happy times once again.

Do Not Be a Prisoner of Your Own Decisions

One of the things that will keep you fresh, current, and always growing in your personal and professional life is to be fluid. Always be open to changing anything and everything, and don't become a prisoner of your own decisions.

Many people do become such prisoners.

They'll think about doing something and finally decide to do it, but they will rarely adjust their plans or change things along the way. Then when success doesn't happen fast enough or they're not getting the results they've wanted, they become frustrated and blame the world—anyone and anything but themselves—for why things aren't happening.

Be different from those people.

Make a decision and take an action, but if it isn't giving you the results you want, change it and keep changing things *until* it does.

Whatever it is, wherever it is, whenever it is, change is good.

"You Jump through My Hoop and I'll Be Happy
to Jump through Yours"

Many people make the mistake of being the nice guy or gal who'll bend over backward to help people in any way possible. All of that is well and good, if they return the favor.

But for lots of people, those who give too freely of their time, talent, genius, and efforts are looked upon as a cheap commodity in the business marketplace and are unjustly undervalued by those who receive their help.

Hold yourself up to a higher standard.

Be kind to people, but let them earn your time and expertise. You are the one who has the skill, talent, and knowledge that will help them, and they need you. Don't give it away or sell yourself too cheaply.

It's Time for You to Become the Person Behind the Plow,
Not the Mule Pulling It

Lots of people go through their entire lives working for someone else and are totally happy. Others have the desire to do their own thing in their own way and start their own business. I think you know which group you belong to.

Regardless of whether you stay an employee or become the president of your own company, always remember that you control your destiny. You may work for a company, but only you can offer that company the unique skills and abilities that can get them the kind of results that only you can bring them.

And if you've started your own business, focus your time, energy, and expertise on the things that pay you the greatest rewards and farm out as much of the rest as you can to others. The most successful CEOs all do this, and there's a good reason for it: Your time is better spent doing the things you're an expert at.

Time to Empty Your Cup

Every 6 to 12 months, take about 15 minutes and make an inventory of where you are and where you're going. Change, throw out, or revise your plans as needed.

This is also the time to take an inventory of the people in your life.

Keep the positive people and let go of those who are bringing you and your business down. No one says you have to keep the same ideas, clients, or other people in your life who are not bringing joy and happiness to it, so let your negative influences go.

The New You: Maverick, Pioneer, Music Success Extraordinaire

Ask 10 people how you should live your life and you'll get 10 different answers. It seems that lots of people who don't know you are out to convince you that they know exactly how you should be living the life you are living.

But let's get real.

No one knows you better than you know yourself. And you don't need anyone telling you what you should do and how you should do it.

Follow your own intuition and gut feeling. It rarely is wrong.

In fact, if you'll look back to the moments when you made decisions that didn't work out as planned, don't be at all surprised to find that those were the times when something inside of you knew better and told you not to proceed, but you didn't listen.

Never let another person's ideas, opinions, and conclusions become your reality unless you know deep down that you are in complete agreement with what they're saying.

Appendix D
Resource Guide

You've read about them in the lessons of the *How to Make It in the New Music Business* book. Here's a quick reference to the resources you'll find helpful.

Lesson 5
Building Your A-Team

Lawyers.com. This is a website devoted to helping you find attorneys anywhere in the United States. It lists those who specialize in various aspects of the law, including entertainment and music—the kind you want. The site has a search engine that lets you choose the type of attorney you need, and once you type in the city where you'd like to find them, the site gives you a listing of attorneys in that area and information about each one. The site also has lots of good tips.

Abanet.org. Another good source of finding attorneys is on abanet.org. This is the official website of the American Bar Association (the granddaddy organization to which all legit lawyers belong). It's easy to find lots of references for your area or for any area you wish. Simply go to the organization's home page, point and click on "General Public Resources," click on "Find Legal Help," and click on any state on the map. You'll then be directed to a listing of local attorney referrals. Look for those who have the ABA Lawyer Referral Logo (since they'll be the ones who meet ABA standards) and it will read "Meets ABA Standards For Lawyer Referral." Once you've found an attorney in the area you're looking, simply click on their website or call the number listed.

Nolo.com. This is an excellent site with loads of information on a variety of legal topics. It also includes reference library of articles, free legal forms, a reference library of articles, dictionaries and encyclopedias, and answers to over 400 of your legal questions.

Legaldocs.com. I'm all for saving you lots of money, so if you're looking for a terrific place to find legal documents that you can simply download, print out, and fill out yourself, look no further than Legaldocs.com. You'll find plenty of free legal documents that you can use, along with others that you can download for a very small fee. This site can save you some serious dinero.

Law.com. If you're looking for a website that can give you a quick and very basic and understanding of the law, your rights, self-representation, and a host of lots of other topics, then check out this site. It has just about everything you could ask for (easy topic menus, links to lots of other law-related sites and information) that will get you up to speed in a hurry.

Lawinfo.com. Let's say that after you've created your music, filed your Copyright Registration, and done all the right things (that I just told you about), you find someone or some company ripping you off. They've sold your song all over the place, without asking or telling you, and now you need an expert who can tell you what that song is worth, and can put a figure on how much they've damaged you. Would you know where to look? Your attorney most likely will (the great ones always do), but how about you? Click on this site and you'll find all the legal expertise you'll need whenever you need it. Let's hope you won't, but dirtbags (people who rip off other people) will always be dirtbags, so keep this web address only a few clicks away.

For more information, answers to questions, resources, documents, and links about copyrights and U.S. copyright laws, check out the following five sites:

Law.cornell.edu. This site is the Legal Information Institute from Cornell Law School. You'll find lots of great information including:

- U.S. Code
- U.S. Constitution
- Code of Federal Regulations
- Federal, state and international laws
- Directories of lawyers, organizations. and journals

Loc.gov. This is the main site of the United States Library of Congress. So much information is on this website, but some of the most useful for you is the United States Copyright database.

Copyright.iupui.edu. This is a site called the Copyright Management Center from Indiana University. You'll find lots of good copyright information here, including:

- Copyright quickguide
- Fair-use information
- Copyright ownership
- Permissions information
- Documents, checklists, and agreements (in pdf format)
- FAQs

Benedict.com. This website covers lots of things, including the law on Fair Use, Copyright Notice, and Public Domain; and the why, what, and how of copyright registration; and interesting cases of copyright use and infringement involving famous celebrities from music, television, and movies.

Weblawresources.com. This website features information on the Internet and protecting your copyrighted works. The site offers packages (e.g., some with more than 50 legal form documents for web, copyrights, etc.) you can purchase for a fraction of what it would cost to have them each created by attorneys. However, the site advises that you secure competent legal counsel to review your documents prior to use.

Lesson 8

Finding the Best Recording & Creating Platform

Sibelius.com

Spectrasonics.net

Glyphtech.com

Studionetworksolutions.com

Motu.com

Digidesign.com

Steinbergusa.net

Apple.com

Sonic.com

Ikmultimedia.com

Native-instruments.com

Cycling74.com

Waves.com

Antarestech.com

Propellerheads.se

Ableton.com

Lesson 11

Launching the Business of "You, Inc."

For more information on The Company Corporation, go to Incorporate.com

For more information on Form SS-4: Application for Employer Identification Number and Form 2553: Election by a Small Business Corporation, go to Irs.gov

Lesson 12
Real World New Music Business Boot Camp

For more information about the Digital Millennium Copyright Act (DMCA) go to Loc.copyright/legislation/dmca/

For more information on copyrights or registering copyrights, and to download free copyright forms, go to Lcweb.loc.gov/copyright/forms.html.

For more information on ASCAP, BMI, SESAC and The Harry Fox Agency go to:

> Ascap.com
>
> Bmi.com
>
> Sesac.com
>
> Harryfoxagency.com

For more information on the National Music Publishers Association, go to Nmpa.org

For more information on The Alliance of Artists and Recording Companies, go to Aarcroyalties.com

For more information on The Recording Industry Association of America, go to Riaa.com

For more information on The International Confederation of Societies of Authors and Composers, go to Cisac.org

Lesson 13
Premiering Your Music to a Global Audience

For more information on Live365, go to Live365.com

For more information on RealAudio, go to RealAudio.com

For more information on DolbyFax, go to Dolby.com

Appendix A
Capturing Niche Markets

For more information on Wal-Mart, go to Walmart.com

For more information on Target, go to Target.com

For more information on K-mart, go to Kmart.com

For a listing of and web addresses for the world's biggest ad agencies, go to Siu.edu/~aaf/agency.html

For more information on *The Indie Contact Newsletter*, go to Indiebible.com

For a listing of names and web addresses for the world's biggest video distributors, go to Dvdverdict.com/studioinfo/index.shtml

Index of Websites to Check Out

Websites change and come and go all the time. But, I've found a few good ones to check out that'll give you lots of information on anything from the latest news and gear, advice from pros and amateurs, great places to buy and sell gear, publishing, A&R, promotions, legal issues that concern you, and much more.

1212.com. Their slogan is "The largest data base of music industry related Web information in over 50 countries." I think you'll agree it's a terrific resource.

Audiomidi.com. Your personal resource for computer music.

Computermusic.co.uk. Latest music and gear news, tutorials, forum, demos, etc.

Crmav.com. Gear and computer news, CD releases, musicians news, message board, and musicians wanted postings, etc.

Futuremusic.co.uk. News, gear, people, making music, desktop, links, audio, A&R area, forum, bid-buy-sell, etc.

Gearbeat.com. The Internet's music gear guide.

Gearpreview.com. Gear previews and reviews for music and film equipment.

Harmony-central.com. A great place to buy new and used gear, get gear reviews, read the latest gear news, links to other music sites, and more.

PeerMusic.com. A different kind of music publisher for those looking for other choices besides Warner-Chappell, EMI, Sony/ATV, etc.

Recordingartistscoalition.com. Their mission statement says, "RAC is a nonprofit, non-partisan coalition formed to represent the interests of recording artists with regard to legislative issues in which corporate and artists' interests conflict, and to address other public policy debates that come before the music industry." A good place to stay informed.

Recordproduction.com. The record producers and studio portal.

Sonicstate.com. News, classifieds, synth site, studio, gear store, latest articles, etc.

Soundonsound.com. They call it "The World's Best Music Recording Magazine" and it's on the Internet.

Studio-central.com. An Internet meeting site for musicians to discuss their home studios, projects, and gear, and ask questions and find answers.

Studioexpresso.com. Artists' gateway to music production services and resources.

Taxi.com. This company has been around for some time now, and they have plenty of success stories for those who've used their services. As they say, "TAXI is the world's leading independent A&R company helping unsigned bands, artists and songwriters get record deals, publishing deals and placement in films and TV shows."

Futureproducers.com

Recordingconsoles.net

Appendix E
Contact Guide

Bob Bradshaw

Customaudioelectronics.com

For a free subscription to *TapeOp* magazine that Bob Bradshaw talks about in the book, go to Tapeop.com

Bob Clearmountain

Mixthis.com

Bob Ludwig

Gatewaymastering.com

Steve Lukather

Toto99.com
Stevelukather.net

Diane Warren

Realsongs.com
Dianewarren.com

ABOUT THE AUTHOR

Robert Wolff's publishing career began more than 20 years ago, when publishing legend Joe Weider (founder and publisher of *SHAPE* and numerous other best-selling magazines) asked him to write for his magazines.

Robert has traveled all over the world and has interviewed some of the biggest names in music, fitness, science, sports, and entertainment, including Simon Cowell, Diane Warren, Jennifer Hudson, Toni Braxton, Jerry Bruckheimer, David Foster, Sharon Stone, two-time Nobel winner Dr. Linus Pauling, World Heavyweight Boxing Champion Evander Holyfield, Arnold Schwarzenegger, and hundreds of others.

At the age of 34, Robert was awarded an Honorary Doctorate of Letters in recognition of his accomplishments in motivating people all over the world to change their lives.

Robert's magazine columns have enjoyed a global reach of more than 7 million readers a month, in 60 countries and in 15 foreign language translations.

His writings have appeared all over the world, including hundreds of internationally published articles in newspapers and such magazines as *Cosmopolitan* and *SHAPE*.

He has interviewed Academy, Grammy, Emmy, Golden Globe, and Nobel award winners and written more than 30 books and has a worldwide following of readers in more than 65 countries.

BOOKS YOU MIGHT ALSO ENJOY

A Final Word…

Just as your life is constantly changing each day, each month, and each year, so too are the lessons and inspiration that can help make positive changes in your life. To help you reach your music dreams that much faster, I'd like to suggest you check out two of my other books available in eBook and print at your favorite book retailer. Enjoy!

If I Only Knew Then What I Know Now

I think it's just the kind of book that can make a big inspiring impact on your life and career.

Think Like an Immigrant

So many of the singers, songwriters, musicians, and hugely successful businesses are immigrants or were started by immigrants. This is a book that gives you their principles for success.

CPSIA information can be obtained
at www.ICGtesting.com
Printed in the USA
LVOW04s2141090117
520375LV00015B/919/P